THE ETHICS OF
INTERNATIONAL
BUSINESS

The Ethics of International Business

□ □ □

THOMAS DONALDSON

New York   Oxford
OXFORD UNIVERSITY PRESS

Oxford University Press

Oxford   New York   Toronto
Delhi   Bombay   Calcutta   Madras   Karachi
Petaling Jaya   Singapore   Hong Kong   Tokyo
Nairobi   Dar es Salaam   Cape Town
Melbourne   Auckland

and associated companies in
Berlin   Ibadan

First Published in 1989 by Oxford University Press, Inc.,
200 Madison Avenue, New York, New York 10016

First issued as an Oxford University Press paperback, 1992

Oxford is a registered trademark of Oxford University Press

Library of Congress Cataloging-in-Publication Data
Donaldson, Thomas, 1945–
The ethics of international business / by Thomas Donaldson.
p. cm.   Bibliography: p.   Includes index.
ISBN 0-19-505874-7
1. International business enterprises—Moral and ethical aspects.
2. Business ethics.   I. Title.
HD2755.5D65   1989   174'.4—dc20   89-9471
ISBN 0-19-507471-8 (pbk)

2 4 6 8 10 9 7 5 3 1

Printed in the United States of America
on acid-free paper

To Paul, Keith and Paige

FOREWORD

The purpose of The Ruffin Series in Business Ethics is to publish the best thinking about the role of ethics in business. In a world in which there are daily reports of questionable business practices, from insider trading to environmental pollution, we need to step back from the fray and understand the large issues of how business and ethics are, and ought to be, connected. We need to integrate the teaching and practice of management more closely with ethics and the humanities. Such an integration will yield both a richer ethical context for managerial decision making and a new set of practical and theoretical problems for scholars of ethics.

During the past 20 years scholarship in business ethics has blossomed. Today, more than ever before, there is a growing consensus among management scholars, ethicists, and business executives that ethics should be a vital part of the teaching and practice of management.

The Ruffin Series will publish both monographs and essay collections of interest to management scholars, ethicists, and practicing managers. Each of these three audiences is important because only through a sustained *dialogue* among management thinkers, philosophers, and managers will lasting progress be made in bringing ethics into the daily business of business.

In 1987, the Peter B. and Adeline W. Ruffin Foundation established a fund at the Darden School, University of Virginia, to create a distinguished lecture series in business ethics. Future books in the Ruffin series will include collections of these distinguished lectures—collections that explore specific topics of professional and scholarly interest.

There can be no better place to begin the series than with Thomas Donaldson's book, *The Ethics of International Business*. This is the first book-length treatment of the moral nature of international business, and it is an innovative, and practical, discussion of the ways that moral theory can contribute to a better understanding of today's global business environment. Readers will be especially interested in the algorithm that the author develops to determine whether certain business practices should transcend national, and cultural, boundaries.

The Ethics of International Business should set a new scholarly standard for business ethics. And it is a standard that we shall try to continue to meet in the Ruffin Series.

R. EDWARD FREEMAN

PREFACE

This book's aim is to advance knowledge about ethics in global business. The book identifies a group of rights critical to global business and develops a broad, normative* framework for use in interpreting ethics in a global market. It also proposes an ethical algorithm for multinational managers to use in resolving conflicts between home country and host country standards.

My intended audience is an eclectic mix of philosophers, business academics, political scientists, economists, theologians, managers, and plain people whose interests intersect with issues of ethics in global business. I hope that some of the book's readers will be managers of multinational corporations. I believe that busy executives who take the time to read this book will be repaid for their efforts by the speed and clarity with which they later identify and analyze moral problems.

A normative framework is sorely needed because scholars have avoided issues of ethics in international business. Indeed, no book has directly undertaken the task of evaluating global business systematically from a moral perspective.

The neglect is a function of predictable but regrettable forces. One is disciplinary inertia. Philosophers, the acknowledged specialists in moral philosophy, preoccupied themselves with theoretical concerns in which the development of factual sophistication—in such areas as psychology, economics and medicine—was recognized, if at all, grudgingly. For business researchers and others, including economists and political scientists, the problem was almost the reverse. Their neglect of moral matters reflected a preoccupation—now happily waning—with "scientific" methodology, a preoccupation which discouraged moral analysis, especially in economics and political science, two of the leading theoretical disciplines through which busi-

---

*I will use the word "normative" throughout the book to refer to concepts that guide choice or conduct. See the two footnotes on page 4 of Chapter 1 for the definitions this book will use for the terms "normative" and "empirical."

ness academics draw sustenance. This scientific turn, with its historical roots in the philosophical positivism of the early twentieth century, was skeptical of any inquiry that could not be readily reduced to facts, numbers, or operational predictions.

Meanwhile, in a related drive for scientific credibility, political scientists have struggled to make their inquiries predictive and manageable. At the international level this trend has sometimes taken the form of embracing crude versions of "realism" (which presume national self-interest as both a descriptive guide and an evaluative norm).

These disciplinary trends have had odd consequences. Philosophy graduate students during the 1960s and 1970s tended to have factual or empirical inclinations trained out of them, while their counterparts in schools of business and departments of political science found their moral observations suspect if not unwelcome.

Recent disciplinary trends, however, are encouraging. Scholars working out of the so-called social issues and business environment perspective in schools of business have produced the best-developed literature in ethics to appear from business schools. Their efforts evolve from the tradition of "business and society" research, itself having roots in the politically turbulent 1960s and early 1970s. (Contributors such as Buchholz, Cochran, Epstein, Frederick, Freeman, and Sethi have made significant advances in developing not only descriptive studies with moral relevance, but nondescriptive, normative hypotheses.[1]) Moreover, political scientists have moved to integrate ethical theory with empirical analysis, not only in domestic but in international contexts (for example, Henry Shue's *Basic Rights* (1980), Charles Beitz's *Political Theory and International Relations* (1979), and James Fishkin's *The Limits of Obligation* (1982).) At the same time, philosophers have made solid contributions in business ethics, medical ethics, and public policy. (In business ethics, philosophers such as Norman Bowie, Richard DeGeorge, Kenneth Goodpaster, and Patricia Werhane have shed light on problems of whistle blowing, employee rights, bribery, and the foundations of corporate legitimacy.)

And yet this unfolding interdisciplinary revolution, one that promises to mix fact and value in the demanding crucible of practice, has yet to reach successfully into the international market place. For while political theorists such as Beitz, Fishkin, and Shue have made substantial contributions, their focus has been almost exclusively on the actions of nation states, not corporations, and they have dealt primarily with political rather than business issues.[2] Similarly, philosophers have been so intensely occupied with domestic issues of business ethics, that global issues have received scant attention.

Finally, even the efforts of business researchers (from the business and society tradition) have tended to bypass international ethics. Only a fraction of their ethically oriented research has found application to multinational corporations, and when it has, the context has been issue-specific, for example, Bhopal or South African divestment.[3] To be sure, business academics have offered a bounty of empirical analysis relevant to multinational corporations, and have conducted detailed inquiries into the structure of global markets and the strategies of multinational corporations. Some of this research has explored the issue of political risk for multinationals,[4] some the nature of multinational decision making from the perspective of basic strategic stances,[5] and some the issue of multinational public policy.[6] Yet virtually none has dealt specifically with multinational decision making from a moral perspective.

Hence, the collective impact of scientifically inspired realism, theoretical enthusiasm, and benign neglect has been to leave the arena of international business largely uncharted, a consequence that exposes starkly the need for developing a normative framework from which we might humanely view the arena.

In attempting to provide such a framework this book adopts positions that not everyone will affirm. In some instances I suggest answers to controversial issues such as the morality of trade with corrupt states such as South Africa, the use of hazardous technology, and the legitimacy of petty bribery. I do this in the belief that moral inquiry must not only raise difficult questions but also formulate plausible solutions. My hope, however, is that even the unsympathetic reader will be able to distinguish the book's application of its principles from the principles themselves and the theories from which they derive. One may agree with the latter while rejecting the former.

Although I am an academic philosopher by training, this book is written for a wider audience. It substitutes ordinary English for philosophical terminology whenever possible. This is not simplification: I am convinced that most important ideas can be communicated in jargon-free language. Nonetheless, writers must attempt to provide a respectable intellectual grounding for what they write and the methods can vary. For social science researchers the grounding usually comes from empirical research. For persons schooled in the discipline of ethics, the grounding comes from moral argument making use of the tradition of ethical theory. This book takes the latter approach, and while I continue to benefit from reading the work of economists, political scientists, and business school academics (and in an earlier life underwent business school training), my habits, strategies, and methods derive largely from philosophy.

Because of the book's interdisciplinary readership, I offer a few remarks by way of guidance. The leading ideas are presented in

Chapters 4, 5, and 6. These chapters deal with the moral foundations of business activity, international rights, and with the resolution
of conflicts among differing cultural norms. They are crucial to my
argument and without them the rest of the book makes little sense.
Readers not given to skepticism about utilizing ethics in a cross-cultural context may wish to skip Chapter 2. This is probably good advice for practicing corporate managers (at least those who do not
doubt about the possibility of ethics in international affairs) since
many will find the detailed arguments necessary to refute realism
and cultural relativism tedious. At the same time, for those prone to
such skepticism, or for philosophers or political scientists with a professional interest in the cultural relativism and "realism" issues (issues dealing with the possibility of transcultural moral values), Chapter 2 is critical. As may be obvious, the remainder of the book presumes that the reader has rejected thoroughgoing moral skepticism,
that is, the view that no moral view is objectively any better than any
other. Even professional philosophers, however, may decide to skip
the first part of Chapter 2, since the refutation of cultural relativism
there proceeds along elementary and traditional lines.

The first draft of this book included a hefty chapter discussing the
moral agency of corporations and nation states. That chapter analyzed and defended the idea that nation states and multinational corporations, just as human individuals, qualify as moral agents; it defended the common sense presupposition, in other words, that nation
states and corporations are capable of possessing genuine moral responsibilities and rights, although not necessarily the same responsibilities and rights as human individuals. Reviewers of the first draft
encouraged me to delete the chapter on the grounds that it was excessively technical and dealt with an issue of interest only to professional philosophers. It was, I think, good advice. In turn I have moved
to a posture of merely assuming throughout the book that nation
states and multinational corporations qualify as moral agents, although my assumption should not be construed to mean that the
issue is a simple one, or that sophisticated arguments are lacking that
attempt to deny moral agency to groups and collectives. Readers interested in the issue of moral agency are encouraged to read from
among the fairly vast literature that has emerged on this topic in the
last decade.[7]

The book reflects the contributions of numerous friends and colleagues in departments of philosophy, political science, economics,
and business. Among those who read the full version of the present
manuscript and made valuable suggestions for change are: Barbara
Ankeny, Norman Bowie, John Coley, Edwin Epstein, R. Ed Freeman, Sherwood Frey, John Matthews, Prakesh Sethi, Robert Solo-

man, and Clarence Walton. Among those who read parts of the manuscript and offered important criticism are George Brenkert, Rogene Buchholz, Richard DeGeorge, Robbin Derry, Jack Donnelly, William Frederick, Raymond Frey, Kenneth Goodpaster, Russell Hardin, Edwin Hartman, Michael Keeley, Terry Nardin, Lynn Sharp Paine, Julius Sensat, Michael Smith, and Manuel Velasquez. Still others heard versions of parts of the manuscript presented at academic conferences and made important contributions, including Gregory Kavka, Christine Korsgaard, and Carl Wellman. The book also reflects the insights of a number of multinational executives with whom I have had the pleasure of working, including Elmer Johnson, Charles Feldberg, and John Jordan. Loyola University of Chicago lent institutional support and encouragement, and Jeanne Huchthausen, secretary of the Loyola Graduate Philosophy program, helped in typing the manuscript. Patricia Bennett of the Olsson Center for Applied Ethics, The Darden School, proofread the manuscript and contributed research information. Finally, my thanks go to Herb Addison and Ann Fishman of Oxford University Press for their encouragement and perceptive editorial advice.

Chicago   T.D.
January, 1989

CONTENTS

THE ETHICS OF INTERNATIONAL BUSINESS

1

Introduction

> Down the road, it is . . . possible to visualize a kind of social science that would be very different from the one most of us have been practicing: a moral-social science where moral considerations are not repressed or kept apart, but are systematically commingled with analytic argument . . . where moral considerations need no longer be smuggled in surreptitiously, nor expressed unconsciously, but are displayed openly and disarmingly.[1]
>
> ALBERT O. HIRSCHMAN

In August of 1987 in Geneva, Switzerland, a group of 3,000 delegates from 141 of the world's developed and developing nations reached a surprising agreement. The occasion was the seventh United Nations Conference on Trade and Development (UNCTAD), a conference that only four years earlier in Belgrade had been marked by bitter disagreement between rich and poor delegates. The developing nations agreed on the importance of stimulating their economies by giving free trade and private enterprise a greater role, and the developed nations agreed to ease the terms of a suffocating debt burden.[2] But for many observers, there was wariness, not confidence. For opinions about global economic "solutions" over the past hundred years—even when marked by consensus among politicians and economists—have been characterized by dramatic volatility. Shifts have occurred from export-led to nonexport-led development strategies, from central planning to decentralized incentives, from capital-intensive to labor-intensive production, from manufacturing-dominated to agriculture-dominated programs, and from strategies emphasizing economic policies to ones emphasizing cultural variables and education.

Yet beneath these shifting currents of economic opinion, almost lost from view, lies a tightly connected set of normative and nonempirical issues surrounded by a remarkably durable collection of moral

3

beliefs. As normative issues, they cannot be reduced to questions of statistically interpretable facts or to the determination of maximally efficient strategies for reaching goals.* Rather, they concern questions of rights, fairness, and justice: they ask what goals should be adopted by economic actors, what rights multinational employees in developing countries should possess, and what obligations and rights corporations should recognize—other than merely legal ones—in their dealings with foreign governments. Such issues, while frequently attracting media attention, have been almost wholly neglected by economists and business researchers who, sensitive to empirical† methodology, often regard them as insolvable. A familiar presumption by such researchers is that they defy serious analysis because of the clash of cultural values.

Yet such issues arise in a broader context characterized by a relatively permanent set of nonempirical beliefs about fairness, human rights, and the need for cooperation in the international economic order. Indeed, these beliefs have been sufficiently persistent in some instances to qualify more as axioms in the ongoing debate than as items within it. They include recognition of the injustice of starvation and chronic malnutrition; of the legitimate rights of a nation, large or small, to economic self-determination; and of the obligations of prosperous, developed countries, however slight, to help their less privileged neighbors. They include recognition of the obligations of multinational corporations to refrain from suffocating local governments while providing at least minimal safety standards for workers, and for those same corporations when confronted with countries such as South Africa where the most basic rights are trampled systematically, to—at a minimum—refrain from conducting "business as usual." Such normative presumptions, indeed, unite all but the most extreme representatives of the various schools of economic development and ideology.

---

*I will use the word "normative" throughout the book to refer to concepts that guide choice or conduct. If a theory or proposition is normative, then it is action guiding, or as moral philosophers often say, "prescriptive." This excludes mere factual assertions, including assertions that certain means will achieve (or maximize) certain ends. Hence the statement "Pull the trigger and you will kill Jones" is a descriptive statement, not a normative one, whereas the statement "You should pull the trigger and kill Jones" qualifies as normative. In contrast to descriptive statements, normative statements need not reflect a present, past, or future state of affairs. For example, one may espouse a normative theory of democracy for the world's nations without believing that all nations will eventually embrace democracy.

†I use the term "empirical" as the opposite of "normative." Empirical concepts are meant to reflect actual facts (the word "empirical" derives from the Greek *empeirikos*, experienced).

Of course, even such generic moral truths as these are not beyond dispute. But their present level of acceptance is at least as high as the most fundamental axioms in theories about the international economy, a fact that encourages the serious exploration of moral issues in a global context. Moreover, it is precisely because one encounters controversy and polemics after passing beyond general ethical precepts either to more specific precepts or to concrete applications, that there arises a need to understand the source, shape, and application of moral concepts in the global market. If we assume that multinational corporations ought not conduct "business as usual" when dealing with states such as South Africa, then what does our assumption mean? Are such corporations required to cut off all business, or merely to conduct activities in accordance with rights-affirming principles? Or, granted that multinationals must observe minimal standards for safety in foreign manufacturing plants, what counts as "minimal standards"—the multinational's home country standards, or the standards of the host country? I hope to help answer such questions in this book.

In assuming that any nonempirical attempt to analyze global business must be wrongheaded, researchers have tended to fail to notice that empirical analyses, especially of economic strategy, ultimately require the use of moral presuppositions. A complete comprehension of facts, including information about maximally efficient means to achieve ends, will be unsatisfactory unless those ends themselves are morally acceptable, since human ends ultimately must pass tests of fairness and justice. The goal of increasing a developing nation's gross national product, assumed by an economic theory of development, may be unsatisfactory if in the attainment of an enlarged national product (as occurred not long ago in the case of Brazil) the poorer half of the population becomes even worse off.

In contrast, then, to mainstream, empirically dominated, analyses of international business, this book focuses on the idea that moral concepts can and should inform international economic activity. My novel and admittedly ambitious project is to establish a moral framework useful for interpreting ethics in the global market. Key to my thesis is the idea that both Hobbesian realists and cosmopolitan moral idealists are wrong. Moral philosophy in application to the international economic realm yields neither a skeptical nihilism in which cross-cultural comparisons are nonsense, nor a roseate extension of one's personal, culture-centered morality. Transnational moral obligations exist, but I argue that they are all too frequently different in kind from ordinary ones. Simply exporting our moral notions abroad paints a false picture of our responsibilities. For example, respect for cultural diversity and recognition of relative levels of technological

or economic development are two values necessary for wisely making global moral trade-offs.

OVERVIEW

The first task is to provide a breathing "space" for moral concepts
in the international realm. Chapter 2 asserts that moral inquiry can
be given meaning in the culturally diverse realm of international affairs where national and corporate self-interest appear to dominate.
It defends this assertion by attempting to unravel and neutralize the
two most salient challenges to the possibility of international morality, namely, cultural relativism and traditional Hobbesianism.

Enhanced power is said to confer enhanced responsibilities, and
with the possible exception of nation-states, multinational corporations are the most powerful organizations in existence. Chapter 3
offers an introductory sketch of the theory and practice of multinational corporations. It describes their powers, the existing codes and
laws influencing their activities, and the infrequent theoretical attempts that have been made to understand their ethical responsibilities. Chapter 3 provides a background for readers unfamiliar with
multinationals and outlines the basis of the moral analysis that follows in later chapters.

Two important concepts provide the moral foundation for the
analysis of these global giants. The first is the notion of a social contract between business and society, and the second is the doctrine of
international rights. In articulating the concept of a social contract
between business and society, Chapter 4 uses a centuries-old philosophical technique that attempts to identify the fundamental responsibilities of large-scale organizations, whether domestic or international, capitalistic or socialistic. The technique is the method of social
contract analysis, a method I have applied to business in an earlier
book, *Corporations and Morality*.[3] This method implies that the moral
foundations of productive organizations can be understood through
a thought experiment in which the terms of a hypothetical contract
are delineated. Productive organizations can be viewed as engaging
in an implied contract with society, a contract not unlike that employed by Locke, Rousseau, and Hobbes in understanding the moral
and political foundations of the state. The intellectual presumption
of the contract is that all productive organizations, including corporations, are artifacts; that they are in part the products of our
moral and legal imagination, and as such, they are to be molded in
the image of our collective rights and societal ambitions. Corporations, as all productive organizations, must have bestowed upon them

by society both recognition as single agents, and the authority to own or use land and natural resources. In return for this, society has the right to expect that productive organizations will, all other things being equal, enhance the general interests of consumers and employees. Society further may expect that in doing so corporations honor existing rights and limit their activities to accord with the bounds of justice. My efforts in *Corporations and Morality* prompted a variety of responses both sympathetic and critical.[4] In this book I attempt to clear up misunderstandings about the nature and design of the social contract, and to utilize the contract in analyzing the ethics of multinational corporations.

Chapter 5 develops a concept of fundamental human rights which is serviceable for international business. The concept is a specification of justified claims from the standpoint of all members of the human community. Such claims constitute a doctrine of rights that all economic actors, including multinational corporations, are bound to observe. One of the chapter's key conclusions is that multinationals are not responsible for honoring rights in precisely the same manner as nation-states or individuals. Hence, Chapter 5 offers guidelines for understanding the varying moral burdens that fall upon different classes of international actors. Ten fundamental international rights, including, for example, the rights to personal security and freedom of association, are advanced which establish bedrock considerations that multinational corporations must respect from the perspective of ethics while operating abroad.

Chapter 6 emphasizes the need to articulate in addition to a doctrine of rights a practical stratagem for applying the home country norms of the multinational manager to the vexing problems arising in developing countries. How should highly placed multinational managers, typically schooled in home country moral traditions, reconcile conflicts between those traditions and ones of the host country? When host country standards for pollution, discrimination, and salary schedules appear substandard from the perspective of the home country, should the manager take the high road and implement home country standards? Or does the high road imply a failure to respect cultural diversity and national integrity? Chapter 6 constructs and defends an ethical algorithm for multinational managers to use in reconciling such normative conflicts; the formula reflects tolerance for cultural diversity as well as an appreciation for a society's relative level of economic development. Multinationals have frequently failed to honor legitimate moral demands in the past, not because of greed or ill will, but because of inattention to the relevant parameters of moral problems.

Yet both the doctrine of rights in Chapter 5 and the algorithm developed in Chapter 6 are inadequate to paint a comprehensive picture of multinational responsibility. Moral concepts must be applied and analyzed in specific contexts, and integrated with particular issues and facts. For this reason Chapters 7 and 8 investigate two specific issues of multinational ethics in detail: namely, hazardous technology in developing countries (Chapter 7) and disinvestment, especially in South Africa (Chapter 8). These surely are not the only issues that warrant detailed analysis, but they serve as key examples of pressing moral problems, and illustrate the application of the normative machinery developed in earlier chapters.

THE LIMITATION OF ISSUES

Should international trade be free or regulated? Are poor countries exploited by their richer neighbors? What is the best strategy for encouraging growth in the developing countries? These issues are largely left aside here. Also left aside are many aspects of the awesome problems of world hunger, international charity, and famine relief. My goals, rather, are to establish the moral bottom line for economic actors, for individuals and multinational corporations in global business, and, to some extent, nation-states insofar as their actions relate directly to global business. In doing so, the book eschews answering the broader question of what each of us *should* ideally do, not as business agents, but as human beings. Instead, it attempts to sketch the minimal duties of global agents and, in what I argue often amounts to the same thing, construes those agents primarily as economic actors subject to moral constraints *as* economic actors rather than as human beings subject to the full duties of charity and brotherly love. What are Exxon, Shell Oil, Dow Chemical, and John Doe permitted or not permitted to do as economic agents pursuing economic ends? For example, are they allowed to buy up land used for primary food production in a malnourished country and turn it to the production of a cash crop for export? Yet this book does not address the broad questions of whether such agents, and especially individual citizens of a First World country, have an obligation to donate a significant portion of their income each year to reduce starvation abroad.

To be sure, these issues left aside are important. But they are discussed in both popular and scholarly literature, whereas the more far-reaching issue of how one should come to understand global events from the standpoint of human rights and responsibilities, especially from the standpoint of global business, has been almost entirely neglected.

In examining the international market, I place considerably more emphasis on corporations than on nation-states. The middle, and largest, section of the book is devoted to corporations. Nonetheless, it has been my explicit aim not to become entangled in the issue of whether multinational corporations have helped more than they have harmed developing countries. Surely, multinationals have engaged in terrible acts: the United Fruit Company's notorious organization of an armed invasion of Honduras in 1910, an invasion that apparently cost only a case of rifles, a few thousand rounds of ammunition, a yacht, and the hiring of a mercenary named Machine Gun Malony, shocks even modern sensibilities.[5] And just as surely, multinationals have brought benefits: many of the remarkable developments of the green revolution, especially the development of seeds requiring little fertilizer but yielding high-protein crops, are the products of multinational corporations. For example, in less than a decade, the area planted by improved species of seeds in Pakistan grew from 50,000 to more than 32 million acres.[6] But whether one believes that multinationals are exploiters, saviors, or neutral participants,[7] there remains a need to clarify the principles to be used in evaluating their day-to-day conduct. And that, not judging the final worth of multinational corporations, is the limited—but still ambitious—task of this book.

2

The Failure of Realism: Obligations Beyond International Boundaries

The aim of this chapter is to unsettle the empirical and Hobbesian foundations of international affairs in a manner that will allow us to perceive those affairs as *moral* phenomena. It is to defend the unpopular but more traditional view that moral concepts should play—as they now do not—a critical role in international economic decisions. Because the same reasons that legitimize ethics as a decision-making factor for multinational corporations apply also to nation-states, our conclusion has implications for nation-states as well as corporate actors, and even for many noneconomic as well as economic decisions. To defend the legitimacy of ethics for global business, it is necessary to challenge not only international business amoralism but the entire school of international thought known as "realism" which denies morality a rightful role in international affairs. Discussing morality's broad application to international issues is thus a propaedeutic, or necessary preparation, for developing a program of normative analysis that can be used later to examine multinational corporations. This chapter counters realist criticisms by showing that the strongest arguments available on behalf of international amoralism, including the proposals of Hobbesians, have difficulty standing the test of rational scrutiny.

I use the terms "ethics" and "morality" as roughly interchangeable expressions, in the broad sense common to moral philosophers, that is, connected to fundamental human values such as rights, freedom, and well-being. These values possess legitimacy beyond the boundaries of simple self-interest, although we leave open for the present whether such extrapersonal extension may be generated from a complex or "enlightened" view of self-interest. Moral or ethical values are also what philosophers call "prescriptive" or "action guiding" because they provide standards for directing human choice. Moral or ethical concepts, then, prescribe from the perspective of either our individual or shared humanity.

REALISM

I apply the label "realist" to anyone opposed to the application of moral concepts to international policy, whether in business or elsewhere. Of course, unreasonable applications of morality to any context are possible; that goes without saying. But realists take one step further: they contend that no matter how careful, any person attempting to apply moral concepts in a normative manner beyond national borders is making a mistake. Realists may be viewed along a spectrum or continuum, ranging from a general skepticism about morality itself, to a more open attitude which, while allowing the possibility of moral truths in some spheres, believes morality to have a radically diminished application in international contexts. The concept "realist" in this sense is a stipulative one; it is not necessarily meant to describe any existing doctrine. Nonetheless, the conclusions we shall derive about realism have clear application to current theories and policies. A key aim of this chapter is to show that any theory which denies morality a rightful place in international affairs, is, at bottom, confused.

Moral doubt in the form of realism has a long tradition. It dates at least from the time of ancient Athens, in Thucydides' account in *The Peloponnesian War* of the dialogue between the Athenians and the Melians.[1] Thucydides describes the Athenian argument that in international politics right must give way to might; that the strong will do what they can, and the weak what they must. The Melians, however, reject this approach and persist in characterizing their dispute with the Athenians in terms of justice. The Athenians, putting their realism into practice, respond by conquering and destroying the Melians.[2] In the 1950s, diplomat George Kennan indirectly supported realism by pointing a finger at what he called the "dangerous moralism" in U.S. foreign policy. Kennan concluded that "the most serious fault of our past policy formulation" lay in the "legalistic-moralistic approach to international problems."[3] It is not that most realists are ruthless defenders of evil or even of amorality; indeed, they sometimes grant that to be human means to be influenced by moral considerations. It is rather that they believe self-help is the only help a state can expect in the relatively uncooperative international community, and that, as a result, morality is either dangerous or hypocritical. It is dangerous when it risks national interests for naive ideals, and it is hypocritical when it clothes self-interest with the appearance of moral legitimacy.[4]

Because naive moralizing in international affairs clearly poses a danger, one form of anti-realism that will *not* be defended here is sometimes called "idealism." As Joseph Nye points out, Hitler's ideology and its catastrophic fulfillment made an entire generation of scholars skeptical about idealism in foreign policy, and since World War II the so-called "realists" have triumphed, at least among specialists writing in the area of foreign policy.[5] In criticizing realism, then, I do not mean to defend the ideology-dominated policies that were popular in the 1920s and 1930s. Simple-minded moralizing, especially when informed exclusively by political ideology, can lead to confusion at best, and dogmatism at worst. Nye and others remind us that the road to World War II may have been paved with the good intentions of the 1930s Oxford students who vowed they would "never fight." In a similar manner, as Jacques Barzun notes, any program attempting to export democratic ideology in a wholesale manner soon faces the challenge of defining those ideals in a manner consistent with tradition and current attitudes. But the annoying truth is that our political ideals, just as the ideals of others, resist definition and contain unsettling inconsistencies.[6] For example, even democracy is an evolutionary phenomenon too elusive for a posed snapshot. "The theorem of democracy still holds," writes Barzun, "but all of its terms have changed in nature, especially the phrase 'the people,' which has been changed beyond recognition by the industrial revolution of the nineteenth century and the social revolution of the twentieth."[7]

Hence, by rejecting both realism and idealism it becomes clear that what we mean by the opposite of realism, or antirealism, is not idealism but something more modest. The antirealist view I shall defend holds that values which are able to stand the tests of rational consistency and compatibility with fundamental moral precepts, and which, moreover, are understood to exist in complex factual surroundings, should play a significant role in international decision making. This is true for decision making related to both political and business ends.

Even the application of well-considered and consistent values to international issues is a precarious pursuit in which the sure-footed often slip. Simple value transference, a maneuver whereby one simply projects one's personal values into the international arena, is a recipe for error and cultural arrogance. Our values are mediated by organizations such as the nation-state and the multinational corporation, institutions necessarily dedicated to a limited range of objectives and which manifest exceedingly narrow personalities. Furthermore, these organizations are forced to operate in a world that plays by an amazing variety of rules. I may be fond of my neighbor and when his house is on fire will rush to help. But there is a strong argument that my country ought not rush in whenever some internal evil threatens a friendly country, not even when the evil may have disastrous consequences. Or, for example, if I believe that Christianity or Judaism is uplifting and socially beneficial, I may encourage my fellow citizens to practice Christian or Jewish tenets. But it is probably true that my country ought not as a matter of government policy promulgate the doctrines of Christianity or Judaism to foreigners or to its nonreligious minority. In each of these instances my personal values are—to use Joseph Nye's metaphor—"off balance."[8]

Like many doctrines, realism's single, unifying skepticism can seek support from a multiplicity of defenses. The two most popular defenses for its claim that the application of moral concepts to the international context lacks legitimacy we shall call "cultural relativism" and "traditional Hobbesianism." Cultural relativism, the more extreme of the two strategies, denies that moral concepts have any international application at all since moral truth is nothing other than internal cultural consensus. In a less nihilistic vein, traditional Hobbesianism reinterprets and rejects the possibility of international morality, first by denying the rationality of behavior motivated by anything other than individual, national, or corporate self-interest, and next by asserting that the basis for morality—the possibility of self-advantage-enhancing cooperation—is nonexistent in the international arena owing to the absence of a sovereign power to enforce compliance.

Both lines of defense of realism can concede that people frequently apply moral terminology to international events; yet from the realist's perspective such terminology has no objective significance. The president of a large multinational corporation can accuse another multinational of "gross immorality and dishonesty" in reneging on a sales contract; or the president of the Republic of South Africa can accuse the leaders of the Common Market nations of encouraging racial violence in South Africa. But from the perspective of both cultural relativism and traditional Hobbesianism, these accusations are confused. It is as if the referee in a game of soccer were to call a foul on a spectator sitting in the stands. The spectator cannot "foul" because she is not subject to the rules of the game.

Cultural Relativism

Cultural relativism asserts that words such as "right," "wrong," "justice," and "injustice" derive their meaning and truth value from the attitudes of a given culture. Moral concepts, insofar as they possess objectivity, gain legitimacy only through the habits and attitudes of a given culture; in turn, all intercultural comparisons of values are meaningless. For example, it makes no sense to claim that the Western practice of locking thieves up is preferable to the Moslem practice of chopping off their hands. As meaningless claims, *transcultural* comparisons are neither true nor false. Meaningless propositions exist one step below even false propositions, since false propositions may be said at least to possess a truth status, that is, there are conditions under which we can imagine them to be true. Meaningless propositions, however, fail even to possess truth status, and hence from the standpoint of cultural relativism the assertion that the imprisonment of thieves as a social practice is preferable to their mutilation constitutes a claim admitting of neither truth nor falsity. The claim, rather, is akin to the nonsensical proposition that "Green ideas think furiously."[9]

Cultural relativists are able to point to the obvious lack of moral consensus in international affairs. Americans moralize about freedom, Shiite Moslems moralize about the revealed truths of Islam, and both Jews and Palestinians moralize about the right to a home land. Hence, the most common question from nonacademic quarters about integrating values with international policy is simply *whose* values should be integrated? Not only do our values differ from those of other cultures, but we differ among ourselves. Suppose I happen to believe as a moral matter that nation-states ought not interfere with the internal activities of sovereign states—even when those activities are themselves immoral—and someone else does not. Which of us is correct?

Yet a number of important arguments advanced against cultural relativism merit consideration. The first derives from an analysis of the nature of moral language[10] and underscores a conspicuous fact about international disagreements. The conspicuous fact is that those engaged in international discussion often use moral language consciously in an attempt to convince their hearers of the truth of their views. For example, when arguing against the claims of capitalism, Soviet Marxists use moral language replete with words such as "exploitation" and "slavery," while defenders of capitalism accuse Marxists of violating basic "rights" and not treating political dissidents "fairly." They believe their arguments are ultimately intelligible and rationally persuasive; were they convinced that moral language is truly empty, they would speak differently. Now of course, some language users may simply employ moral terminology for its calculated effect; they may simply wish to provoke anger or psychological acceptance from the individuals or countries accused; or, perhaps they wish simply to utter words with an eye to domestic impact, hoping to gain approval from local followers. But often something deeper happens. Often, citizens of one country, whether world leaders or not, talk to citizens of another country in an attempt to *convince* those persons of the correctness of their normative views. A citizen of the United States in 1989, for example, might attempt to convince a Soviet citizen by using reasons and facts that more Jews should be allowed to emigrate to Israel, or attempt to convince a Chinese citizen that social criticism ought never be censored by the state.

The point is that if cultural relativism is correct these individuals cannot even be said to be "arguing" with one another. If moral language is truly empty, the exercise of argument itself would be pure nonsense. No true argument, as such, between representatives of different cultures could occur because an argument requires at least the logical possibility of resolution. An implication of cultural relativism would be that exchanges such as this are merely a series of utterances, attempts, perhaps, to express subjective feelings, or perhaps calculated to achieve a certain psychological effect, but not arguments. A further implication is that the person who finally succeeds in expressing his feelings, or in achieving his psychological effect—even if he has failed to *convince* his hearers—should simply stop talking.

This is what appears to make a moral dispute between one culture and another quite different from the instance in which a soccer referee assigns a spectator a "foul." For in the odd and hypothetical instance of the soccer referee, the referee cannot, unless he is insane, believe that the spectator will be brought on the basis of true facts and good reasons to accept his assignment of "foul": indeed, he will expect just the reverse, knowing that the rules of soccer do not claim "facts" or "reasonableness" for their legitimacy, but only convention. But when a citizen argues with a foreign citizen, she *does* presume that facts and reasons are relevant to judging the matter; she presumes that argument may not be entirely futile, and she hopes that in the end she may be successful in bringing the other to "see" the correct alternative. So by the very logic of international debate, by the very act of language that classifies the convictions of advocates in the global struggle, reference appears to be made to some common, if not absolute, framework for resolving moral disputes. (The argument, of course, is a standard one against the doctrine of emotivism, a doctrine popular in English philosophical circles in the 1930s.

If moral language is nothing more than the expression of emotion, it is asked, then what can be the point of moral argument?)

Let us take a moment to note that some people mistakenly endorse cultural relativism because they confuse it with cultural tolerance. Cultural relativism, however, bears little resemblance to tolerance. If a culture disagrees with the Shiite Moslem practice of having women wear veils, yet owing to its tolerance believes nonetheless that it should refrain from forcing its views on Shiite Moslems, then tolerance counts as a *moral,* not relativistic, value. Suppose the U.S. belief in tolerance leads it to reject the call of U.S. fanatics to employ military force in compelling a Moslem change of custom—even though most U.S. citizens believe the wearing of veils unfairly discriminates against Moslem women. Now certainly a corollary of the U.S. belief is that any country that disagrees, and believes it *should* force a change in custom, is *wrong.* Were the Soviet Union to invade Moslem countries in order to improve the status of women, the U.S. citizenry would, in this instance, deny the moral validity of the Soviet's rationale. Such implications stamp the U.S. defense of tolerance in this instance as inconsistent with cultural relativism. In turn, were a cultural relativist asked whether culture A's belief in tolerance is any better than B's belief that values should be forced down peoples' throats, the relativist would be forced to deny it. The relativist could not endorse tolerance over intolerance.

Another argument against cultural relativism takes the form of a *reductio ad absurdum.* The claim is that virtually no person can live with cultural relativism's severe consequences because consistent cultural relativism demands jettisoning more than naive relativists imagine. Granted, when toying with the prospect of relativism, most are willing to allow that prejudice and custom infect many cultural norms. It is only custom that makes English rules of etiquette requiring, for example, the fork to be used in the left hand, "better" than U.S. rules of etiquette. And one may even argue that it is only prejudice that condemns the practice of polygamy, or the torture of animals (practiced by American Hopi children and accepted by Hopi parents). But for most people the moral buck stops somewhere. Consider two instances of practices once common in "civilized" societies. First-century Romans followed a law under which, if a slave owner was killed by one of his slaves, *all* of his slaves were executed, even ones entirely innocent of the murder, and the law was applied strictly to households of 300 and more slaves. Or consider the practice of Japanese Samurai warriors in earlier centuries. A new sword would be tested by murdering a complete stranger. When the sword had been forged, the Samurai would find a stranger in the road, confront him face to face, and without warning swing the sword down in a diagonal arc. If the sword cut neatly from the side of neck to the waist on the opposite side, it was of adequate quality. If not, it was unfit for a warrior.

Now perhaps some can grit their teeth and declare that however shocking, such practices are not objectively "wrong." It all boils down, they may add, to how one defines "wrong," or perhaps even to how important one thinks it is to discourage murder or test swords. But even such a person as this must be subject to one further test to conclusively establish her relativism. She must be unable to imagine even a single *hypothetical* instance which counts as objectively evil. No limits are placed on the person's imagination; practices may be imagined, for example, that serve no purpose other than mere amusement. In other words, the person must consider the worst practices her most hideous nightmares can concoct.

Now we may predict that most people engaging in the thought-experiment will back down. But what if one or two holdouts remain? What are we to say of a person who thinks, for example, that the torture of babies for mere amusement is not objectively wrong? That the rightness or wrongness of torturing infants for sport is only a matter of cultural taste? Here one may be reminded of Aristotle's answer to the question of how we should respond to a person who refuses to accept the law of noncontradiction. How, the question goes, should we respond to a person who claims to deny the most elementary proposition in logic, the principle that a statement or proposition cannot be both true and not true at the same time and in the same respect. Artistotle's succinct answer is that we should regard such a person as a "vegetable."

If it is true that there are practices which, however hypothetical or unlikely, a reasonable person would regard as wrong no matter *what* the surrounding beliefs system decreed, then cultural relativism cannot be true. For cultural relativism requires the absence of any objective ground whatsoever for morality. Hence it is noteworthy that very few persons indeed—from whatever culture—are willing to accept Draconian practices of the sort we have been describing. Moreover, for most people the line is drawn long before this; for them there exists a fundamental intuition that political torture, the systematic denial of human freedom, and the persecution of the homeless and hungry is wrong no matter where it occurs.

It is not altogether surprising, then, that cultural relativism has fared poorly as a philosophical doctrine. Indeed, one would be hard pressed to name a single recognized contemporary or classical philosopher who espouses it. One can find a great many philosophers defending what might be called "modified relativism," the notion that although some objective cross-cultural points of comparison exist, significant gray areas exist that are best called regions of moral "taste," for which no rational method can give the "right" answer. But, then, most of us allow the intrusion of personal taste into ethics at some point or other. For those who do, but who stop short of cultural relativism, the issue of modified cultural relativism versus nonrelativism is simply that of how broadly one should paint the area of taste in morals. On this interpretation, the salient issue is no longer simply whether any objective cross-cultural comparisons are possible, but how many and to what degree. As should be obvious, modified relativism is actually a form of constrained objectivism rather than genuine relativism.

The central reasons for professional philosophy's rejection of cultural relativism do not lie in some positive defense of absolutism, the doctrine that there are eternal, universal, ethical principles capable of being formulated. The rejection arises from relativism's own failure to defend itself through more than guilt by association. Relativism relies on the fact that cultural norms differ: that sexual customs in the Trobriand Islands are different from those in Sioux City, and that while nepotism may be acceptable in India, it is unacceptable in England. But this can be only the beginning, not the end of the argument. For as Richard Brandt has noted, if cultural relativism were correct, it must not only be true that transcultural disagreements exist, but that each side of a transcultural argument has an equally valid perspective, and, further, that the reason for the equal validity of perspective lies not in the content or relative content of the various views, but in the nature of all transcultural disagreements.[11] Given the ordinary understanding of the expression "equally valid," this would mean showing either that no rational method exists whereby one moral view can be shown to be preferable to another (on moral grounds), or that, if such a method exists, it fails in a trans*cultural* context even as it succeeds in a trans*individual* context. It also means demonstrating that some transcultural ethical disagreements exist such that their resolution cannot be achieved through the resolution of factual misunderstandings.

For example, suppose culture A disagrees with culture B's view that infants should be punished for crying at night. But suppose that culture B is the Apache tribe of earlier centuries, a culture whose nomadic ways and almost constant state of warfare with other tribes meant that a child's cry in the night could doom its members by disclosing the tribe's location to attackers. Culture A may come to agree that, *under factual circumstances similar to that of B's, infants should* be punished for crying at night. Or suppose in another instance that culture A defends the practice of human sacrifice, and B does not. A member of culture A may learn that B practices human sacrifice because it believes that it is necessary to appease the gods, and to prevent the destruction of humankind. Culture A may be willing to grant that if B's factual belief about the gods were true, then human sacrifice would be justified, but it may insist on denying that B's factual belief is true. So in this instance again, if one clears up the factual misunderstanding, the ethical disagreement vanishes. Now if all moral disagreements among cultures turned in this manner on factual disagreements, then making the case for cultural relativism would be impossible. Relativism would be merely a reflection of transcultural factual confusion, not a deeper relativity of values. Hence, it is necessary for the defenders of cultural relativism both to deny such a possibility, and to prove either that no rational method for settling moral disputes exists, or that if one does exist, it is strangely impotent in transcultural contexts.

These tasks, and especially the latter of the two, are sufficiently foreboding that philosophers have generally concluded that cultural relativism—at least in its unmodified form—is intellectually untenable. And, in the absence of serious attempts to undertake these tasks—attempts that we might evaluate and analyze for their validity—we seem forced to agree. In rejecting the claims of cultural relativism for purposes of this book we do not thereby imply that a single, shining code of transnational ethics is possible. Indeed, it is not necessary to assume any potential transcultural agreement beyond a bare ethical minimum—for example, of respect for human life, eschewing indiscriminate torture, and so on. The possibility, hence, shall be left open that the region of "taste," or the region of behavior in which there is no objective right and wrong beyond cultural disposition, encompasses far more than most even imagine. But in rejecting cultural relativism we *do* mean that the doctrine of cultural relativism fails to establish that the international arena exists as a pure moral "free zone." We mean that cultural relativism offers no persuasive reason for seeing the international realm as a moral free-for-all in which anything goes.[12]

Traditional Hobbesianism

The argument of choice for most modern realists is usually the moral theory, or a close copy thereof, of the seventeenth-century philosopher Thomas Hobbes. In contrast to cultural relativism, this defense of realism constitutes an intellectually formidable view with no lack of devotees. Hobbes believed that nations exist in a "state of nature" characterized by the absence of binding moral obligations and the unfettered pursuit of self-interest. Hence, power, not right, must be the operative principle for nations in international affairs just as it is for individuals not yet rescued from their state of nature. But while individuals are capable of escaping their state of nature by establishing a sovereign capable of enforcing rules, nations are captive to their very autonomy: they lack both the ability and the opportunity to establish a world sovereign.[13]

Charles Beitz's distinction regarding the import of Hobbesian theory for international affairs is useful here. The distinction concerns the Hobbesian state of nature analogy, and divides that analogy's "analytical" from its "prescriptive" application.[14] In the analogy's analytical application, empirical predictions are at stake, in particular, the crucial prediction that global actors will not come to develop reliable expectations concerning, for example, treaties, promises, and cooperative institutions. Such cooperation is said to be impossible in the absence of an overarching world authority.[15] But in the analogy's prescriptive application it is moral precepts, not empirical predictions, that are at stake. Here the theory entails both that the moral requirements on action must ultimately find their justification through appeal to agents' rational self-interest, and, closely related to this, that the justification of international norms must occur in terms of the interests of states and not of individuals.[16]

Hobbes believed that in a world lacking a global sovereign, all pacts, promises, and treaties are uncertain and ephemeral. As Terry Nardin writes, "The dilemma of the treaty is thus little different from that of the private contract: it is an *ad hoc* device for reducing uncertainty that is itself uncertain because effective means for authoritatively interpreting its terms and securing their enforcement are lacking."[17] Locke and Rousseau, too, underscore the uncertainty existing in the absence of a systematic enforcer. For Locke, such a situation implies that there is no "umpire" to administer common rules. He writes that "it is a condition in which there may be found elements of society—agreements, transactions, cooperation on the basis of shared interest—but not 'settled standing rules' or 'an established, settled, known law,' impartially applied."[18] Rousseau agrees that permanent law regulating national conduct is impossible in the absence of sanctions: indeed, he calls the very notion a "chimera."[19]

But although traditional Hobbesianism is the principal line of defense for most contemporary realists in international policy, it has been subjected recently to increasing criticism. The view's somber and technically conceived pessimism about international morality— which applies also to international law—strikes many as excessive. They doubt whether the absence of a supreme power to generate and enforce norms automatically invalidates norms themselves. Is it true, for example, as the analytical application suggests, that anticipating arrangements of reciprocal compliance and cooperation is impossible without a world sovereign? As Beitz, Nardin, Kavka, and others have noted this seems *prima facie* to clash with formidable level of cooperation that presently occurs on an international level.[20] For example, international documents such as the Universal Declaration of Human Rights (1948) specify lists of basic rights common to citizens of its signatory nations, and international law plays a significant, if insufficient, role in regulating international affairs.[21]

Further, it is argued that existing international law cannot be understood exclusively through national self-interest, as the prescriptive aspect of the theory claims, for the simple reason that the concept of genuine law refers to a practice that has value in itself apart from the ends it can secure from its participants. If that were not so, they argue, then a shifting of interests might of itself negate law. What individual people or nations want to achieve, even what the majority of them want to achieve, cannot stand as the sole basis of law, and this is the meaning of the ancient maxim "Let justice be done though the heavens may fall." Hence, to make use of a domestic analogy, even if someone could persuade the U.S. judiciary that general interests would be best satisfied by the hanging of an innocent person, or by the FBI's systematic violation of the constitutional right to citizen privacy, law and justice (at least as presently formulated) forbid it. And the same must be true for international law insofar as it is relevantly similar to domestic law: Even if Ayatollah Khomeini in Iran in 1979 believes that the future of the world would be enhanced by violating diplomatic immunity and making captives of American diplomats—even if, God forbid, he happens to be *right* about it—international law properly forbids it. This basis for international law, a basis that allows it to override even collective considerations of international interests, is viewed by many as a reflection of morality itself, expressed in the requirements of legal justice.

Nonetheless, defenders of realism may balk at such reasoning. They assert that it begs the question by defining "international law" in a controversial manner, and then presuming that existing international law fits the definition. Were international law "genuine" law in this sense, then of course it frequently would need to revere principles at the expense of consequences; but whether it is genuine is precisely the issue. What is more, the argument may exaggerate the degree of international cooperation. The sphere of international relations is clearly not so rosy as anti-Hobbesians sometimes want to imagine it. Even if the assumption that human nature and human sociability can be used to derive common norms and interests is correct, world history paints a discouraging picture of international cooperation. As historian Stanley Hoffmann has observed, in many periods in history there simply are no, or very few, common norms or common interests. Furthermore, a significant problem is that each state tends to pursue its *own* interests, not those of other states; and sociability itself, as Rousseau reminds us, can be the source of considerable mischief.[22]

Yet in response to the realist it must be granted that significant cooperation at least sometimes occurs, and it is not always true that the statesman is knocked to the ground whenever his guard is lowered. Although international law may not be "genuine" in the sense of maintaining all the characteristics of its domestic counterpart, it seems clearly to contain within itself the seeds of the distinction between ends and principles necessary to ground a moral conception of justice. This is the point made by Terry Nardin. Nardin grants that the classical interpretation of international law, the idea of nations pursuing common interests in concert, is inadequate to serve as a critique of realism. In turn, he rejects it and introduces a different interpretation that relies on shared values rather than ends.

> International society as such—that inclusive society of states, or community of communities, within which all international association takes place— is not a purposive association constituted by a joint wish on the part of all states to pursue certain ends in concert. It is, rather, an association of independent and diverse political communities, each devoted to its own ends and its own conception of the good, often related to one another by nothing more than the fragile ties of a common tradition of diplomacy. The common good of the inclusive community resides not in the ends that some, or at times even most, of its members may wish collectively to pursue but in the values of justice, peace, security, and coexistence, which can only be enjoyed through participation in a common body of authoritative practices.[23]

Nardin demonstrates that international law consists of more than explicit treaties and agreements. The World Court in The Hague, Netherlands, the various treaties involving the use of the sea and other resources, and similar compacts, he argues, do not exhaust the meaning of "international law." International law also consists in, and depends upon, certain fundamental principles of association, principles discovered in custom where they play the role of moral arbiters and reference points in international affairs. Included among such principles are those of "legal equality [among states], the right to national self-defense, the duties to observe treaties and to respect human rights, the concepts of state sovereignty and non-intervention, and the duty to cooperate in the peaceful settlement of disputes."[24] With background concepts such as these, then, international law may be seen to presume aspects of international morality.

From this vantage point, international law properly interpreted

becomes a means for expressing many of the genuinely moral commitments that ought to, and frequently do, bind nations together in
common practices. Such notions change over time, but they are not
infinitely malleable. Listen to Voltaire describing the practices of international relations of his day: "That the European nations never
make their prisoners slaves; that they respect the ambassadors of
their enemies; that they are agreed concerning the preeminence and
particular rights of certain princes, . . . and that, above all, they are
agreed on the wise policy of preserving, as best they can, an equal
balance of power among themselves."[25]

Even if one doubts Nardin's claims about the force of shared values in contrast to interests as underlying international law, the bare
notion of shared interest is, in itself, probably sufficient to account
for a surprising amount of un-Hobbesian cooperation, and hence to
undo much of Hobbes's analytical pessimism. Hobbes argues that as
forward-looking creatures, vulnerable to the violence of almost any
of their fellows, persons existing in the state of nature will move to
establish not a limited or divided authority, but a sovereign one, that
is, an authority with unlimited power. But an essential drawback, as
Kavka notes, it that this argument fails to explain why the options
for the inhabitants of the state of nature are restricted in this manner. Why are they restricted to either the state of nature or to unlimited sovereignty, and why, in particular, is there no third alternative,
namely, developing defensive pacts with others?[26] Why could not
individuals, states, or organizations existing in a Hobbesian state of
nature join with others in a defensive coalition, thus securing protection for their vital interests without assuming the additional risks
associated with the nearly total abandonment of their rights under
an unlimited sovereign?

At this juncture—especially when considering the issue from the
perspective of shared interests—some modern defenders of traditional Hobbesianism in international affairs have sought refuge in
the concept of the Prisoner's Dilemma, although this is becoming an
increasingly uncertain refuge. The concept of Prisoner's Dilemma
appears to blunt the arguments just offered, and, in turn, to support
Hobbes's pessimism about cooperative strategies short of absolute
subjection, by pointing to noncooperation as the preferred, or rational, strategy for participants in an international state of nature.
But everything turns on whether the state of nature is properly viewed
as a elementary example of Prisoner's Dilemma.

In the Prisoner's Dilemma, the payoffs for each of two players are
determined by the combination of their moves, a consequence over
which neither has complete control.[27] Hence, with the choices for
each player limited to one of two moves, either cooperation or non-

Table 2.1. Prisoner's Dilemma

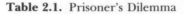

	Person A (payoffs in upper right corners)	
	Cooperate	Defect
Cooperate	3 3	4 1
Defect	1 4	2 2

Person B (payoffs in lower left corners)

cooperation (defection), it follows that four possible payoffs are possible for each player, as indicated in the matrix (Table 2.1).

The dilemma consists in this: whereas the rational move for each player is clearly defection or noncooperation, the outcome for each turns out to be worse than it would have been had each made the irrational move of cooperation.

A pressing question for our purposes is whether the Prisoner's Dilemma accurately describes the situation of persons or organizations in international affairs, for if it does, then given Hobbes's assumption about the inevitably self-interested motives of nations and individuals, the possibility of any cooperative strategy short of submission to absolute authority appears undermined. If the Prisoner's Dilemma is applicable, cooperation is foreclosed in part because, without the all-embracing ability to impose sanctions granted to a sovereign, the cooperation of others is uncertain and depends upon their perception of their self-interest. Gregory Kavka, however, correctly answers that the Prisoner's Dilemma does not apply to international affairs for two reasons: first, because it presumes a single-play, or "uniterated" context, where international events occur in a repeatable, or iterated, context; and second, because it presumes merely two-party rather than multiparty play.[28] In other words, when play is iterated and players know that there will be future games against identical players, the opportunities for cooperation increase; similarly, when many more than two players engage in play, possibilities for coalitions—and hence at least limited cooperation—also increase.

Now in *theory* neither of these considerations may finally defeat the pessimistic conclusion of the Prisoner's Dilemma, but in *practice* the effect especially of iterated play is to encourage cooperation. One reason why pessimism appears justified in theory is the following: suppose that both players understand that the game is to be played again and again for n number of times. Now it is important to see that from the perspective of theory alone, iteration of play in itself may not encourage cooperation. Keep in mind that each player is presumed to know that the other knows that play will be repeated for n number of times, and that the other knows that he knows it, and so on.[29] Kavka explains:

> Given the assumptions of self-interest and rationality, and the dominance of noncooperation on a single play, it follows that a player will cooperate on a given play only if he believes so doing may induce his opponent to cooperate on some later play or plays. Since each party, being rational, knows this, each party knows his opponent will not cooperate on the nth [i.e., last] play. But then each party knows that a cooperative move on the $n-1$st [i.e., the next to the last] play will be to his disadvantage and to the advantage of his opponent. But his opponent, knowing this, will have no reason to cooperate on the $n-2$nd [i.e., the play before the next to the last] play and will not so cooperate. Thus . . . we conclude that each party will make the noncooperative move on every play.[30]

If we add that this general argument can be extended to *multiparty* versions of Prisoner's Dilemma, then we appear to have a argument pointing to the hopelessness, at least in theory, of cooperation in the state of nature.

That nothing of the sort is true in practice is instructive, especially for the prospects of international cooperation. When flesh and blood people are asked to play an iterated Prisoner's Dilemma game, substantial cooperation is achieved. In fact, many players achieve cooperative strategies for most plays in a finite string of plays.[31] But why? As Kavka points out, it probably has little to do with theoretical inadequacies in the argument, and much to do with inevitable inadequacies in human reason as it anticipates the rationality of others. The parties, from the perspective of the argument, must be rational in a dramatic and calculative manner. Each is assumed to follow the line of argument advanced earlier in its full complexity and to believe that each of the others is doing the same. But the assumption that each player can and will predict the absolute rationality of other players is itself irrational, although in this instance the "irrationality" is practical, not formal. It is unrealistic to suppose that real actors will either manifest perfect rationality or suppose its existence in others as a condition for their own deliberation, and, not surprisingly, people frequently fail to do so in the real world.[32] This is at least one explanation of why players often achieve cooperation even in the face of cooperation's theoretical irrationality and why, even if the international political arena were viewed as a Hobbesian state of nature, the existence of cooperative pacts can be explained.

However interpreted, then, Hobbes's state of nature reveals flaws in its conception which give added support to cooperative possibilities. Indeed, it may be that such cooperative possibilities extend both to Nardin's conception of shared, nonpurposive values and to the traditional conception of coordination to achieve shared interests. In any event, the existence of such possibilities undo the analytical claims of traditional Hobbesianism and hence its argument on behalf of realism.

To all of this should be added that Hobbes's own theory includes question-begging assumptions. For example, the statesman is not, as Hobbes would have it, involved in a life or death struggle. The presupposition that survival and security are the exclusive national motives driving international affairs, thus reducing all other considerations to ones of means for national ends, exaggerates matters. Lesser concerns frequently intervene as considerations in their own right, and even when survival or security are at stake, moral questions not only *can* be raised, but more important, *are* raised about the means taken to achieve them.[33] "Does the survival of Israel require reconciliation with the Arabs and insertion in the Middle East—Nahum Goldmann's vision," asks Stanley Hoffmann, "or a tough, annexationist stance—Ben Gurion's vision as long as he was in power?"[34]

And so we are brought to an important conclusion about traditional Hobbesianism. In what has been called its "analytical" application, the state of nature hypothesis fails to predict the actual cooperation that occurs in situations without a sovereign, in particular, the existing international realm. Rather, as we have seen, significant international cooperation is predictable even on the assumption that many international situations approximate the Prisoner's Dilemma.[35] It follows that even if Hobbes were right that morality reduces to mere self-interest, and that in consequence trusting others is often dangerous, the thoroughgoing international pessimism of realism is not justified since the self-interest of states directs them toward cooperative strategies, at least in instances where it is reasonable, if not formally "rational," to predict cooperative attempts by others.

NEO-HOBBESIANISM

Some of Hobbes's admirers have been reluctant to adopt his entire theoretical package, especially his pessimism about international cooperation. Contemporary philosophers David Gauthier and Gregory

Kavka, for example, utilize the essential, ingenious twist Hobbes gave to the analysis of morality and self-interest while denying that it results in international realism. David Gauthier, in particular, offers a striking example of what we may call "Neo-Hobbesianism" in his book *Morals by Agreement*.[36] His view is significant for our purposes because it replaces much of Hobbes's pessimism with optimism, and promises to show how international morality is possible not despite, but because of, Hobbesian considerations.

Relying upon two prominent twentieth-century paradigms, the economist's notion of rationality, and the emerging field of decision theory, Gauthier mounts a new and striking defense of rational prudence. He updates Hobbes by utilizing concepts of "maximizing" and "economic rationality" and argues that moral norms can have transnational application, at least when the term "moral" is construed to include rational principles of self-interested cooperation.[37] Such applications are possible at the international level, he argues, even in the absence of a global sovereign enforcer, since the very presumption against morality entailed by the competitive market concept (the idea that rational agents choose optimally by making direct calculations designed to maximize preference satisfaction) is defeated by adding to that concept the possibility of "contracting" or "agreeing" with one another about constraints on the maximization of individual interests. The title of his book, *Morals By Agreement,* reflects this strategy.

Yet even this novel attempt to generate international ethics from the concept of refined self-interest fails in the end. Gauthier's strategy is to assume the economic model of rationality, a model that ties rationality to anticipated benefit to the reasoner, or to be more precise, to the maximization of utility conceived of as preference satisfaction. The model, then, is used to generate morality, or at least a rational morality—the morality of the economic human being. Morality, almost magically, appears to be extracted from a seemingly nonmoral source. In this story it is a happy accident that the fruits of interaction are significantly great to compel enormous constraints on the actions of individuals. This happens because isolated man is productively impotent without the aid of his fellows.

But a major problem for Gauthier's theory in application to international contexts is that an individual nation is not so impotent as an individual person. In international contexts the fruits of interaction are less certain, and for the first time the possibility that a nation or people may choose simply not to maximize on the basis of an anticipated cooperative surplus is realized. The basis that the fruits of interaction provide, it turns out, is simply too weak to sustain even commonly accepted truisms about international behavior, for ex-

ample, requirements to rescue foreigners from starvation in instances where it costs the rescuing nation virtually nothing, as well
as to refrain from exploiting life and property. (I analyze and clarify
Gauthier's position and argue against it in considerably greater detail in the Appendix.) Interestingly enough, Gauthier himself is driven
in the end to acknowledge the relevance of a morality broader than
the rational, contractarian theory he constructs in *Morals By Agreement*. Hence, Gauthier's neo-Hobbesianism promises to turn the baser
metal of national interest into international morality. Yet while demonstrating the striking extent to which certain forms of international
cooperation can find a rationale in the predictable, albeit refined,
pursuit of self-interest, the alchemy is ultimately unsuccessful.

A related problem—relevant to domestic as well as international
levels—rests in the general Hobbesian assumption that morality is
defensible only to the extent that it coincides with the enlightened
self-interest of rational actors. This is the "prescriptive" rather than
"analytic" side of the Hobbesian question. Both neo-Hobbesians and
traditional Hobbesians thus appear to pull moral rabbits from a rational, self-interested hats. But as with more mundane magic, we
must ask whether what is pulled from the hat is a real rabbit. To put
the matter differently, do the conclusions generated by self-
interested man in the Hobbesian state of nature or in the maximizing models used by Gauthier, add up to real morality? I am per-
suaded that they do not, and while not pretending to prove my point
here, I note that such a view reflects the skepticism of moral common sense in rejecting the idea that morality is fundamentally a matter of calculated self-interest—even when "self-interest" is interpreted through the relatively sophisticated concept of maximizing
one's preferences. Most moral agents do not attribute their reasons
for behaving morally to some happy coincidence that aligns self-interest with moral behavior. This is why even if were we to accept
Adam Smith's vision of a world characterized by a happy parallel
between people's individual interests and the public good, the parallel itself—the "invisible hand"—cannot count as our *reason* for acting morally.

We have examined the two principal realist philosophical strategies, cultural relativism and traditional Hobbesianism, and find that
neither succeeds in barring the application of morality to international affairs. Neither, in short, is successful in defending realism.
This holds true whether defensible "morality" is defined as enlightened self-interest or, as I have implied it should be, something
deeper. We are led to conclude, then, that realism, at least when
understood as the doctrine that morality has no proper application

to international affairs, lacks solid support from each of the two directions most likely to provide it. Accordingly, in the following chapters we shall presume the existence of a moral "space" for international affairs.

What remains is the task of showing more concretely what happens when moral concepts are applied to international affairs, and, in particular, showing the precise form such concepts should take when applied to the new international leviathan, the multinational corporation.

3

The Global Corporation

This chapter will offer an introductory sketch of the theory and practice of the multinational firm. Of necessity it will be a still image of a moving, elusive phenomenon. The sketch will be drawn, moreover, from a moral angle; it highlights the vast powers of multinationals, the existing codes and laws influencing their activities, and the rare theoretical attempts that have been made to understand their ethical responsibilities. Yet it attempts almost no moral analysis. Its aim is descriptive; it is to serve as a preliminary for the moral analysis that will follow.

The multinational corporation has been defined as "a national company in two or more countries operating in association, with one controlling the other in whole or in part."[1] The definition suggests correctly that although global companies are multinational in doing business in more than one country, their composition and character reflects significant uninationality. They are chartered in a single country; typically a majority of their stock is owned by citizens of their home country; and their top managements are dominated by citizens of their home country.

The modern multinational is a product of the post–World War II era. Its dramatic success has stemmed from, among other factors, spiraling labor costs in developed countries, increasing importance of economies of scale in manufacturing, improved communication and transportation systems, and rising worldwide consumer demand for new products.[2] A host of ethical issues has dogged the evolution of the multinational. These fall in at least eight major categories: bribery and corrupt payments, employment and personnel issues, marketing practices, impact on the economy and development of host countries, effects on the natural environment, cultural impacts of multinational operations, relations with host governments, and relations with the home countries.[3]

Such issues are often subtly distinct from similar issues arising in domestic contexts and require global rather than domestic solutions. Consider the issue of bribery and the specific controversy surrounding the United States Foreign Corrupt Practices Act (S.305). The FCPA was passed in 1977 in the wake of the Lockheed bribery scandal, in which Lockheed officers bribed Japanese government for a lucrative plane contract. The FCPA prohibits U.S. corporations from offering or providing payments to officials of foreign governments.[4] Yet whatever U.S. corporate officers happened to think of the ethics of bribery (or "sensitive payments"), they were quick to recognize upon the passing of the FCPA that if they refrain from bribery while their West German, Japanese, and English competitors persist, they are saddled with a stark competitive disadvantage. Legislators who drafted the act hoped that other countries would follow the U.S. lead and establish antibribery acts of their own. But years after passage of the act their hope remained a dream, and U.S. industries continued to suffer from "less ethical" competition. The point is simply that for multinational problems of this kind, effectiveness and fairness require global, not domestic, solutions.

We should not be surprised that multinational activities often spawn ethical controversy. The usually reliable backdrop of national law, the local legal order which tends to ensure a minimum level of compliance for domestic corporations in domestic markets, is missing in the international scene. Domestic law is usually less effective in regulating the activities of home-chartered corporations abroad than at home, and often also is less effective—especially when it is the law of a small, developing country—at regulating the activities of large, foreign multinationals.

Then there is the fact of corporate power. Philosophers note that enhanced power confers enhanced responsibilities, and for this reason it is significant that both critics and defenders of the multinational corporation view it as one of the world's formidable repositories of power. Richard Barnet and Ronald Muller, well-known critics of multinationals, have remarked that the global corporation is the "most powerful human organization yet devised for colonizing the future."[5] And in the same vein, business analyst P. P. Gabriel, writing in the *Harvard Business Review*, has characterized the multinational as the "dominant institution" in a new era of world trade.[6] Such claims reflect the fact that, with the exception of a handful of nation-states, multinationals are alone in possessing the size, technology, and economic reach necessary to influence human affairs on a global basis. National boundaries themselves are often merely doorways to trade for multinationals: IBM operates in 126 countries, communicates in 30 languages, has twenty-three overseas plants, and since 1970 the U.S.-based company has received over one half its total net income from overseas business.

Multinational power is not a wholly new phenomenon. We are reminded of the British East India Company, which hundreds of years ago deployed over forty warships, possessed the largest standing army in the world, was lord and master of an entire subcontinent, had dominion over 250 million people, and even hired its own church bishops.[7] In more recent history, the U.S. company ITT purchased a significant interest in the Focke-Wulf Company a few years before the outbreak of World War II. The Focke-Wulf Company turned out bombers for Hitler's war machine which were used to attack Allied forces shipping throughout the war. Some thirty years later ITT was able to collect 26 million dollars from the U.S. government as compensation for damage done to the Focke-Wulf Company by Allied bombing.[8]

Attributing power to multinationals is not the same as attributing immorality. Power itself is morally neutral. Great power enhances the possibility of effecting great evil, but similarly enhances the possibility of effecting great good. Indeed, it is from the latter perspective that many observers, including the liberal economist John Kenneth Galbraith, see the multinational as the most potent force for world peace and cooperation. This perspective extends the insight of William Robertson in the eighteenth century that "commerce softens and polishes the manners of men."[9] Power may define and enhance certain responsibilities, but it does not decree moral outcomes. In the end, the multinational corporation is probably something less than a savior, and less than a corruptor, but, as mentioned earlier, determining the multinational's worth is not an aim of this book.

Let us analyze multinational power by drawing a distinction between what might be called "first-order" and "second-order" power. First-order power is direct, exercised through a multinational's political or financial strength. Second-order power, in contrast, is indirect, derived from a multinational's organizational know-how, technological prowess, and status as a representative of cultural values or dominant market ideology.

One reason for the extent of first-order multinational power is the relative weakness of national power in certain spheres. George Ball, himself a frequent employee of multinationals, once remarked that the nation-state unfortunately "is a very old fashioned idea and badly adapted to our present and complex world."[10] Nation-states are linked necessarily to specific geographic locations; multinationals are not. Nation-states, especially those with democratic political regimes, are often unwitting victims of the disorganization brought about by attempting to answer a plurality of domestic voices, and their decisions reflect international issues only with difficulty. The multinational firm, in contrast, can plan centrally and act globally. It acts unrestricted by the messy considerations of equity and democracy. Money, not political ideology, empowers its decisions. The power of money in an international environment was recognized by both Adam Smith and Karl Marx.

When we remember that in the United States more than 25 percent of the employees of its largest firms work outside the United States, we realize that even the power of the U.S. government to effect a stable overall employment policy is severely limited. Even attempts by the government to institute monetary policy have been weakened in a multinational economy. In 1986 the U.S. government in concert with the other leading developed nations agreed to devalue the dollar, and it was assumed that the U.S. trade balance would improve because U.S. goods would be relatively cheaper. But by 1988 the value of the dollar relative to a basket of foreign currencies had lost over a third of its value even as the trade balance refused to shrink. This unpredictable result occurred largely because multinationals outside the United States failed to raise the price of goods entering the United States because of their desire to retain market share.

World financial organizations such as the International Monetary Fund (IMF) and the World Bank are disposed to reflect multinational concerns and interests, which also enhances first-order impact. Since the most successful multinationals are based in the countries that shape the voting of the IMF and World Bank, those companies are in the position of having their interests reflected in the very mechanism of the organizational voting process.

Almost by definition, the multinational firm seeks an optimum allocation of its resources on a worldwide basis.[11] This means utilizing all economic advantages, which often includes playing off tax and salary expectations in one country against those in another. Whereas domestic firms must pay for capital and labor at the prevailing national rate, the multinational, other things being equal, pays the lowest rate it can find in the international market.[12] In turn, the restraints that the labor movement once could place on domestic industries have significantly weakened, since multinationals can simply move their manufacturing capacities abroad. Moreover, multinationals are sometimes able to utilize tax havens and to shift income from high-tax to low-tax countries. Bizarre events can occur as a result. In 1971 a loan of 120 million dollars was made to the Nassau Branch of the Fidelity Bank of Philadelphia. It was made despite the fact that the Nassau Branch of the Fidelity Bank of Philadelphia was nothing more than a desk and a telephone.[13]

In addition to its direct, first-order power, a multinational corporation may be said to wield significant second-order power. This
power is indirect, related to its technology, organizational skills, and
status as a representative of the dominant market ideology. For example, it was the organizational skills of the multinational which in
Brazil made U.S. executives the leading sponsors of the Business-
men's Council Brazil-U.S., an organization that was said to have been
the principal representative for many years of the total Brazilian private sector.[14] Similarly, the accounting know-how of the multinational firm allows it to maintain complex records, and to respond
effectively to host country tax initiatives.

But the multinational is more than a locus of specialized skills and
information. It is also, to use Barnet and Muller's memorable phrase,
an "exporter of dreams." From the standpoint of a developing country, the multinational serves as the legitimate representative of the
ideal life-style. By the beginning of the 1970s, the two leading ad-
vertising agencies in the United States, J. Walter Thompson and
McCann Erickson, were earning well over 50 percent of their profits
outside the United States.[15] It is said that shoe-shine boys in Beirut
save their piasters to buy the real thing, Coca-Cola, instead of the
other brands that sell for half the price.[16]

Most evidence suggests that both the first- and second-order power
of the multinational will continue to increase. One reason is that
multinationals often benefit from economic incentives offered by home
governments, such as the foreign tax credit.* Moreover, forces at
work in the international economy push multinationals toward geo-
centricity. "The ultimate modal form of multinationalism if it is allowed to take its own course unhampered by the parochial intervention of nation states," writes Terutomo Ozawa, "is geocentric, the
final stage being one in which the multinational corporation has no
country to which it owes more loyalty than any other, nor any country where it feels completely at home."[17]

The very life cycle of a product helps explain this evolution. In
the beginning a new piece of technology, such as the home computer, is the product of research and development in a developed
economy. Then domestic latecomers enter the market, competing
with the original group of companies. Concurrently, an export market develops in which competing producers are forced to seek other
geographic areas where profit margins are higher. Still later, as profit
margins begin to shrink again, it is necessary to reduce labor costs
by tapping cheaper labor markets in developing countries. Compa-

---

*In the United States the foreign tax credit serves to relinquish U.S. tax on income
earned abroad up to the amount of the foreign tax.

nies such as Zenith simply cannot remain competitive by manufacturing radios and television sets in the United States and avoiding multinationalism. Rather, they are driven to multinationalism by the very forces that underlie the product life cycle.

INTERNATIONAL LAWS, CODES, AND GUIDELINES

The formal responsibilities of multinationals as defined in domestic and international law as well as in codes of conduct are expanding dramatically. While many codes are nonbinding in the sense that noncompliance fails to trigger sanctions, these principles taken as a group are coming to exert significant influence on multinational conduct.

A number of specific reasons lie behind the present surge in international codes and regulations. To begin with, some of the same forces propelling domestic attempts to bring difficult-to-control activities under stricter supervision are influencing multinationals.[18] Consider, for example, hazardous technology, a threat which by its nature recognizes no national boundaries yet must be regulated in both domestic and foreign contexts. The pesticide industry, which relies on such hazardous technology (of which Union Carbide's plant in Bhopal, India, is one instance), in 1987 grossed over $13 billion dollars a year. Pesticide industries are mushrooming, especially in the developing countries.[19] It is no surprise, then, that the rapid spread of potentially dangerous technology has prompted the emergence of international codes on hazardous technology, such as the various UN resolutions on the transfer of technology and the use of pesticides.

Furthermore, just as a multiplicity of state regulations and laws generates confusion and inefficiency and stimulates federal attempts to manage conduct, so too a multiplicity of national regulations stimulates international attempts at control. Precisely this push for uniformity lies behind, for example, many of the international codes of ethics, such as the World Health Organization (WHO) Code of Marketing Breast Milk Substitutes. A well-known case illustrates the need for uniformity. This incident involved the collision of French and U.S. law in the sale of equipment by U.S.-based Dresser Industries to the Soviets for the planned European pipeline. United States law forbade the sale of such technology to the Soviets for reasons of national security while French law (which affected a Dresser subsidiary) encouraged it in order to stimulate commercial growth. It was neither to the advantage of Dresser Industries, nor to the advantage of the French or the U.S. governments, to be forced to operate in an arena of conflict and inconsistency. For months the two governments engaged in a public standoff while Dresser and Dresser's public image were caught in the middle.

National laws, heretofore unchallenged in authority, are now being eclipsed by regulatory efforts. As Lee E. Preston has shown, these efforts fall in four categories: interfirm, intergovernment, cooperative, and world-organizational efforts.[20] The first category of "interfirm" standards reflects initiatives from industries, firms, and consumer groups, and it includes the numerous interindustry codes of conduct for international business, such as the Sullivan Standards for fair business practice in South Africa, the WHO Code on Pharmaceuticals and Tobacco, and the World Intellectual Property Organization's Revision of the Paris Convention for the Protection of Industrial Patents and Trademarks. The second category of "intergovernment" efforts includes specific-purpose arrangements between and among nation-states, such as the General Agreement on Tariffs and Trade (GATT) the IMF, and the World Bank.[21] "Cooperative" efforts, the third category, involve governments and industries in reciprocal arrangements that regulate international commerce. The European Community (EC) and the Andean Common Market (ANCOM) are two notable examples of such cooperative efforts.[22]

Finally, the fourth or "world-organizational" category includes efforts from broad-based global institutions such as the World Court, the International Labor Organization (ILO), the Organization for Economic Cooperation and Development (OECD), and the various subentities of the United Nations. This category is exceptionally varied. For example, OECD guidelines are directed at both private businesses and governments, and the OECD published its *Declaration on International Investment and Multinational Enterprise* in 1976, in which it laid down the so-called national treatment principle which insists upon equal treatment for all businesses in a given nation, regardless of home country. Another world-organizational entity, the International Labor Organization, is, like the World Court, an outgrowth of the defunct League of Nations, although since 1946 it has been formally affiliated with the United Nations. The ILO has 150 member nations and informs its activities through the maintenance of groups of delegates drawn from government, management, and labor. It has over the years generated hundreds of declarations of policy— more than 300 of which remain in place today—and is responsible for more than 5,000 ratifications by governments.[23] Among its more notable contributions are two principles from the ILO's "General Policies" section of the *Tripartite Declaration of Principles Concerning Multinational Enterprises and Social Policy* (1977): namely, its endorsement of "host-country" authority as the locus of legal control and the final arbiter in conflicts between host and home country; and its application of the "national treatment" principle to multinational issues, a principle which, like that promulgated by the OECD, demands equal, noncountry-specific treatment of businesses within a host country context.

Nonetheless, controversy is a hallmark of world organizational efforts, and disagreement constantly arises over the proper interpretation of regulatory principles. The interpretation of the "national treatment" principle is a good example. Some countries complain that a strict interpretation deprives them of the flexibility necessary to construct effective domestic policy. Others defend a strict interpretation as essential for fairness and economic efficiency.

Similarly, controversy has plagued the United Nations and allowed it to achieve only mixed success in international business regulation. On the one hand, insofar as it has contented itself with smaller issues and matters of technical clarification, it has been surprisingly successful. Consider, for example, the many General Assembly actions such as the Law of the Sea Treaty (1982), the Resolution of Restrictive Business Practices (1980), and the Moon Treaty (1980). Projects emanating from its many agencies also have successfully established guidelines in the areas of safety, environmental pollution, ocean shipping, and consumer protection. Yet more ambitious and radical U.N. attempts to regulate international business have failed, largely because they have tended to pit the developed against the developing countries, and to promulgate policies upon which no clear coincidence of interest and ideology exists. The call for a "new international economic order," which demanded substantial transfers of wealth from developed to developing nations, and which has been broadly supported by developing countries since its formal appearance in 1974, serves as the best-known case in point. The developed countries, as might be expected, have staunchly opposed significant transfers of wealth, while the developing countries have demanded them in the name of justice. Similarly, a conflict of ideology and interests has been chiefly responsible for the failure of the United Nations to approve or finalize its long-projected "UN Code of Conduct for Transnational Corporations."[24]

Most world-organizational policies also depend almost exclusively on national government implementation, and this constitutes a serious and sometimes fatal weakness in their application. As the actions of the United States in the conflict during the mid 1980s with the World Court over Nicaragua prove, countries sometimes thumb their noses at international rules when the rules lack the power of sanction. Virtually all of the guidelines of the OECD and the ILO rely exclusively upon the discretion of individual governments (which do possess the power of sanction) for their adoption and implementation. Because of this, even if the United Nations had been successful in adopting its much-touted code for transnational corporations, it is doubtful how extensive international compliance would have been.

Without sanctions and an effective means of interpreting and imposing them, certain types of disputes have lessened chances of resolution. Take, for example, the case investigated by the OECD at the behest of the Belgian government involving a U.S. corporation, Badger, Inc. Badger decided to shut its doors without paying compensation to terminated Belgian employees as required by Belgian domestic law, asserting in its defense that it lacked sufficient funds. Yet Badger (U.S.) is a subdivision of the much larger Raytheon, Inc., a company with a deeper pocket. The Belgian government used Raytheon's deeper pocket as its key argument in making its case against Badger to the OECD. Negotiations between the Belgian government and Raytheon-Badger under the auspices of the OECD finally did lead to small compensation payments from Badger, but most believe that it was political and moral suasion, not the authority of the OECD, that prompted the resolution.

The question of sanctions has affected the definition as well as the application of "law" in international contexts. Because sanctions are regular accompaniments of domestic law, but not of "international law," some critics have come to regard "international law" as a misnomer. For example, the well-known legal theorist of the nineteenth century, John Austin, defines "law" so as to exclude principles without sanctions, and a number of respected twentieth-century theorists have followed suit. A similar issue arises regarding international guidelines affecting multinational corporations: the question is whether those guidelines qualify as "laws" or merely moral "obligations."

From one perspective, the dispute in both its commercial and political manifestation is trivial—a mere matter of words. That is to say, it makes little difference whether one uses the word "law," "obligation," "precept," or whatever, so long as one understands by the concept what other language users understand. Moreover, it is important to note that precepts can often be effective in securing compliance even without explicit sanctions. One of the more important sets of norms governing international conduct, diplomatic protocol, is typically backed neither by sanction nor by formal decree. Its norms include rules governing the treatment of ambassadors and of embassies; they are unconnected even to what the World Court decrees or what signed international documents specify.[25] They concern, rather, what nations operating in the international arena regard as reasonable practice. And, notably, they command almost universal compliance (although exceptions, such as Iran's treatment of U.S. diplomatic hostages in 1979, sometimes occur).

INTERPRETATIONS OF MULTINATIONAL CORPORATE RESPONSIBILITY

Although little writing by business academics confronts issues of international ethics directly, some writers deal with such issues obliquely. The area of research known as "business strategy" intersects frequently with questions of moral relevance. The intersection is predictable since, as one might expect, strategy forces one to prescribe action in a comprehensive and integrated manner, and causes one, in turn, to confront ethical claims.

We may distinguish "nonpolitical" from "mixed" strategic theories. Nonpolitical strategies emphasize economic advantage through the use of economic concepts. Michael Porter's well-known three generic strategies of overall cost leadership, differentiation, and focus fit the "nonpolitical" niche nicely, and much of the debate over international business strategy is cast in precisely such a mode.[26] In contrast, the "mixed" theories entail explicit political strategies and possess greater relevance for moral issues than purely economic ones. As it happens, the "mixed" strategic advice given by business academics to multinational corporations ranges from humanely motivated attempts to incorporate moral thinking into multinational decision making on the grounds of its long-term competitive payoffs, to blatant endorsements of political "hardball." Almost all the "mixed" literature tends to assume that multinational managers are well aware of the existence of political risks of operating in host countries, but that such managers often fail to approach risks systematically.[27] In other words, the assumption is that managers realize that once a company locates in a developing country the rules of the game may be changed, but the managers are confused about what to do about it. This assumption appears justified, and examples of rule switching abound. A well-known example occurred in India when corporate board membership requirements were suddenly altered in the wake of the Bhopal chemical disaster. By changing board membership requirements, the Indian government made it more difficult for Union Carbide and other U.S. companies to predict and limit their potential liability. Representatives of U.S. corporations in India were caught unawares; they were accustomed to the relatively constant pattern of the Securities and Exchange Commission in the United States. With such uncertainties in mind, the "mixed" strategic literature helps executives "manage" risk by isolating relevant variables and proposes

methods for anticipating and responding to risk in practice. Sometimes considerations of an obviously moral nature, such as "good
citizenship" requirements, are advanced on the nonmoral basis that
they will reduce eventual political risk.

In a few instances, however, just the reverse occurs. In what might
be called "crassly political" theories of political strategy, obviously
questionable practices are endorsed on the grounds of competitive
efficiency. For example, J. J. Boddewyn, a professor of international
business at the City University of New York, has asserted that a
"winning strategy of influencing public opinion, lobbying, entering
into alliances with other firms, bribing officials, and other forms of
'political action' . . . is probably legitimate under certain circumstances."[28] In discussing what he calls an "International Political
Strategy" Boddewyn boldly asserts that the guiding principle of such
a philosophy is that "if a firm cannot be a cost, differentiation, or
focus leader, it may still beat the competition on another ground,
namely, the non-market environment." Specific examples of political
behaviors that presumably may attain legitimacy are offered, including an aerospace company bribing foreign government leaders to
secure an order, and a tractor company investing in a less developed
country to obtain a monopoly market position from the government
in return.[29]

The analysis used to support Boddewyn's perspective is distress-
ingly inadequate for anyone trained in moral theory (and, if my intuition is correct, it would shock the moral intuitions of most business academics as well). For example, while granting that the ordinary
conception of "legitimacy" includes law-abiding behavior as well as
conformity to either local values and customs or home country morality, Boddewyn proceeds to observe that "law obedience is to a considerable extent a matter of costs and benefits," and that problems
of cultural relativity make value judgments difficult if not impossible. Boddewyn does grant that the ethical issues surrounding the
"political" strategy he outlines deserve further, and rigorous analysis. But the style of his own analysis is less than rigorous and frequently relies on suggestion and innuendo. At one point, for example, when speaking of business dealings with centrally planned
economies, Boddewyn merely asks rhetorically, "How can protec-
tionism be fought if not through political action—fire with fire—or
even through such illegal marketing behavior as smuggling?"[30]

Most "mixed" strategic literature, however, wisely avoids this approach and offers help in understanding the international backdrop
against which moral problems arise. One well-known study, for example, deftly divides multinationals into three separate strategic

stances, which characterize three distinct kinds of multinational corporations.[31] Properly understood, these stances can be used to derive morally useful insights. The first such stance, employed by the so-called *Multidomestic Multinational,* uses plants in a number of host countries to service the markets that exist in those countries. The vicissitudes of the host country's economic and political environment demand considerable tailoring of the company's activities, and of its product, to the local context, so that significant decision-making authority must be retained at the local level. Often, the company headquarters serves primarily as a financial umbrella for what is, in fact, a series of separate operations.[32] The second, employed by the *Global Multinational,* contrasts with the first by utilizing standardization, economy of scale, and volume to compete in a global competitive environment. Subsidiaries in various countries specialize in production, and each subsidiary obtains from the others what it needs but does not produce. Typically, the overflow from one subsidiary is transferred to another. This form of management requires considerable coordination and hence is integrated and global. Finally, *Administratively Controlled Multinationals* reflect a mixture of the *Multinational* and *Global* strategies. In such a corporation both local and broader economic factors play a role in decision making, without the presence of an explicit, integrating strategy.[33]

Clearly, the strategic status of the multinational, whether it is a multidomestic, global, or administratively controlled corporation, will affect the character of organizational decision making, including decision making with a moral component, undertaken by the company (although to my knowledge no analysis of the moral implications of such strategies has yet been offered). For example, we might infer that a multidomestic firm will not only have a more diverse culture of values than will a global multinational, but it will also receive and process morally relevant information in a different manner. Because a multidomestic firm is forced to adapt more directly to the nuances of the host country environment, one would expect local managers to have a clearer perception of host country cultural values, and, in turn, for the company to have more difficulty formulating a companywide stance on principles for international business. Proctor and Gamble, a multidomestic firm, must have a local management in Nigeria that is in touch with Nigerian attitudes about hair care, eating habits, and hygiene. This demands a more cautious and systematic monitoring of societal habits and mores than would be needed for, say, the motorcycle division of Honda, a global multinational. On the other hand, one would expect Honda to reflect a uniform corporate culture, and a more uniform set of values, than Proctor and Gamble.

Other "mixed" strategy literature is helpful in providing statistical information relevant to ethical issues confronting multinationals. Bribery is a good example. Some research implies that bribery is not only more likely in certain countries, but more likely in certain industries and companies.[34] Other research attempts to predict the likelihood of bribery by determining whether certain managerial philosophies and characteristics are operative in a corporation.[35] Still other research has debated the costs and benefits of bribing in particular circumstances. With regard to the issue of costs and benefits, some researchers assert that the costs of bribery generally outweigh the benefits, citing in support considerations of efficiency in the market, and the backlash of mistrust and cynicism regarding business ethics.[36] Others take the opposite side and claim that red tape, delays, and the prospect of losing multimillion dollar contracts to rival competitors can make bribery cost-effective.[37]

For the moment let us sidestep the substantive issue of bribery (we shall return to this topic in Chapters 5 and 6) to make a critical point about research into ethical issues generally. While enormously helpful, much existing empirical research misses the *normative* dimension. Consider the instance of bribery and the empirical research just discussed. Suppose it should turn out that we could know with certainty that the costs of bribery, at least for some corporations in some situations, fail to outweigh the benefits. Or suppose, instead, that we come upon conclusive evidence showing just the reverse. In either event, would it follow without additional argument that bribery in certain instances is justified? Or that it is *not* justified? No, something more—and of a different sort—would be needed to draw such normative conclusions. What if we could conclusively predict the occurrence of bribery given certain managerial characteristics? Certainly such an ability would be vital in attempting to curb immoral bribery. Yet we should not forget that having such an ability tells us nothing about *what counts* as immoral bribery. This point may be applied broadly to any instance of a purely empirical conclusion. Determining what counts as an immoral practice is a philosophical and normative task that involves, but is not exhausted by, empirical inquiry.

In general, as suggested by the preceding remarks, the research of international business experts succeeds in offering a wealth of strategic and empirical information, but those experts have been somewhat less successful in interpreting the moral implications of their research and in providing an integrated moral view of the multinational. This is not to say that business researchers have failed to do their job, only that empirical research methodology—in which business researchers are experts—is less than omnipotent. Empirical methodology cannot answer each and every question that humans find worth raising. The first step in augmenting a purely empirical perspective of international business is to analyze the moral foundations of the multinational corporation, a task that is the focus of the next chapter.

4

The Moral Foundations
of Multinationals

> Now what I want is, Facts. Teach these boys and girls nothing
> but Facts. You can only form the minds of reasoning animals
> upon Facts.
>
> MR. GRADGRIND, IN DICKENS, *Hard Times*

In Chapter 2 we rejected realism and affirmed the existence of a
moral "space" for international affairs. But in order to make sense
of the responsibilities of corporations operating in such a moral, international space, we must inquire first about the foundations of corporate responsibility in general. For example, is it possible to ground
the moral legitimacy of the corporation? And if so, how?

For present purposes we shall assume that corporations, including
multinational corporations, qualify as moral agents at least in the
minimal sense that they and their actions may sometimes be characterized by moral concepts. Characterizing a corporation as "blame-
worthy" or "morally responsible" is neither a conceptual failure nor
a failure to use moral language properly. We shall also assume that
the responsibilities of multinationals extend beyond merely obeying
the law and maximizing profit. Both propositions are ones that I
have argued for at length elsewhere [1] and they represent dominant
opinion in corporate and business ethics circles.

The principal question here concerns the shape and source of corporate obligations. Granted that corporations *have* obligations, what
form do they take? And what is their grounding?

The usual point of entry to understanding corporate responsibility
is the so-called stakeholder model of corporate social responsibility.
This plain-speaking, normative model views the corporation and especially the managers of the corporation as agents representing the
interests of a variety of constituencies, including but not limited to
shareholders, employees, suppliers, consumers, and members of the

44

general public. The stakeholder model is a genuinely normative, in contrast to empirical, model because it is prescriptive or "action guiding." When provided with reasonable empirical assumptions, this model offers valuable insights. The model reveals that shareholders and other investors are not the only parties with stakes in management's actions, and it holds managers responsible for weighing and balancing the interests of the various stakeholders in their decisions.

The model strikes a blow against corporate Neanderthalism of the kind associated with Milton Friedman. Friedman has written that "there is one and only one social responsibility of business—to increase its profits."[2] (He is willing to add, however, that the corporation must at least stay within the rules of the competitive "game," meaning that it must compete freely and openly without deception or fraud.)[3] And a small but significant minority of business executives continue to espouse such a philosophy—with morally pernicious consequences. The attitude is exemplified by the U.S. corporate raider T. Boone Pickens who once remarked that he is "amused by people who say that if an arbitrager bought a stock an hour ago, he should not have the right to decide what happens to 40,000 employees."[4] The stakeholder model both denies Friedman's myopic view of corporate responsibility and explains why many employees fail to appreciate Pickens's humor. The model states clearly that corporate responsibility cannot be reduced to the interests of a *single* group of stakeholders.

The model's implication that the managerial constituency extends beyond even shareholders and employees gains credence whenever we glimpse the panoramic effects of corporate actions. Corporate decisions do not occur in a social vacuum. For example, when Chevron closed Gulf's Pittsburgh headquarters in the 1980s, it did more than dismiss or transfer 5,800 people. It ravaged the local community. Gulf had given charitable support to fifty local institutions and was supplied by countless local companies.[5]

Despite its important insights, the stakeholder model has serious problems. The two most obvious are its inability to provide standards for assigning relative weights to the interests of the various constituencies, and its failure to contain within itself, or make reference to, a normative, justificatory foundation.

No serious attempt has been made by defenders of the model to devise a principle for making trade-offs between the interests of shareholders, suppliers, employees, consumers, members of the general public, or anyone else who might qualify as a stakeholder. But it is here that the toughest problems of ethics usually emerge. The stakeholder model implies that IBM ought not merely serve the interests of shareholders; it implies that it should do more than focus on maximal return on investment while neglecting the interests of the general public. But we are left wondering how to weigh and balance the interests at stake. Consider the issue of whether IBM should sell its computers to the Chilean government when it believes the government will use the computers to track down and torture political dissidents. Or consider whether the U.S.-based USG Corporation should pay lower wages to nonwhite South African workers (and hence commit an act of racial discrimination) if it believes it will benefit stockholders to do so.* Here it is of little help to note that the interests of Chilean dissidents and of South African nonwhites are relevant to corporate decision making. What we need to know is just *how* relevant they are.

Nor will a simple "utilitarian" calculation, based on the assessments of consequences and indicating which of the available alternative actions will bring about the very best results by maximizing aggregate welfare, solve the problem. In the first place, it is generally agreed among defenders of the stakeholder model that the interests of shareholders are to be given greater weight in the decision making of corporate managers than those of, say, suppliers or members of the general public—and this conflicts with the utilitarian moral premise which asserts that in assessing consequences each person's interests count equally. ("Each person," according to the standard formula, "counts for one and no more than one.") Further, even if some weighing mechanism could be devised that would play the interests of one set of stakeholders off against those of another, morality is often said to involve more than the calculation and weighing of interests. Should we, as managers confronted with whether or not to engage in racial discrimination, *weigh* the interests of South African blacks against those of our stockholders? Should we not, rather, simply refuse to discriminate altogether? This implies the concept of a moral right—in this case the moral right not to be discriminated against—in setting an absolute minimum below which behavior ought not fall.[6]

Furthermore, the stakeholder model lacks any explicit theoretical moral grounding. In the business literature where it flourishes, it is *asserted* as the correct model, and when defended, the defense relies on the empirical assertion that it more accurately describes actual business decision making than alternative "pure" models of economic maximization. But the search for normative insight is not, as I shall explain in more detail shortly, a primarily empirical task. We want to know how the modern manager *ought* to behave, not how he

---

*By the way, USG has been scrupulous in attempting to pay equal pay for equal work in South Africa.

does behave. Perhaps he *ought* to do nothing other than maximize profits; in any event, if we happened to establish conclusively (as empirical evidence strongly suggests) that most managers go beyond merely maximizing profits, that in itself would be insufficient to prove that they *ought* to do so. In fact, it would be insufficient to draw any significant normative conclusion. This explains why the stakeholder model is especially vulnerable to the Friedman-like cynic who denies its conclusion and simply asserts (also without moral argument) that the social responsibility of business is nothing other than, and nothing more than, the maximizing of return on investment for shareholders.

Perhaps the stakeholder model could be fitted with a consequential, or utilitarian, theory that would give it moral grounding.[7] But whatever the prospects of such a project, no such grounding to my knowledge has been provided to date. This is reason to look elsewhere.

THE SOCIAL CONTRACT MODEL

For purposes of either replacing or augmenting the stakeholder model, I wish to recommend a "social contract" approach, one with application both to multinational and domestic corporations. While I have defended this approach in more detail elsewhere, I will offer a brief sketch here.[8] The point of social contract thinking is not to dig up the historical causes of, say, the Sumerian or Egyptian kingdoms. It is, rather, to clarify the proper moral presuppositions of organizational existence. The strategy is to engage people in a thought-experiment that will utilize reason and intuition in a manner calculated to achieve moral insight. The point of applying social contract reasoning to business is to clarify the moral foundations of productive organizations, of which corporations happen to be one kind. As we look at the moral foundations of business, we are to presume that rational individuals living in a state of "nature"—in which everyone produces without benefit of the direct cooperative efforts of others—attempt to sketch the terms of an agreement between themselves and the productive organizations upon which they are considering bestowing status as legal, fictional persons, and to which they are considering allowing access both to natural resources and the existing employment pool.

All productive organizations, then, are viewed as engaging in an implied contract with society, not unlike that employed by Locke, Rousseau, and Hobbes in understanding the moral and political foundations of the state. The raison d'être for the productive organization turns out to be its contribution to society, tempered by a set of reciprocal obligations existing on both sides of the organization/society divide. The principal, although not the sole, reason why members of society should want to have productive organizations rather than a state of nature is the enhanced contribution made possible by productive organizations, organizations in which people combine their labor with others to create a given product or service. The net increase in productivity that results from moving away from individual production is beneficial to social contractors because it promises to enhance the welfare of two overlapping classes of people, namely, those who participate in the productive process (employees) and those who consume its products or services (consumers).

Adam Smith's allegory of the pin factory helps explain why cooperative labor promises to enhance productivity. By specializing and working in concert with others, each person becomes able to produce far more pins than he or she could as an isolated worker. Similarly, by cooperating to produce toasters, space shuttles, scientific experiments, and legal advice, persons working within productive organizations increase greatly their net per capita productivity. This informs, in turn, the productive organization's principal responsibility: to produce efficiently in order to enhance the welfare of employees and consumers. Hence from the standpoint of the social contract, complaints about inefficient U.S. industries, about insulated and entrenched corporate leaders, and about the detrimental effects of trade restraints upon efficiency—whether correct or not—exhibit not only an economic but a moral dimension.

Hypothetical contractors in a state of nature will demand that the obligations of productive organizations extend not only to consumers and employees, but to all those affected by the organization's activities. They will demand, in turn, that corporate activities remain within the boundaries of justice and human rights. This implies that if I own a South African corporation and pay nonwhite workers less than whites for the same work, even if I happen to do it in 1988 when it is legal, I violate the business social contract because I violate the nonwhites' right to nondiscriminatory treatment. Of course, which theory of justice or which list of human rights one embraces may be controversial. But insofar as the business social contract is valid, it cannot be denied that a corporation must respect fundamental human rights, and—which amounts to nearly the same thing—it must accord its activities with principles of justice.

The moral justification for the existence of productive organizations does not directly affect the responsibilities of shareholders because the concept of the productive organization is broader than that of the jointly held corporation. Society would no doubt find it necessary to maintain productive organizations even if they failed to adopt the form of the jointly held, investor-owned corporation; and however immoral a socialistic or communistic society might be for denying the right to own property to its citizens, it, like capitalistic society, will possess productive organizations that have many of the same obligations to society as their capitalistic counterparts.

Rather, to understand why in capitalistic society the social contract demands that managers owe moral duties to shareholders, we must move beyond the general conception of the social contract to examine a different, supplementary source for business responsibility. This source is free agreement in the context of human rights and it generates what we shall call "derivative" obligations. Such "derivative" obligations include personal agreements, specific contracts and laws; these obligations are "derivative" because it is from agreements in the context of certain rights that they take on, or derive, their shape and legitimacy. To illustrate: the rights to private property and freedom, rights that are expressed in one's control over money and goods, constitute an enabling foundation which in the context of a particular agreement generates most of management's duties to shareholders. I own a sum of money. I have a moral right to it, and a moral right—within specific limits—to husband and control it. I then enter into an agreement with a corporation wherein the corporation pledges to manage that money, always attempting to serve my interests by maximizing return on investment. Here it is the moral right to property and freedom, exercised in this instance by the corporation and me, along with the ethical sanctity of promises and contracts, that constitutes the moral foundation of the corporate manager's obligation to pursue my interests, and of the company's obligation incidentally, to reward the manager as agreed.*

An important but utterly different set of derivative duties are those constituted by the laws of society. Our shared right of democratic participation, expressed in the laws that our democratically elected representatives shape and apply, constitute the enabling foundation that underlies the moral validity of the laws of society.

---

*This does not give the manager the right to lie, murder, steal, or violate valid moral rights in her efforts; nor does it give a manager the right to bribe a publicly elected official of the democratic government of a developing country. In addition to the fact that the manager is bound as an individual to respect the rights of others, she, as an agent of the corporation, is bound by the social contract's requirement that all productive organizations both respect rights and limit their actions to the bounds of justice.

All "derivative" duties are more flexible than those generated by the basic form of the business social contract. Whereas the business social contract lays down a minimal floor of responsibility—which is virtually constant over time—derivative duties are almost infinitely plastic. Because they depend upon the substance of agreements, including even political agreements in the form of laws and legislation, their formal range covers the substance of all logically possible agreements that do not violate existing obligations. Barring unusual circumstances, people have a moral as well as a legal duty to obey the law, and thus, for example, managers operating in legal jurisdictions are morally bound to avoid illegal pollution. But were the law to change, they might also be bound to do other things, such as to refuse to collect money for Political Action Committees (PACs), or to hire the hard-core unemployed. Similarly, the agreements that create and legitimate corporations may take many forms: managers of for-profit corporations are morally bound to advance the interests of their shareholders and this means improving or maximizing return on investment (statistical surveys of for-profit shareholders show that shareholders perceive their interests to be almost exclusively aligned with maximizing return on investment). But in the instance of nonprofit corporations such as the Red Cross, managers are bound to serve quite different ends—goals explicitly identified with social welfare. The plasticity of derivative duties is almost unlimited: under hypothetical circumstances we can imagine managers morally obliged to encourage bird watching, to collect elliptical basketballs, or to promote the cause of rock opera.

It is worth noting that although the stakeholder model reflects much of what is contained in the concepts of the social contract and derivative duties, it has difficulty distinguishing between them and thus frustrates the finding of solutions in some practical contexts. By assuming that managers must weigh and balance the interests of a variety of stakeholders (employees, stockholders, suppliers, consumers, and people in the surrounding community), the stakeholder model correctly apprehends the possibility of conflict between, say, a manager's duty to her shareholders and that to her consumers. But consider, for example, the issue of whether management should tolerate noise levels in a Third World plant substantially higher than allowed by First World regulations—levels that over the long term will cause some hearing loss among employees, at least among those unable to wear protective equipment. Assume that the Third World country either has no regulations governing sound levels or has inadequate ones, and that a conflict arises between management's duty to serve shareholders' interests (the interests of one set of stakeholders) and its duty to enhance employees' interests (the interests of another set of stakeholders). We need only assume that long-term profits will be enhanced by tolerating existing noise levels (say, by refusing to install sound-muffling equipment), and that doing so will damage the long-term interests of employees.

Now in such an instance the social contract model would agree with the stakeholder model that a conflict exists between satisfying two sets of interests. But the social contract model proceeds to mark a distinction between the duties at issue, that is, between the social contract-related duties and those that are supplementary and derived. Because the manager's duty to employees in most instances is contract-related, it is formally identical to the duty of any producer to his employees: that is, whether he is a guild tradesman, a manager of IBM, or the inspector at a communal Soviet tractor works, a manager must show concern for his employees' interests and undertake only actions that respect the bounds of rights and justice, for this is how society frames the legitimacy of the organization he manages. On the other hand, a manager's duty to shareholders is for the most part derivative, that is, dependent upon such things as the laws and regulations governing the system in which he operates, the securities laws, the nature of the corporate charter, and the nature of any other agreements struck by him, fiduciary or otherwise, with investors.

The next step, then, is to note that the basic rights denoted in the contract-related duties override derivative duties because they constitute the ground or moral basis for the legitimacy of derivative duties. This happens because, as mentioned earlier, the right of a shareholders to have a corporate manager serve her financial interests is derived from a set of agreements made against the backdrop of such basic rights as the right to own and enjoy private property. That is to say, were the moral right to private property not more fundamental than the duty of the manager to pursue the interests of the shareholder, then the right could not be used to justify the duty. Because the duty is dependent upon the right for its moral legitimacy, it takes a privileged position.

In the noise level case, management's derivative duty to serve shareholders, when considered in isolation, implies refusing to install sound-muffling equipment (assuming that there are no explicit or implied agreements with either shareholders or employees to the contrary). But insofar as the refusal involves the violation of a fundamental right, the problem has an easy solution. For if refusing to install muffling equipment violates the worker's right to physical security (something that appears likely if management anticipates long-term damage to workers' hearing), then as we have seen, the right must be regarded as superseding management's derivative duties. Again, the fundamental rights referred to in the contract-related duties outweigh the derivative duties of managers to shareholders.* It follows that the manager is obliged in this instance to place the interests of employees before those of investors and take steps to reduce or eliminate ear-damaging sound levels. Such an example shows the importance of analyzing multinational situations and isolating the particular types of rights and duties at issue. (Chapter 5 offers a key tool for such analysis, especially in multinational contexts, namely, the concept of a "fundamental international right.")

In analyzing derivative duties it is also important to understand that the "derivative duties" of managers may extend considerably beyond the simple obligation of management to increase shareholders wealth; in addition to explicit duties to shareholders and employees defined in corporate charters, employee agreements, and union contracts, derivative duties can include *implicit* commitments. Employing the economic theorist R. H. Coase's concept of a firm as a substitute for expensive modes of transacting, Cornell and Shapiro argue that a firm's claimants go beyond stockholders and bondholders to include obligations from implied agreements with other groups such as customers and employees.[9] Here the argument is that by entering into an implied agreement, certain persons may make claims based on the derivative obligations implied by the agreement. The authors distinguish between explicit contractual claims that firms issue, such as wage contracts and product warranties, and implicit claims, such as "the promise of continuing service to customers and job security to employees." The distinguishing feature of implicit claims is that they are "too nebulous and state-contingent to reduce to writing at a reasonable cost."[10] For example, Apple Computer introduced the Macintosh in January 1984, promising that a file server would be available in the near future. "Because the [file server] disk was not yet fully developed the costs to Apple of explicitly stating what future characteristics the disk would have were very high. Consequently, Macintosh customers were sold an implicit claim."[11] The authors continue,

> Implicit claims are purchased by other corporate stakeholders as well. . . .
> When a firm hires a new employee, he or she frequently receives promises
> about the work environment, the evaluation process and the opportunity
> for advancement, as well as an explicit employment contract. Similarly,
> managers typically have no formal employment contract, but often per-

---

* It should be confessed, however, that not all practical problems are so easily resolved by invoking the derivative versus contract-related distinction, and certainly not all clearly involve the potential violation of a fundamental right. For example, does firing workers as a mere matter of convenience during an economic downturn necessarily violate a fundamental right?

ceive an implicit contract that guarantees lifetime jobs in exchange for competence, honesty, loyalty, and hard work.

These implicit claims typically do not have legal status and, what is more, cannot be unbundled and sold separately.[12]

Important for our purposes is the fact that certain implicit agreements carry moral weight that influences management decisions. If there are implicit agreements between the corporation and its employees in a developing country, for example, then, although it may not be true that a manager is obliged to honor each and every such agreement to perfection, the implicit agreements constitute significant moral factors in her decisions. Consider, for example, the decision to retain or lay off workers in an economic downturn. If it can be shown that an implicit agreement exists between employees and shareholders under which dismissal is expected by both parties only in the event of personal incompetence or deterioration in a company's profitability, then a decision to dismiss simply as a result of a relatively mild economic downturn must be regarded as unfair.[13]

We should grant, nonetheless, that the most important derivative obligations tend to be explicit ones. Although they include the broad range of contractual and legal arrangements entered into by a firm, including commitments to pension funds, unions, and suppliers, the most notable of such obligations are the fiduciary commitments of managers to shareholders. The not infrequent violations of such agreements by modern managers, through "greenmail," "golden parachutes," shareholders-abusing "shark repellents," and excessive executive perks, then, clearly count as *moral* violations, even if they are not *legal* violations.

APPLYING THE CONTRACT

Let us proceed to highlight the social contract-related obligations relevant to the international context. Clearly the methodology of the social contract is no less relevant to the international than the domestic context. For just as it makes sense to undertake a thought-experiment in which we imagine the members of *our* society living in a state of nature and, in turn, considering the terms under which those members will grant to productive organizations benefits necessary for them to produce efficiently, so too it makes sense to imagine the members of *any* society undertaking such a thought-experiment. If it is reasonable to justify morally the existence of General Motors in the United States in terms of certain implied conditions, then, it is reasonable to interpret the moral existence of Nestle in Switzerland in terms of the same conditions—provided that the conditions are sufficiently neutral from the standpoint of culture. What culture-neutral conditions, then, will be imposed by rational inhabitants of the state of nature upon productive organizations? The following three conditions apply.

1. *That a productive organization should enhance the long-term welfare of employees and consumers in any society in which the organization operates.*

Explanation: Such enhancement is likely to occur through the productive organization's exploiting its peculiar advantages as a productive organization, such as increased efficiency of production. It should be noted that this condition reflects both a fixed and a fluctuating dimension. The fixed dimension is it that it denies to any productive organization the moral right to exist and operate if that organization has a negative long-term welfare effect (a net welfare decrease) for employees and consumers relative to the level hypothetically existing in the state of nature (individual production). The fluctuating dimension is that it demands that even a certain degree of positive long-term welfare enhancement is not sufficient to satisfy the contract. It implies, in other words, that productive organizations are bound morally to strive for higher and higher levels of relative welfare enhancement.

2. *That a productive organization should minimize the drawbacks associated with moving beyond the state of nature to a state containing productive organizations.*

Explanation: From the standpoint of the interests of consumers and the general public, this condition includes minimizing pollution and the depletion of natural resources, as well as minimizing the destruction of personal accountability and the misuse of political power. From the standpoint of the interests of employees, it requires organizations to minimize worker alienation, lack of control over working conditions, and technologically induced monotony and dehumanization.

3. *That a productive organization should refrain from violating minimum standards of justice and of human rights in any society in which it operates.*

Explanation: Theories of rights and of justice vary. Nonetheless it is worth noticing that whether one's theory of justice is Nozickian, Rawlsian, or Sandelian—or, is for that matter any modern, respected theory attempting to define justice—one's theory shares common elements with all of the other theories. While defining the limits of justice may be controversial, justice itself is not an infinitely flexible concept. As mentioned earlier, the next chapter attempts to provide a working consensus on the issue of rights in multinational business through the concept of a "fundamental international right."

For present purposes, perhaps the most important feature of this summary list of corporate responsibilities is the groundwork it provides for the normative analysis later in the book. That analysis will attempt to spell out the duties of multinational corporations in respecting rights in foreign operations. Later chapters will specify *what* it means for a multinational corporation to be moral, based on what is said in this chapter about *why* a corporation should be moral. The analysis of the subsequent chapters must be grounded upon a deep level of justification; it must answer the question "Why be moral?" when directed at a corporation. By demanding that productive organizations honor rights, enhance the welfare of workers and employees, and minimize the drawbacks associated with productive organization, the social contract of this chapter answers that question.

Let me illustrate. Why should a multinational corporation resist the temptation to pay its workers in the Philippines below subsistence level? Now the most immediate answer, and the one that will be provided in Chapter 5, is "Because workers enjoy a right to subsistence." In Chapter 5, an appeal will be made to a fundamental moral principle which, in this instance, takes the form of a right. But then it must be asked, "But why should corporations respect rights at all?" To this question the answer cannot be a simple appeal to rights, for that would be circular. The question asks for something deeper: "Why should a corporation—just the same as an individual person—be rights-respecting at all?" Nor can the answer be simply, "The corporation qualifies as a kind of moral agent," for although we presumed at the outset of this chapter that the corporation is a moral agent of *some* kind, we did not specify *what* kind. We did not, in other words, presume that the corporation is precisely analogous to a human being, and, indeed, we have no warrant to infer (at least without argument) that the duties of individuals *are* identical with the duties of corporations.

Here the social contract frames an answer. A multinational corporation should honor rights because the terms of the contract demand that it honor rights as a condition of its justified existence. That is to say, it is possible through a thought-experiment in which rational contractors are imagined in a state of individual production to see clearly the legitimacy of society's demand that corporations honor rights. And this, in turn, is the final stage of the answer to the question "Why should a multinational corporation resist the temptation to pay its workers in the Philippines wages below subsistence level?" It should resist because *in* so doing it is honoring a right, and honoring valid rights is something it is required to do under the terms of the social contract.

One tangential implication of the social contract should not pass unnoticed. It is that the very concept of a contract implicitly assumes, as Rawls's own hypothetical contract makes explicit, that parties have a right to decide what happens to the fruits of their cooperative endeavors. This implies a right of social self-determination, and constitutes an important consequence of the contract in application to international business. Societies have a right to self-determination, and it is a right implied by and endorsed through the social contract. The contract thus falls in line with (although it is not so broad as) the principle that has gained long-standing acceptance in international political relations: namely, the right of self-determination and concurrent protection from military invasion, even for noble purposes, by other nations.[14]

FICTIONAL CONTRACTS AND REAL OBLIGATIONS

An important avenue of criticism against social contract theory turns on the oddity of deriving *actual* duties from a *hypothetical* contract. It is an obvious criticism trading on the simple distinction between fact and fiction. Over the centuries this criticism has been directed both at the tradition of social contract thinking in general and at specific applications of contract methodology. Recently the criticism has been aimed at my own attempt in *Corporations and Morality* to apply social contract thinking to business, and if correct it would scuttle the conclusions in the foregoing paragraphs.[15]

The criticism questions the contract's existential status. Any social contract, the argument goes, is fiction, not fact; it is an imaginary agreement, an ideal of the imagination, a merely heuristic device. "If metaphysical abstractions impose concrete obligations," one critic writes, "Donaldson could advance his imagery SCB [Social Contract for Business] as a hypothesis about this particular abstraction." But of course metaphysical abstractions do no such thing. Consequently, short of bringing flesh and blood people together to sign an actual pen and ink contract, the social contract for business must "remain a minor heuristic exercise."[16]

Interestingly enough, one can agree with part of this criticism but reach exactly the opposite conclusion. Indeed, as we shall show, if the contract were something *other* than a "fiction," it would be inadequate for the purpose at hand: namely, revealing the moral foundations of productive organizations.

In its most prominent form this criticism applies to any version of the social contract; to that of Hobbes, Locke, Rousseau, and Rawls (all of whom were attempting to understand the foundations of political concepts such as authority and distributive justice), as well as to the business social contract. The strategy of the criticism is to highlight a dilemma: the contract itself must either be a mere heuristic device—something only useful in a process of learning or discovery—or it must exist as an actual agreement. The dilemma, then, lies in asserting that the first alternative provides no basis for maintaining that corporations or political states have genuine obligations, while the second rests on an unsupported existential claim.

Let us grant outright that the "contract" referred to in social contract analysis is not an existing, pen and ink contract. It is not even a tacit, mutually understood, agreement. Indeed, as already suggested, *were* it such a thing, it would fail utterly in its purpose. It would fail because once negotiated, it could no longer lay claim to having exposed the moral foundations of productive organizations. Were it an empirically discoverable contract, then it would count as one existing social arrangement among others, and would, in turn, be subject to further moral evaluation. The underlying point is that existing social arrangements are not *self-validating* from a moral perspective. This amounts to saying that they cannot serve as the last step in a series of moral justifications, or to put it another way, they cannot serve as their *own* moral justification. Even the U.S. Constitution cannot serve as its own moral justification, as the justification for having the particular kind of constitution that it is. Rather, something beyond itself is needed—something like, although perhaps not identical to, Locke's notion of the social contract. For who is to say that any particular existing contract is fair simply because it was agreed to by all existing and interested parties? Existing power disparities may fail—indeed some would say are bound to fail—to yield fair agreements. Think, for example, of the contract that might have been negotiated between sixteenth-century sovereigns and their subjects. Would it have circumscribed even the limits of sovereign power that the Hobbesian social contract lays down—limits that today seem shockingly inadequate?

Some have asserted that an actual and "nonfictional" contract would be self-validating, but only on the condition that it is freely negotiated. Fairness here would be ensured by the freedom of the process, by the absence of coercion of the negotiating parties. The view might explain why the subjects of sixteenth-century sovereigns could not have negotiated fair social contracts; they simply were not free to bargain. The problem here is that to justify such a claim, one would need at a minimum an argument to the effect that freely negotiated contracts are necessarily fair ones, and this argument is suspicious *prima facie* since it entails the counterintuitive conclusion that all freely negotiated contracts in history have been fair. It is a problem similar to the flaw infecting economic notions of Pareto Optimality. By definition, a state is Pareto Optimal if no one can be made better off without making someone else worse off; and as economists have been wont to show, perfectly free exchange generates (with a few assumptions thrown in) a Pareto Optimal state. The catch, however, is that Pareto Optimal states can be truly awful. If, for example, a single person or small group of persons owns all or most of the property in a society, all transactions may be "free," and the state may be Pareto Optimal (the only way the dispossessed will be made better off is through worsening the relative position of the privileged) while at the same time the society reflects a grossly unjust distribution of wealth and other goods. Can one honestly believe that any contract mutually negotiated and acceptable both to the privileged and the poor in such a society would be self-validating?

Let us remind ourselves again, then, of the dilemma that presumably confronts the social contract. The dilemma is that the contract is either a mere heuristic device or it actually exists. What can be shown, however, is that in the most important sense the contract *is* both a heuristic device *and* an "existing" entity—although in keeping with the preceding discussion, we must interpret its existential status quite differently from that of tables and chairs.

What might be meant by saying that the contract is a mere "heuristic device," and why do heuristic devices provide no basis for grounding obligations? Given that heuristic concepts are helpful in making discoveries, perhaps we may view the problem in this manner: the concepts in the social contract are analogous to animal footprints for the hunter; they are useful in tracking and discovery, but sharply distinguishable from the animals themselves. Yet in terms of this analogy, the question then becomes whether one can distinguish the animals of the social contract from their tracks.

The objects of moral inquiry that we are hunting—the concepts to be discovered—are rights and obligations. Now, according to the "heuristic" horn of the dilemma, the social contract may serve as a clue in discovering such rights and obligations, but cannot aspire to any genuine existential status. It cannot contain real obligations within itself, says the criticism, but perhaps it can put us on the trail to a few. The problem, however, is that this criticism assumes that rights and obligations are "real" in some sense in which the social contract is not. It assumes, in other words, that rights and obligations "exist" in some more tangible world than that in which the social contract "exists."

Just how "real" are rights and obligations? Most intellectual historians agree that the term "right" did not appear in print until the sixteenth century as part of the phrase the "rights of Englishmen." (The expression "rights" literally referred to the rights of English *men,* not English women, and was further restricted to those men who were landed property owners.) These and other considerations underscore the fact that rights and obligations possess an existential status quite different from that of tables and chairs. Indeed, if viewed as existing in the material world at all, such moral entities could only be said to exist through participation in specific laws and practices. Nonetheless, when laws and practices fail fully to protect, for example, when they fail to guarantee the values of freedom and tolerance (as, unfortunately, they fail to do in many societies today) we should still want to say that those people without freedom *have* a right to freedom, and those people who persecute their neighbors *have* an obligation to show tolerance. Now the question arises: in what sense are we able to say that a nonwhite in South Africa possesses the right to freedom of expression despite being denied it by the white South African state? Can the black's right be pointed to? Is her inherent right the result of some fair and free agreement? Further, would it be a cogent defense of the South African status quo to say that the black's right simply does not *exist?* Would it be a valid objection to say that since it is not written down or implicitly agreed to by the relevant parties, it therefore can be nothing but a fiction?

Clearly this is nonsense. It is nonsense because fundamental rights, obligations, duties, and liberties, as well as the common good, the general will, the kingdom of ends, the unalienated man, the reasonable man (in the law), equal treatment, cruel and unusual punishment, the social contract, and a host of other fundamentally prescriptive concepts are not descriptive of existing states of affairs at all. If there is any point to G. E. Moore's notorious Naturalistic Fallacy, it is this.[17]

Notions such as that of "reasonable man" in the law, or of a hypothetical "social contract" may be misguided, inconsistent, or dead wrong. These notions may fail to clarify moral problems and, if cognitivists (moral philosophers who believe that ethical judgments are true or false) are correct, these notions may be labeled "false." We can even advance arguments for and against individual concepts being discarded from use altogether. All such concepts may even be fictions of a sort. But, and here is the point, they are not for that reason to be discarded. For if they were not "fictions" in at least one important sense of that term, they could not also qualify as fundamentally prescriptive concepts.

Having said this, let us grant that the notion of a "social contract" is more abstract than the concept of a right or obligation in the sense that it is "analogical." This means that it is an "as if" moral construct: its logical form is "One should behave *as if* such and such were the case." In the present context, this means that the social contract advises individuals and corporations to act *as if* the members of society had agreed to define the rights and obligations of productive organizations in a certain manner. In turn, critics may attack the social contract for being analogical in this sense.

Such a criticism, would be difficult to mount, however, since not only are a host of other analogical moral concepts in use, but analogical concepts need not be simply clues in the business of moral discovery; they need not be merely heuristic tools for discovering nonanalogical concepts.

Let us take these points separately. For the philosopher Immanuel Kant the very notions of God and freedom were analogical concepts.[18] But of course for Kant the notions were not thereby accorded secondary moral status; indeed for him freedom was the sine qua non of morality. Here is another notion employed often by social reformers: the human "brotherhood" or "sisterhood." We are, according to this concept, to treat others, even strangers in distant lands, *as if* they were brothers or sisters. But whether we should or should not, the epistemological point remains: the moral notion of universal brotherhood or sisterhood is not to be undone simply on the grounds that it is analogical. The concept may be excessively ambitious in its expectations for human sentiment; it may be vague or even dead wrong; but if it is to be rejected, it is not rejected simply because it is analogical.

Analogical moral notions may serve as heuristic tools to discover nonanalogical concepts, and a social contract may inform the discovery of rights and obligations. But this is not necessarily the order of moral discovery. We might instead first ask what specific persons' rights or obligations are, and then use our findings to generate the outline of an analogical concept, for example, of a social contract. Indeed, this is Locke's order of discovery when he begins by assuming the existence of certain rights in the state of nature and then proceeds to specify the terms of the social contract.

We may conclude, then, that the dilemma is illusory. The social contract has among its many uses a heuristic function, but this does not preclude speaking of the "existence" of the social contract so long as we are careful to specify the specific sense of existence we have in mind. Moreover, the interpretation of the status of the social contract here is consistent with the main lines of the social contract tradition, and in particular of those versions of the contract offered by Hobbes, Locke, Hume, Rousseau, Kant, and Rawls. As Ernest Barker remarks when discussing the remarkable efficacy and durability of the social contract in history, "Even if there had never been a contract, men actually behaved 'as if' there had been such a thing; and behaving and acting in terms of quasi-contract—or what the lawyers call 'contract implied in law,' an idea which may be extended to cover the case of 'contract implied in government'—they made those terms of quasi-contract serve good and admirable purposes."[19] The point of social contract thinking, again, is not to dig up and describe historical events; it is, rather, to clarify the proper moral presuppositions of institutional power by asking what rational contractors would likely do under certain circumstances. Once the thought-experiment of the contract is complete, one may express the results in various ways: one may speak of the fundamental rights and obligations of the parties involved, or one may speak, and do so without committing moral error, of a tacit moral agreement or "contract" between parties.

We are close to recognizing this when we see that the contract serves as an "ideal." But even the term "ideal" is ill-suited to our task, for it carries too much linguistic baggage. The social contract for business we have been discussing is not an "ideal" in the ordinary sense of the term, for it is not the best possible agreement one can imagine. Were it so, it would need to demand the best efforts that the affected parties could muster, for example, by way of sympathy and charity. Instead, the business social contract is intended only to be a *fair* contract, one that is reasonably just for all parties and which condemns no representative person to systematic unfairness. Productive organizations and society should act *as if* they had struck a deal, the kind of deal that would be acceptable to free, informed parties acting from positions of equal moral authority (one person, one vote); but they are not required by the contract to act as if they were saints.

Critics perform a vital service by raising key ontological and existential puzzles about social contract thinking.[20] Their questions demand answers. Yet talking of a business social contract is not at all like talking of unicorns; and while such talk is prescriptive, and analogical to boot, it is fully meaningful. The language of the business social contract may be perceived as describing a "fiction." But this "fictional" language is in at least one important sense the only means we have for discussing the deeper moral reasons that underlie the existence of business organizations. For if we define fiction to be whatever falls outside the boundaries of empirical reality, then our only route to the independent evaluation of reality is fiction.

MINIMAL AND MAXIMAL DUTIES OF MULTINATIONALS

If multinational corporations may be said to be subject to a social contract, it remains to delineate their responsibilities. This requires at the outset distinguishing between responsibilities that hold as minimal conditions and those that exceed the minimum. Such a distinction is reminiscent of Immanuel Kant's distinction between perfect and imperfect duties. Perfect duties are those owed a specific class of persons under specified conditions, such as the duty to honor promises. They differ from imperfect duties such as the duty of charity which allow considerable discretion as to when, how, and to whom they are fulfilled.[21] But the perfect-imperfect distinction is not wholly appropriate for corporations, since we have already argued that as a productive organization, corporations do not have responsibilities identical to those of individual persons.

For this reason let us instead draw a distinction between "minimal" and "maximal" duties. A minimal duty is a duty of which the persistent failure to observe would deprive the corporation of its moral right to exist. A maximal duty is one whose fulfillment would be praiseworthy but not absolutely mandatory. The distinction, then, is between duties that must be observed in order to preserve a corporation's very moral right to exist, and those whose performance goes beyond this minimum.

Consider, for example, the application of this distinction to multinational corporations in their dealings with developing countries. We assumed for decades that technology allied with ongoing First World investment in the Third World could, even if it did not make everyone well-off, at least satisfy everyone's basic needs. Today that assumption looks increasingly doubtful. A pressing concern, then, is what obligations do multinational corporations have to citizens who are affected by their actions and who live in developing countries.

To give substance to the meaning of "maximal" duties, we have only to look at the increasingly articulate series of requests from developing countries themselves. Some countries have asked corporations to shoulder maximal duties by way of making straightforward donations of resources, capital, and technological expertise to the host economy. Often such requests sound more like a demand for justice than a plea for help, and many speak from the standpoint of what is called the "revolution of rising frustrations."[22] Host nation representatives complain that international trade perpetuates the role of developing countries as producers of raw materials and unsophisticated products, thus reinforcing inferior division of labor relationships. They complain that the price ratio between sophisticated products sold by developed nations and unsophisticated ones sold by developing nations continues to change to the disfavor of the latter. In response, they call for a "New International Economic Order," a call which, as noted earlier, was reflected in a special declaration by the United Nations General Assembly. Reduced to its simplest underlying meaning, it is a request for the transfer of resources from rich to poor nations. It is a call for nations to enhance their economic aid to underdeveloped countries, and for corporations to support needed developmental programs. From the point of view of corporations, it is an appeal at the minimum for special treatment, and at the maximum for economic philanthropy.* Such philanthropy, in contexts where the donating corporation does not expect economic rewards for its efforts, would not count as a "minimal" duty; that is, if it counts as a duty at all, it is a "maximal" duty.

Now at the broadest moral level, it is impossible to doubt the need for an overall transfer of resources. Half of the world's population lives in countries where the per capita annual income is less than $400.[23] In those countries, 15 percent of all children die before reaching the age of five, and those who live often suffer the permanent effects of malnutrition. Almost a billion people, about 800 million are said by respected UN sources to live below standards prescribed by any "rational definition of human decency."[24] Years ago *Fellowship* magazine drew a succinct analogy: "If the world were a global village of 100 people, 70 of them would be unable to read, and only one would have a college education. . . . Over 50 would be suffering from malnutrition. 6 of them would be Americans. These 6 would have one half of the village's entire income." "How," the author asks, "would the wealthy 6 live in peace with their neighbors?"[25] Many people agree with Ronald Muller's statement that "the proposition that developed and underdeveloped countries will get rich together is at best exactly half true."[26] Even with overall global output expanding, many dare hope only that bigger crumbs will be produced by a bigger pie.

But it may be asked whether this implies any *minimal* duties for multinationals. Just as we praise a U.S. corporation's attempt to help clean up a local slum, without regarding the action as a fixed duty, so I suspect we should praise the multinational that attempts to alleviate global economic disequilibrium, without regarding it as a sine qua non of its moral right to exist. Or, to take another example, we should praise the Ford Motor Company's policy in South Africa of providing free legal and financial assistance to employees who are civilly disobedient without demanding the company's actions as the

---

*It is most certainly not a libertarian appeal for the "mutually beneficial changes" endorsed by President Ronald Reagan at the Cancun Summit in the early 1980s.

fulfillment of a minimal duty. Even when such actions are not instances of outright charity and contain overtones of corporate self-interest, they deserve our applause, not our courteous nod. They fall in the class of what I have called "maximal" not "minimal" duties.

The pressing task, thus, is to define acceptable minimal standards for multinationals. In doing so the door must be left open to the possibility that acceptable minimal standards vary over time and in different societal contexts. Today, for example, we should hold corporations to a stricter standard for the sale and distribution of carcinogens than was done in 1900 when little was known about chemicals and cancer.

The most popular moral language in the Western world for establishing minimal obligations, and a language with special appeal in the United States, is that of "rights." It is a language we encountered earlier when spelling out the terms of the social contract. This complex language is, moreover, especially suited to the important task of emphasizing the claims of the individual over that of the collective good. And it is this language that we explore, refine, and apply in the next chapter.[27]

5

Fundamental Rights and Multinational Duties

Child labor, almost eradicated in developed nations, continues to plague developing countries. Though not the worst example, Central America offers a sobering lesson. In dozens of interviews with workers throughout Central America conducted in the fall of 1987, most respondents said they started working between the ages of twelve and fourteen.[1] The work week lasts six days, and the median salary (for all workers including adults) is scarcely over a dollar a day. The area is largely nonunionized, and strikes are almost always declared illegal. There is strong similarity between the pressures compelling child labor in Central America and those in early nineteenth-century England during the Industrial Revolution. With unemployment ranging from a low of 24 percent in Costa Rica, to a high of 50 percent in Guatemala, and with families malnourished and older breadwinners unable to work, children are often forced to make growth-stunting sacrifices.[2]

What obligations, if any, do multinational corporations have in such a context? Chapter 2 demonstrated that international actors cannot claim immunity from morality, and Chapter 3 identified the need to identity the "minimal," rather than the "maximal," duties of multinational corporations. But how are we to conceive such minimal duties? Do they encompass a foreign multinational's obligation to refuse to hire children in a Guatemalan assembly plant, even if doing so harms the company's competitive position? Furthermore, if the duties of multinational corporations are not reducible to those of nation-states and individuals, then how are they different?

This chapter will frame and answer these questions by appeal to the concept of an international human right. After reviewing some of the more important attempts to analyze rights in an international context, I identify ten rights that multinationals are bound to respect, including the minimal duties that must be observed in respecting them. The chapter shows that multinationals are not responsible for honoring international rights in the same manner as nation-states or individuals, and offers guidelines for understanding the varying moral burdens that fall upon different classes of international actors. Multinationals have sometimes failed to honor legitimate moral demands in the past, not because of greed or ill will, but because they lacked a clear vision of their responsibilities.

RIGHTS

Rights establish minimum levels of morally acceptable behavior. One well-known definition of a "right" construes it as a "trump" over a collective good, which is to say that the assertion of one's right to something, such as free speech, takes precedence over all but the most compelling collective goals, and overrides, for example, the state's interest in civil harmony or moral consensus.[3]

Rights are at the rock bottom of modern moral deliberation: Maurice Cranston writes that the litmus test for whether something is a right or not is whether it protects something of "paramount importance."[4] If I have a right to physical security, then you should, at a minimum, refrain from depriving me of physical security (at least without a rights-regarding and overriding reason). It would be nice, of course, if you did more: if you treated me charitably and with love. But you must at a minimum respect my rights. Hence, it will help to conceive the problem of assigning minimal responsibilities to multinational corporations through the question, "What specific rights should multinationals respect?"

Notice that the flip side of a right typically is a duty.[5] This, in part, is what gives aptness to Joel Feinberg's well-known definition of a right as a "justified entitlement to something from someone."[6] It is the "from someone" part of the definition that reflects the assumption of a duty, for without a correlative obligation that attaches to some moral agent or group of agents, a right is weakened—if not beyond the status of a right entirely, then significantly. If we cannot say that a multinational corporation has a duty to keep the levels of arsenic low in the workplace, then the worker's right not to be poisoned means little.

Often, duties fall upon more than one class of moral agent. Consider, for example, the furor over the dumping of toxic waste in West Africa by multinational corporations. During 1988, virtually every country from Morocco to the Congo on Africa's west coast received offers from companies seeking cheap sites for dumping waste.[7] In preceding years, the United States and Europe had become enormously expensive for dumping, in large part because of the costly safety measures mandated by U.S. and European governments. In February of 1988, officials in Guinea-Bissau, one of the world's poorest nations, agreed to bury 15 million tons of toxic wastes from European tanneries and pharmaceutical companies. The companies agreed to pay about 120 million dollars, which is only slightly less than the country's entire gross national product. And in Nigeria in 1987, five European ships unloaded toxic waste containing dangerous poisons such as polyclorinated biphenyls, or PCBs. Workers wearing thongs and shorts unloaded the barrels for $2.50 a day, and placed them in a dirt lot in a residential area in the town of Kiko. They were not told about the contents of the barrels.[8]

Who bears responsibility for protecting the workers' and inhabitants' rights to safety in such instances? It would be wrong to place it entirely upon a single group of agents such as the governments of West African nations. As it happens, the toxic waste dumped in Nigeria entered under an import permit for "non-explosive, nonradioactive and non-self-combusting chemicals." But the permit turned out to be a loophole; Nigeria had not meant to accept the waste and demanded its removal once word about its presence filtered into official channels. The example reveals the difficulty many developing countries have in formulating the sophisticated language and regulatory procedures necessary to control high-technology hazards. It seems reasonable in such instances, then, to place the responsibility not upon a single class of agents, but upon a broad collection of them, including governments, corporate executives, host country companies and officials, and international organizations. The responsibility for not violating the rights of people living in West Africa to be free from the dangers of toxic waste, then, potentially falls upon every agent whose actions might harm, or contribute to harming, West African inhabitants. Nor is one agent's responsibility always mitigated when another "accepts" responsibility. To take a specific instance, corporate responsibility may not be eliminated if a West African government explicitly agrees to accept toxic waste. There is always the possibility—said to be a reality by some critics—that corrupt government officials will agree to accept and handle waste that threatens safety in order to fatten their own Swiss bank accounts.

In wrestling with the problem of which rights deserve international standing, James Nickel recommends that rights that possess international scope be viewed as occupying an intermediary zone between abstract moral principles such as liberty or fairness on the one hand, and national specifications of rights on the other.[9] International rights must be more specific than abstract principles if they are to facilitate practical application, but less specific than the entries on lists of rights whose duties fall on national governments if they are to preserve cosmopolitan relevance. Nickel says little about which criteria should distinguish rights appropriate at the national level from rights appropriate at the international level, except to mention the relevance of a given nation's "historical era." But the difference he has in mind seems obvious: one nation's particular social capacities or social traditions may favor the recognition of certain rights that are inappropriate to other nations. Citizens of a rich, technologically advanced nation, for example, but not of a poor, developing one may be viewed as possessing a right to a certain technological level of health care. A citizen of the United States may have the right to kidney dialysis; a citizen of Bangladesh may not.

As a first approximation, then, let us interpret a multinational's obligations by asking which *international rights* it should respect. We understand international rights to be the sort of moral precepts that lie in a zone between abstract moral principles and national rights specifications. Multinationals, we shall assume, should respect the international rights of those whom they affect, especially when those rights are of the most fundamental sort.

But whose list of fundamental rights shall we choose? Libertarians sometimes endorse well-pruned lists of liberty-centered rights, ones that resemble the first ten amendments to the U.S. Constitution (the Bill of Rights) without the subsequent historical additions. Welfare liberals sometimes endorse lush, intertwined structures that include entitlements as well as freedoms. Who is to say that a given person's list, or a given country's list for that matter, is preferable to another's?

One list receiving significant international attention, a list bearing the signatures of most of the world's nations, is the Universal Declaration of Human Rights.[10] However, it and the subsequent International Covenant on Social, Economic and Cultural Rights, have spawned controversy despite the fact that the Universal Declaration of Human Rights was endorsed by virtually all of the important post–World War II nations in 1948 as part of the affirmation of the U.N. Charter. What distinguishes these lists from their predecessors, and what serves also as the focus of controversy, is their inclusion of rights that have come to be called "social," "economic," "positive," or "welfare" rights. Nuances separate these four concepts, but they need not detain us; all formulations share the feature of demanding more than forbearance from those upon whom the right's correlative duties fall. All four refer to rights that entail claims by rights holders to specific goods, where such goods must at least sometimes be provided by other persons (although sometimes by unspecified others). The goods at issue are typically such things as food, education, and shelter. For convenience, we shall use the term "welfare right" to refer to all claims of this kind. Some international rights documents even specify *as* rights claims to goods that are now regarded as standard benefits of the modern welfare state. For example, Articles 22 through 27 of the Universal Declaration of Human Rights assert rights to social security insurance, employment, protection against unemployment, health care, education, and limits on working hours.[11]

Many have balked when confronted with such lists, arguing that no one can have a right to a specific supply of an economic good. Can anyone be said to have a "right," for example, to 128 hours of sleep and leisure each week? And, in the same spirit, some international documents have simply refused to adopt the welfare-affirming blueprint established in the Universal Declaration. For example, the "European Convention of Human Rights" omits mention of welfare rights, preferring instead to create an auxiliary document ("The European Social Charter of 1961") which includes many of what earlier had been treated as rights as "goals." Similar objections underlie the bifurcated covenants drawn up in an attempt to implement the Universal Declaration: one such covenant, entitled the "Covenant on Civil and Political Rights," was drawn up for all signers, including those who objected to welfare rights, and a companion document, entitled the "Covenant on Economic, Social and Cultural Rights," was drawn up for welfare rights defenders. Of course, many countries signed both; but some signed only the former.[12]

A number of philosophers have offered eloquent defenses of welfare rights, and have used them to analyze the obligations of developed to less developed countries. James Sterba argues that "distant peoples" (for example, people in developing countries) enjoy welfare rights which members of the developed countries are obliged to respect.[13] Welfare rights are defined as rights to whatever is necessary to satisfy "basic needs," needs "which must be satisfied in order not to seriously endanger a person's health and sanity."[14] It is Sterba's principal thesis that the welfare rights of distant peoples and future generations may be justified by the concept of a right of all persons to life and fair treatment.[15] The thesis means—to take only one application—that multinationals are obliged to avoid work place hazards that seriously endanger workers' health.

Henry Shue advances a similar notion, but does so in a far more detailed and comprehensive manner, in his book *Basic Rights*. His analysis has special relevance for our purposes. Shue asserts that his principal purpose is to "try to rescue from systematic neglect within wealthy North Atlantic nations a kind of right that . . . deserves as

much priority as any right: rights to subsistence."[16] The substance
of a basic right is "something the deprivation of which is one standard threat to rights generally," and basic rights include welfare rights.
They include, in particular, the right to subsistence, which Shue defines as a right to "minimal economic security," entailing, in turn, a
right to, for example, "unpolluted air, unpolluted water, adequate
food, adequate clothing, adequate shelter, and minimal preventative
public health care."[17]

The chief examples of basic rights other than a right to subsistence, for Shue, are the rights of freedom of physical movement,
security, and political participation. The right to freedom of physical
movement is a right to not have "arbitrary constraints upon parts of
one's body, such as ropes, chains, . . . and the absence of arbitrary
constraints upon the movement from place to place of one's whole
body, such as . . . pass laws (as in South Africa)."[18] The right to
security is a right not to be subjected to "murder, torture, mayhem,
rape, or assault"; and the right to political participation is the right
to have "genuine influence upon the fundamental choices among
the societal institutions and the societal policies that control security
and subsistence and, where the person is directly affected, genuine
influence upon the operation of institutions and the implementation
of policy."[19] This later concept underlies the cherished idea in the
United States, defended from the Revolutionary War to the present,
that everyone has a right to affect his or her national destiny.

For Shue, the essence of a basic right is its status as a prerequisite
for the enjoyment of other rights. Thus, being secure from beatings
is a prerequisite for the enjoyment of, for example, the right to freedom of assembly, since one's freedom to hold political meetings is
dependent upon one's freedom from the fear of beatings in the event
one chooses to assemble. Shue insists correctly that benevolent des-
potism cannot ensure such basic rights. One's rights are not protected even by the most enlightened despot in the absence of social
institutions that guarantee that basic rights will be preserved in the
event such benevolence turns to malevolence.[20] Illusions, as the saying goes, are not liberties.

Accordingly, Shue considers it a "minimal demand" that "no individuals or institutions, including corporations, may ignore the universal duty to avoid depriving persons of their basic rights."[21]

Shue is no doubt correct in thinking that the seeming "strange-
ness" of welfare rights reflects a blind spot in Western liberalism for
severe economic need. Notably, nowhere does U.S. law affecting foreign policy mention subsistence rights, and though the State Department is required by law to note formally human rights violations, it
resists listing the nonfulfillment of vital needs as rights violations.[22]

Shue's analysis, moreover, provides a formidable argument on behalf of such rights.

His strategy is successful in part because it unpacks the sense in which it is contradictory to support any list of rights without at the same time supporting any specific right upon whose preservation the list can be shown to depend. It is a strategy with direct application to the controversy between defenders and critics of welfare rights, for if he is correct, even a list of *non*welfare rights ultimately depends upon certain basic rights, at least a few of which are welfare rights. His argument utilizes the following, simple propositions:

1. Everyone has a right to something.
2. Some other things are necessary for enjoying the first thing as a right, whatever the first right is.
3. Therefore, every one also has rights to the other things that are necessary for enjoying the first thing as a right.[23]

We can grasp Shue's point more easily by considering on the one hand a standard objection to welfare rights, and on the other, a response afforded by Shue's theory. Many who criticize welfare rights utilize a traditional philosophical distinction between so-called negative and positive rights. A "positive" right is said to be one that requires persons to act positively to *do* something; a "negative" right requires only that people not deprive directly. Hence, the right to liberty is said to be a "negative" right, whereas the right to enough food is said to be a "positive" one. With this distinction in hand, it is common to proceed to make the point that no one can be bound to improve the welfare of another (unless, say, that person has entered into an agreement to do so); rather, at most they can be bound to *refrain* from damaging the welfare of another.

Shue's argument, however, reveals the implausibility of the very distinction between negative and positive rights. Perhaps the most-celebrated and best-accepted example of a "negative" right is the right to freedom. Yet the meaningful preservation of freedom requires a variety of positive actions: for example, on the part of the government it requires the establishment and maintenance of a police force, courts, and the military, and on the part of the citizenry it requires ongoing cooperation and diligent (not merely passive) forbearance. And the protection of another so-called negative right, the right to physical security, necessitates "police forces; criminal rights; penitentiaries; schools for training police, lawyers, and guards; and taxes to support an enormous system for the prevention, detention, and punishment of violations of personal security."[24]

This is compelling. The maintenance and preservation of many nonwelfare rights (where, again, such maintenance and preservation is the key to a right's status as "basic") requires the support of certain basic welfare rights. For example, certain liberties depend upon the enjoyment of subsistence, just as subsistence sometimes depends upon the enjoyment of some liberties. One's freedom to speak freely is meaningless if one is weakened by hunger to the point of silence.

Although it establishes the legitimacy of some welfare rights, Shue's argument is nonetheless flawed. In the first place, from the standpoint of moral logic, his methodology appears to justify the more important in terms of the less important. That is to say, insofar as a basic right is defined as one whose preservation is necessary for the preservation of all rights generally, the determination of what counts as "basic" will occur by a process which takes as fundamental all rights, including nonbasic ones, and then asks which among those rights are rights such that their absence would constitute a threat to the others. Not only does this fail to say anything about the moral grounding of rights in general, it also hinges the status of the basic rights on their ability to support all rights, including nonbasic rights, and this appears to place the justificatory cart before the horse.[25] This problem enlarges when we notice that many of the so-called nonbasic rights such as freedom of speech at least appear to be of equal importance to some so-called basic rights. One is left wondering why a few of the world's most important rights, such as the rights to property, free speech, religious freedom, and education, are regarded as "nonbasic."

Shue himself acknowledges that status as a basic right does not guarantee that the right in question is more important. At one point, while contrasting a nonbasic right, such as the right to education, to a basic right, such as the right to security, he writes, "I do not mean by this to deny that the enjoyment of the right to education is much greater and richer—more distinctively human, perhaps—than merely going through life without ever being assaulted." But he next asserts the practical priority of basic rights by saying, "I mean only that, if the choice must be made, the prevention of assault ought to supersede the provision of education."[26] So while denying that basic rights are necessarily more important than nonbasic ones in all respects, he grants that they are more important in the sense that probably matters most: they are given priority in decisions in which a choice must be made between defending one right and defending another. He concludes, "Therefore, if a right is basic, other, nonbasic rights may be sacrificed, if necessary, in order to secure the basic right."[27]

But what Shue leaves obscure is the matter of which rights *other* than basic rights are deserving of emphasis. For Shue, every right must occupy one of two positions on the rights hierarchy: it is either basic or not. But then how are individuals, governments, and corporations to know which rights should be honored in a crunch? Shue clearly believes that individuals, governments, and corporations must honor *basic* rights, but what of the remaining nonbasic rights? What of the right of freedom of speech, to property, or to a minimal education? And if they are to be recognized as significant, then why? Surely, Shue will agree that all *nation-states* must honor the right to freedom of speech, but is the same true of all individuals and corporations? Does it follow that corporations must tolerate all speech affecting the work place and never penalize offending workers, even when the speech is maliciously motivated and severely damages profitability? And are all *states* similarly responsible for defending *all* other nonbasic rights?

We may seek help in a different direction, this time an attempt to wrestle with the status of international rights made by James Nickel. Nickel helps alleviate the problems arising from Shue's formulas by moving beyond Shue's simple specification of basic rights to the establishment of four conditions that *any* would-be international right must pass:

1. The right must protect something of very great importance.
2. The right must be subject to substantial and recurrent threats.
3. Evidence must be provided that observance of a political right is required for an adequate response to the threats in number 2.
4. The obligations or burdens imposed by the right must be affordable in relation to resources, other obligations, and fairness in the distribution of burdens.[28]

The first condition recognizes that if claims are made to things which have little or only moderate importance, then even if those claims happen to be valid, they cannot aspire to the status of "rights." Again, rights lay down minimal, not maximal, conditions upon the behavior of others, and are allowed to trump even collective social goods. Hence, they refer to goods of critical importance and impose duties that are not to be taken lightly. We are reminded of Maurice Cranston's "paramount importance" test cited earlier for bona fide rights.

Rights, argues Nickel, also must be subject to substantial and recurrent threats (condition number 2). He notes that this is true largely because the list of claims centering on interests of fundamental importance would otherwise expand indefinitely (the would-be right to digest one's food, like many other would-be rights, concerns a matter of fundamental importance, but is seldom threatened). It is worth noting, however, that even without this condition, the list would be eventually cut by the remaining two conditions.[29]

In condition number 3, Nickel asserts that to qualify as a *political* right, that is, one that nation-states are bound to protect, a moral claim against the government should be necessary for countering the threat mentioned in number 2. In some instances, nongovernmental measures may be satisfactory: for example, in a given social context, either self-help or voluntary social action may be adequate to fend off a given threat to a fundamental interest. His view appears to assume that, all other things being equal, less government interference in the lives of citizens is preferable to more. But that things are seldom "equal" in this sense appears to be his personal belief.[30]

In condition number 4, Nickel draws attention to what might be called a "fairness-affordability" criterion by stating that rights must impose obligations or other burdens that are affordable in relation to available resources, and they must be compatible with other genuine obligations. Part of the jurisdiction for this condition, although not articulated by Nickel, appears as simple as the time-honored dictum in moral philosophy that "ought implies can," or, in other words, that no person or entity can be held responsible for doing something if it is not in their power to do it. Nickel's interpretation of "fairness" also adds the reasonable proviso that sometimes a duty may be of a kind that is discouraged for moral reasons, either because it conflicts with another bona fide obligation or because it constitutes an unfairness in the distribution of burdens.

Nickel's explicit purpose in advancing these four conditions is to clarify which purported claims can impose valid obligations upon the governments of nation-states. Because our purpose is different, and because we intend shortly to analyze *corporate*, not *government* obligations, we need to revise Nickel's four conditions.

Nickel's primary concern, again, is with the obligations of nation-states. This makes the application of his third condition problematic for the two other major types of international moral agents, namely, individuals and multinational corporations. By placing governmental obligations in relief, Nickel's condition generates rights that are insufficiently ambitious. The condition eliminates rights whose protection can be assured by voluntary, nongovernment-coerced, behavior on the reasonable presupposition that coercion is an evil, albeit one that can be frequently overridden as a decisive criterion in the establishment of a right. But when asking which rights corporations and individuals ought to observe as a matter of moral obligation, we need not concurrently raise the issue of coercion. Whether individuals and corporations ought not act in ways that violate persons' rights to, say, speak their minds freely, is one thing; whether, given that such a right exists, individuals and corporations ought to be coerced by the government into respecting the right (say, by passing whistle-blowing laws applicable to corporations) is another. The two issues are related but not identical.

The distinction between these two issues relates to the familiar distinction between moral and legal rights. Moral rights exist without the formal endorsement of the law, while legal rights require it. One's moral right to not be enslaved may or may not also be a legal right: in ancient Greece and pre–Civil War United States it was not. And some moral rights perhaps ought not be enforced as *legal* rights: consider a person's right not to be discriminated against on the basis of race by prospective marriage partners. If John Jones decides not to marry Frieda Smith because she is white and he is black, do we want a law court to intervene on Smith's behalf? Should the court either punish Jones or coerce him to marry Smith?*

Because Nickel's third condition is apropos of legal but not of moral rights, and because we shall construct a list of moral rights applicable to all international moral agents, including the three most perspicuous of these—individuals, nation states, and corporations—his condition is irrelevant or our purposes. (If, for example, one wishes to include among the class of international moral agents clans, tribes, groups of elders, etc., then it follows that they too will be subject to the moral rights being defined.) Hence, eliminating the third condition, the revised list reads as follows:

1. The right must protect something of very great importance.
2. The right must be subject to substantial and recurrent threats.
3. The obligations or burdens imposed by the right must satisfy a fairness-affordability test.

Let us further stipulate more precisely for our own purposes what shall be meant by the fairness–affordability test in condition number 3. The affordability part of the test implies that for a proposed right to qualify as a genuine right, all moral agents (including nation-states, individuals, and corporations) must be able under ordinary circumstances, and after receiving any share of charitable help due them, to assume the various burdens and duties that fairly fall upon them in honoring the right. "Affordable" here implies literally being *capable of paying for;* it does not imply that something is necessarily unaffordable because paying for it would constitute an inefficient use of funds, or would necessitate trading off other more valuable economic goods.

---

*Even if we say "no" to this, however, it is worth noting that virtually all the more important legal rights, such as to freedom, property ownership, and personal security, are also moral rights; and, indeed, one of the two rival schools of jurisprudence holds that law is grounded generally, if not in each specific instance, by morality.

This use of the term "affordability" means that—at least under unusual circumstances—honoring a right may be a fundamental moral duty* for a given multinational even when the result is financial loss to the particular firm. For example, it would be "affordable" in the present sense for multinational corporations to employ older workers and to refuse to hire eight-year-old children as full-time, permanent laborers, and hence doing so would be mandatory even in the unusual situation where a particular firm's paying the higher salaries necessary to hire older laborers would result in financial losses. By the same logic, it would probably not be "affordable" for either multinational corporations or nation states around the world to guarantee kidney dialysis for all citizens who need it. This sense of the term also implies that any act of forbearance (of a kind involved in not violating a right directly) is "affordable" for any moral agent.[31] To put the last point another way, I can always "afford" to let you exercise your right to vote, no matter how much money it might cost me.

Turning to the "fairness" side of the test, the extent to which it is "fair" to distribute burdens associated with a given right in a certain manner will be controversial. We assume, however, that for any right to qualify as a genuine right, some "fair" arrangement for sharing the duties and costs among the various agents who must honor the right exists, and that such an arrangement makes it possible (although not necessarily probable) for the right to be enjoyed by most people in most instances.

Next, let us stipulate that satisfying all three of the revised conditions qualifies a prospective right as what we shall call a "fundamental international right," and, in turn, as a right that must be respected by the three major types of international actors: individuals, nation-states, and corporations. This definition does not mean that individuals, nation-states, and corporations must "respect" the rights in precisely the same manner. That is, it does not entail that the correlative duties flowing from the rights are the same for each type of actor.† It entails only that each such actor must "respect" fun-

---

*Not all contractual or legal duties will qualify as "fundamental moral duties" in this sense. Furthermore, fundamental moral duties take precedence over legal or contractual duties. Hence, the duty to forbear from killing the innocent (associated with honoring people's right to physical security) is not to be canceled by one's having signed a contract to kill an innocent person; nor is it to be canceled by a law commanding the killing of innocents.

†Indeed, even for the same actor the duties associated with honoring a right vary depending upon circumstances. My duties to honor your right to physical security when you are drowning 10,000 miles away in the Indian Ocean are minimal or non-

damental international rights in some manner, and that they possess some duties, however minimal, in consequence. Later we shall attempt to specify the particular correlative duties possessed by corporations in contrast to other agents. (Additional "limitation principles" may be necessary to tailor a list of fundamental rights to specific agents.)

THE COMPATIBILITY PROVISO

The "compatibility" proviso presumes that so long as a right satisfies the conditions just outlined, honoring it is compatible with honoring *all other* fundamental international rights. This proviso simplifies our project, for it denies that sacrificial trade-offs must be made between rights, in which right is sacrificed for the sake of honoring another; it also eliminates the need to establish a rights pecking order of the sort that plagues Shue's account.

But, one may reply, do not rights conflict with one another frequently? And if so, what is the point of positing a compatibility proviso? Does not one right sometimes outweigh another right? Does not the storekeeper's right to his property "outweigh" the robber's right to her liberty in instances where the robber is convicted of theft? And are we not justified in locking the robber away?

The compatibility proviso does not preclude the possibility that rights will sometimes conflict in the traditional sense that the impact of one fundamental right must sometimes be weighed against that of another. Certainly we are justified in jailing thieves, but it does not follow that the rights to property and liberty are incompatible. By the compatibility proviso we mean only that rights may be understood in a way that removes the necessity of *abandoning* one right in favor of another. Rights in the context of a legal tradition typically achieve such compatibility through a detailed legislative process in which they are defined with greater and greater specificity. If, for example, vaguely defined rights such as the right to liberty or property are given greater precision, as usually happens in the annals of law, then we may justify the act of jailing a thief without denying the thief's right to liberty. In other words, properly defined, the thief's liberty does not include the right to steal, or even to be at liberty following a theft in the event a properly constituted court of law judges her guilty.

---

existent; but barring unusual circumstances, my duties when you are drowning 10 feet away include throwing you the nearest lifeline.

We reject the view, then, that simply formulated rights, such as the right to liberty or property, exist in some simple, eternal, moral firmament. It is a view sometimes engendered by the "inalienable" and "self-evident" language of the U.S. Declaration of Independence, but is quite at odds with reality. It is an oversimplification that the framers of our government themselves rejected. To say that people possess the right to property or liberty is merely the first step in a moral process which, when asked to interpret a specific instance of conduct, will either appeal to a more detailed and specific phrasing of such a right, or, at a minimum, to a procedure for weighing various rights claims against one another.

By this understanding we thereby bias the process of international rights definition in the direction of more rather than less complexity; but this is not a bad thing. Edmund Burke was not alone in noting the dangerous simplicity inherent in naive views of human rights. Furthermore, in so doing we allow that at the margin it may be impossible for any weighing procedure, or any detailed description of rights—say, in international covenants or international law— to comprehend rights and their application to specific situations with sufficient precision to settle all controversies. But, then, no moral language can aspire to such practical omniscience.

The compatibility thesis is at odds, rather, with any conception of rights that professes impotence in the face of certain practical dilemmas, and which in such dilemmas is forced to resort to the sacrifice of one or more fundamental rights. The conception we reject is, interestingly enough, advanced—though in different forms—by both Shue and Nickel. We remember, for example, Shue's remark that "if a right is basic, other, non-basic rights may be sacrificed, if necessary, in order to secure the basic right."[32]

But why have writers such as Shue and Nickel denied the compatibility thesis? Their reasons lie deeper than an aesthetic preference for generally versus specifically phrased rights. Their reasons are connected to a certain conception—which I hold to be a misconception—about the relationship between traditional and welfare rights. They suppose that in the context of scarce resources, trade-offs must sometimes be made between welfare rights and traditional rights.[33] Nickel, for example, argues that when scarce resources allow for the satisfaction of some among a bundle of competing rights, certain tests must be used to determine whether welfare rights should be abandoned in favor of more traditional, "negative," rights, or vice versa. He sets up, in other words, a potential conflict between supplying bread *and* justice. If, in a South American country, the government can give its population either enough food to eat or political freedom, then it must decide whether to do the former or the latter. This move occurs against the backdrop of Nickel's general belief—shared by Shue—that welfare rights do not automatically possess second-class status in the context of such trade-offs, and that welfare rights have often been given short shrift by political leaders in developing countries.

Yet even granting that welfare rights have been undervalued, the very supposition that trade-offs between bread and justice must occur seems confused.[34] Such a supposition may be accurate when considering marginal analysis problems in microeconomics. But whereas it makes sense to construct problems in which rational decision makers undertake trade-offs between buying books and loaves of bread when constrained by limited incomes, it fails to make sense to construct problems in which nations must make trade-offs between protecting welfare rights and nonwelfare rights. The reason is that the protection of nonwelfare rights—civil and political liberties—is not subject to analysis as a simple "economic commodity." Insofar as the protection of civil and political liberties is subject to economic analysis at all, its cost is anomalous.

Nickel speaks of the relative costs of a system of justice (of police, law courts, and so forth) compared to those of providing adequate nutrition. The argument has a convincing ring when we think of countries such as Chile in 1989. Most of us would have preferred to see fewer helmets of the Chilean police and national guard and more poor Chileans tilling their redistributed plots of land. But we must remind ourselves that in Chile in 1989, as in many poor, authoritarian countries today, the costs of maintaining the military police are often not the costs of maintaining a system of true justice, but of protecting the special interests of a select group of privileged persons. Indeed, the large expenditures for police forces in such countries are usually counterproductive to the cause of justice.

A proper system designed to protect justice is remarkably inexpensive; indeed, it probably has a *negative* cost; that is, its costs in terms of overall national economic resources are sufficiently low that the price of abandoning it is still greater. This should be no surprise. Imagine an underdeveloped country engaged in Nickel's thought-experiment. Imagine that it finally decides—no doubt for bad reasons—to withdraw resources from its legitimate institutions used to protect civil liberties and political rights. It decides, in other words, to shut off funds for trials, for police protection, and for general elections. As a result, disputes between citizens, with no arbitration in courts, would need to be settled by economic power or violence. Because of the absence of police protection, robbery, vandalism, and larceny would escalate even as the class of nonproductively employed thieves, burglars, and con-men also increased.

The absence of fair elections would tend to encourage the elite to garner political and economic power disproportionate to their social or economic contributions, and it would tend to drive others to the destructive alternative of organized revolution. The economic costs alone of abandoning or weakening such civil and political institutions could be staggering. Of course, there are exceptions. Unfair elections may not immediately destabilize society (this seems especially true for countries, like the Soviet Union, with no history of democratic process), and free elections may produce tyrannical leaders, such as Hitler in Germany. But history implies that even in the short term the protection of basic civil and political rights tends to enhance and sustain a country's gross national product, not to retard it. The real problem is not that developing countries are forced because of scarce resources to choose between bread and justice; it is that they find it difficult to protect adequately the specific class of rights known as welfare rights. Whereas the protection of basic liberties and freedoms carries negative short- and long-term economic costs, the same is not necessarily true for welfare rights, whose protection requires considerable initial expenditures for educational institutions, nutritional sustenance, and employment. Even welfare rights probably carry negative economic costs in the long term. But the payoff from such rights is less immediate, and the relatively massive expenditures necessary to secure them in underdeveloped countries can be postponed in a way in which expenditures for police protection and law courts cannot.

Hence, if there are trade-offs to be made between supporting one class of right and another, they are trade-offs to be made between different *welfare* rights in the *short term,* and not in the long term between welfare rights on the one hand and traditional rights on the other. No fundamental right need ever be sacrificed from the perspective of the long term, and neither welfare nor traditional rights need be sacrificed on behalf of the other. This, then, is the meaning of the compatibility proviso.

Support of the compatibility proviso, furthermore, is in line with the logical definition of a right. Rights are usually defined to be more than means toward good ends; to use technical language, they are usually defined as nonutilitarian entities whose justification turns on more than merely assessing consequences in specific situation. They represent not means, but minimal conditions that must be met in moral conduct; they are, to use Ronald Dworkin's expression, "trumps" over collective goals. Because they are minimal conditions, it follows that one ought never sacrifice one kind of right for the sake of another.

FUNDAMENTAL INTERNATIONAL RIGHTS

We are now prepared to identify some of the items that should appear on a list of fundamental international rights, as well as to lay the groundwork for interpreting their application to multinational corporations. To review quickly: we have defined a fundamental international right as satisfying the three conditions that emerged from a revision of Nickel's original list, and which must be respected by all international actors, including nation-states, individuals, and corporations. (We may abbreviate the expression "fundamental international right" to "fundamental right.") The first and second of these conditions concern the need for the right to protect something of great importance, and to be subject to substantial and recurrent threats. The third condition establishes limitations upon the duties associated with the prospective right. We have interpreted this third, "fairness–affordability" condition to mean that for a proposed right to qualify as a genuine right, all moral agents must be able under ordinary circumstances, and after having received any charitable aid due them, to assume the various burdens and duties that fairly fall upon them in honoring the right, and, further, that some "fair" arrangement exists for sharing the duties and costs among the various agents who must honor the right. This arrangement, moreover, must allow the possibility (although not necessarily the probability) that the right will be enjoyed by most people in most instances. In addition a "compatibility proviso" serves to eliminate the need to establish a rights pecking order.

Though probably not complete, the following list contains items that appear to satisfy the three conditions and hence to qualify as fundamental international rights:

1. The right to freedom of physical movement
2. The right to ownership of property
3. The right to freedom from torture
4. The right to a fair trial
5. The right to nondiscriminatory treatment (freedom from discrimination on the basis of such characteristics as race or sex.)
6. The right to physical security
7. The right to freedom of speech and association
8. The right to minimal education
9. The right to political participation
10. The right to subsistence

This is a minimal list. Some will wish to add entries such as the right to employment, to social security, or to a certain standard of living (say, as might be prescribed by Rawls' well-known "difference" principle). Disputes also may arise about the wording or overlapping features of some rights: for example, is not the right to freedom from torture included in the right to physical security, at least when the latter is properly interpreted? We shall not attempt to resolve such controversies here. Rather, the list as presented aims to suggest, albeit incompletely, a description of a *minimal* set of rights and to serve as a beginning consensus for evaluating international conduct. If I am correct, many would wish to add entries, but few would wish to subtract them.

The list has been generated by application of the three conditions and the compatibility proviso. Each reader may decide whether the ten entries fulfill these conditions; in doing so, however, remember that in constructing the list one looks for *only* those rights that can be honored in some form by *all* international moral agents, including nation-states, corporations, and individuals. Hence, to consider only the issue of affordability, each candidate for a right must be tested for "affordability" by way of the lowest common denominator—by way, for example, of the poorest nation-state. If, even after receiving its fair share of charitable aid from wealthier nations, that state cannot "afford" kidney dialysis for all citizens who need it, then the right to receive dialysis from one's nation-state will not be a fundamental international right, although dialysis may constitute a bona fide right for those living within a specific nation-state, such as Japan.

Even though the hope for a definitive interpretation of the list of rights is an illusion, we can add specificity by clarifying the correlative duties entailed for different kinds of international actors. Because by definition the list contains items that all three major classes of international actors must respect, the next task is to spell out the correlative duties that fall upon our targeted group of international actors, namely, multinational corporations.

This task requires putting the "fairness-affordability" condition to a second, and different, use. This condition was first used as one of the three criteria generating the original list of fundamental rights. There it demanded satisfaction of a fairness-affordability threshold for each potential respecter of a right. For example, if the burdens imposed by a given right are not fair (in relation to other bona fide obligations and burdens) or affordable for nation-states, individuals, and corporations, then presumably the prospective right would not qualify as a fundamental international right.*

---

*It is worth noting that fundamental international rights are not the only type of rights. In addition there are legal rights and nation-specific moral rights. For ex-

In its second use, the "fairness-affordability" condition goes beyond the judgment *that* a certain fairness-affordability threshold has been crossed to the determination of *what* the proper duties are for multinational corporations in relation to a given right. In its second use, in other words, the condition's notions of fairness and affordability are invoked to help determine *which* obligations properly fall upon corporations, in contrast to individuals and nation-states. The condition can help determine the correlative duties that attach to multinational corporations in their honoring of fundamental international rights.

As we look over the list of fundamental rights, it is noteworthy that except for a few isolated instances multinational corporations have probably succeeded in fulfilling their duty not to *actively deprive* persons of their enjoyment of the rights at issue. But correlative duties involve more than failing to actively deprive people of the enjoyment of their rights. Shue, for example, notes that three types of correlative duties are possible for any right: (1) to avoid depriving; (2) to help protect from deprivation; and (3) to aid the deprived.[35]

While it is obvious that the honoring of rights clearly imposes duties of the first kind, to avoid depriving directly, it is less obvious, but frequently true, that honoring them involves acts or omissions that help prevent the deprivation of rights. If I receive a note from Murder, Incorporated, and it looks like it means business, my right to security is clearly threatened. If a third party has relevant information which if revealed to the police would help protect my right, it is not a valid excuse for the third party to say that it is Murder, Incorporated, and not the third party, who wishes to kill me. Hence, honoring rights sometimes involves not only duties to *avoid depriving,* but to *help protect from deprivation* as well. Many criticis of multinationals, interestingly enough, have faulted them not for the failure to avoid depriving, but for the failure to take reasonable protective steps.

The duties associated with rights often include ones from the third category, that of *aiding the deprived,* as when a government is bound to honor the right of its citizens to adequate nutrition by distributing food in the wake of a famine or natural disaster, or when the same

---

ample, the right to sue for damages under the doctrine of strict liability (where compensation can be demanded even without demonstrating negligence) is a legal right in the United States, although it would not qualify as a fundamental international right and is not a legal right in some other nation-states. Similarly, the right to certain forms of technologically advanced medical care such as CAT scanning for cancerous tumors may be a nation-specific moral right in highly industrialized countries (even when it is not guaranteed as a legal right) but could not qualify at this point in history as a fundamental international right.

government in the defense of political liberty is required to demand that an employer reinstate or compensate an employee fired for voting for a particular candidate in a government election.

Nonetheless, the honoring of at least some of the ten fundamental rights by multinational corporations requires only the adoption of the first class of correlative duties, that is, only the duty to avoid depriving. The correlative duties for corporations associated with some rights do not extend to protecting from deprivation or to aiding the deprived, because of the "fairness-affordability" condition discussed earlier. (Certain puzzles affecting the application of the fairness-affordability condition are discussed later in the chapter in the context of the "drug lord" problem.)

It would be unfair, not to mention unreasonable, to hold corporations to the same standards of charity and love as human individuals. Nor can they be held to the same standards to which we hold civil governments for enhancing social welfare—since many governments are formally dedicated to enhancing the welfare of, and actively preserving the liberties of, their citizens. The profit-making corporation, in contrast, is designed to achieve an economic mission and as a moral actor possesses an exceedingly narrow personality. It is an undemocratic institution, furthermore, which is ill-suited to the broader task of distributing society's goods in accordance with a conception of general welfare. The corporation is an economic animal; and as noted in Chapter 4, although its responsibilities extend beyond maximizing return on investment for shareholders, they are informed directly by its economic mission.

The "minimal/maximal" distinction from Chapter 4 mirrors the application of the "fairness-affordability" criterion; both imply that duties of the third class, to aid the deprived, do not fall upon for-profit corporations except, of course, in instances in which a corporation itself has done the depriving. Barring highly unusual circumstances,* both distinctions imply that whatever duties cor-

---

*Extraordinary conditions are capable of creating exceptions to the principle. For example, suppose that an earthquake devastates a host country and that thousands of local residents are dying for want of blood. Suppose further that the branch of a multinational corporation happens to possess the means to provide blood on a short-term basis and hence save thousands of lives, while the local government does not. In such an instance, the company may have a minimal duty to aid in the rescue; that is, it may have a correlative duty (correlative to the right of persons to physical security) to aid the deprived. Such exceptions have analogues in the realm of individual action. For example, normally we do not consider helping a particular person in distress a "perfect" duty—a duty that one must perform. Although we may regard helping people in distress a duty, we allow considerable discretion as to when and how the helping occurs. But if one happens to be walking on a lonely mountain trail and discovers a hiker who has slipped and clings precariously to a ledge, it becomes a perfect duty to help short of risking one's own personal security.

porations may have to aid the deprived are "maximal," not "minimal," duties. They are duties whose performance is not required as a condition of honoring fundamental rights or of preserving the corporation's moral right to exist.

The same considerations are relevant when sorting out the specific correlative duties of for-profit corporations according to the fairness-affordability criterion as when distinguishing between minimal and maximal duties. For example, it would be strikingly generous for multinationals to sacrifice some of their profits to buy milk, grain, and shelter for people in poor countries, yet it seems difficult to view this as one of their minimal moral requirements, since if anyone has such minimal obligations, it is the peoples' respective governments or, perhaps, better-off individuals. This is another way of saying that it is an unfair arrangement—and hence would conflict with the fairness-affordability criterion—to demand that multinational corporations, rather than national governments, shoulder such burdens. As noted in Chapter 4, these are maximal, not minimal, duties, and a given corporation's failure to observe maximal duties does not deprive that corporation of its moral right to exist. Furthermore, from our analysis of rights in this chapter—in which we noted that rights impose demands of minimal conduct—it follows that when a corporation fails to discharge a maximal duty to aid the deprived, the failure does not necessarily constitute a violation of someone's *rights*. A corporation's failure to help provide housing for the urban poor of a host country is not a *rights* violation.

The same, however, is not true of the second class of duties, to protect from deprivation. These duties, like those in the third class, are also usually the province of government, but it sometimes happens that the rights to which they correlate are ones whose protection is a direct outcome of ordinary corporate activites. For example, the duties associated with protecting a worker from the physical threats of other workers may fall not only upon the local police, but also to some extent upon the employer. These duties, in turn, are properly viewed as correlative duties of the right—in this instance, the worker's right—to personal security. This will become clearer in a moment when we discuss the correlative duties of specific rights.

Table 5.1 lists correlative duties that reflect the second-stage application of the "fairness-affordability" condition to the earlier list of fundamental international rights. It indicates which rights do, and which do not, impose correlative duties of the three various kinds upon multinational corporations.

A word of caution should be issued for interpreting the table: the first type of correlative obligation, not depriving directly, is broader than might be supposed at first. It includes *cooperative* as well as in-

Table 5.1. Correlative Corporate Duties

Fundamental Rights	Minimal Correlative Duties of Multinational Corporations		
	To avoid depriving	To help protect from deprivation	To aid the deprived
Freedom of physical movement	X		
Ownership of property	X		
Freedom from torture	X		
Fair trial	X		
Nondiscriminatory treatment	X	X	
Physical security	X	X	
Freedom of speech and association	X	X	
Minimal education	X	X	
Political participation	X	X	
Subsistence	X	X	

dividual actions. Thus, if a company has personnel policies that inhibit freedom of movement, or if a multinational corporation operating in South Africa cooperates with the government's restrictions on pass laws, then those companies may be said to actively deprive persons of their right to freedom of movement, despite the fact that actions of other agents (in this example, the South African government) may be essential in effecting the deprivation.[36]

Still, the list asserts that at least six of the ten fundamental rights impose correlative duties upon corporations of the second kind, that is, to protect from deprivation.* What follows is a brief set of commentaries discussing sample applications of each of those six rights from the perspective of such correlative duties.

---

*It is possible to understand even the remaining four rights as imposing correlative duties to protect from deprivation by imagining unusual or hypothetical scenarios. For example, if it happened that the secret police of a host country dictatorship regularly used corporate personnel files in their efforts to kidnap and torture suspected political opponents, then the corporation would be morally obligated to object to the practice and to refuse to make their files available. Here the corporation would have a correlative duty to protect from deprivation the right not to be tortured. The list of rights identified as imposing correlative duties of protection was limited to six, however, on the basis of the fact that their protection is directly related to activities frequently undertaken by corporations in the real world.

SAMPLE APPLICATIONS

Discrimination

The obligation to protect a person from deprivation of the right to freedom from discrimination properly falls upon corporations as well as governments insofar as everyday corporate activities directly affect compliance with that right. Because employees and prospective employees possess the moral right not to be discriminated against on the basis of race, sex, caste, class, or family affiliation, it follows that multinational corporations have an obligation not only to refrain from discrimination, but in some instances to protect the right to nondiscriminatory treatment by establishing appropriate procedures. This may require, for example, offering notice to prospective employees about the company's policy of nondiscriminatory hiring, or educating lower-level managers about the need to reward or penalize on the basis of performance rather than irrelevant criteria.

Physical Security

The right to physical security similarly entails duties of protection. If a Japanese multinational corporation operating in Nigeria hires shop workers to run metal lathes in an assembly factory, but fails to provide them with protective goggles, then the corporation has failed to honor the workers' moral right to physical security (no matter what the local law might decree). Injuries from such a failure would be the moral responsibility of the Japanese multinational despite the fact that the company could not be said to have inflicted the injuries directly.

Free Speech and Association

In the same vein, the duty to protect from deprivation the right of free speech and association finds application in the ongoing corporate obligation not to bar the creation of labor unions. Corporations are not obliged on the basis of human rights to encourage or welcome labor unions; indeed they may oppose them using all morally acceptable means at their disposal. But neither are they morally permitted to destroy them or prevent their emergence through coercive tactics; for to do so would violate their workers' international right to association. The corporation's duty to protect from deprivation the right to association, in turn, includes refraining from lobbying host governments for restrictions that would violate the right in question, and perhaps even to protesting host government measures that do violate it. The twin phenomena of commercial concentration and the globalization of business, both associated with the rise of the multinational, have tended to weaken the bargaining power of labor. Some doubt that labor is sharing as fully as it once did from the cyclical gains of industrial productivity. This gives special significance to the right of free speech and association.

Minimal Education

The correlative duty to protect the right of education may be illustrated through the very example used to open this chapter: the prevalence of child labor in developing countries. A multinational in Central America is not entitled to hire an eight-year-old for full-time, permanent work because, among other reasons, doing so blocks the child's ability to receive a minimally sufficient education. What counts as a "minimally sufficient" education may be debated, and it seems likely, moreover, that the specification of the right to a certain level of education depends at least in part upon the level of economic resources available in a given country; nevertheless, it is reasonable to assume that any action by a corporation which has the effect of obstructing the development of a child's ability to read or write would be proscribed on the basis of rights.

Political Participation

Clearly in some instances corporations have failed to honor the correlative duty of protecting from derpivation the right to political participation. Fortunately, the most blatant examples of direct deprivation are becoming so rare as to be nonexistent. I am referring to cases in which companies directly aid in overthrowing democratic regimes, as when United Fruit Company allegedly contributed to overthrowing a democratically elected regime in Guatemala during the 1950s.

A few corporations continue indirectly to threaten this right by failing to protect it from deprivation, however. Some persist, for example, in supporting military dictatorships in countries in which democratic sentiment is growing, and others have blatantly bribed publicly elected officials with large sums of money. Perhaps the most famous example of the latter occurred in 1972 when the prime minister of Japan was bribed with 7 million dollars by the Lockheed Corporation to secure a lucrative Tri-Star Jet contract. Here, the complaint from the perspective of this right is not against bribes or "sensitive payments" in general, but to bribes in contexts where they serve to undermine a democratic system in which publicly elected officials hold a position of public trust.

Even the buying and owning of major segments of a foreign country's land and industry has been criticized in this regard. As Brian Barry has remarked, "The paranoia created in Britain and the United States by land purchases by foreigners (especially Arabs, it seems) should serve to make it understandable that the citizenry of a country might be unhappy with a state of affairs in which the most important natural resources are in foreign ownership." At what point would Americans regard their democratic control threatened by foreign ownership of U.S. industry and resources? At 20 percent ownership? At 40 percent? At 60 percent? At 80 percent? The answer is debatable, yet there seems to be some point beyond which the right to national self-determination, and national democratic control, is violated by foreign ownership of property.[37]

Subsistence

Corporations also have duties to protect from deprivation the right to subsistence. Consider the following scenario: a number of square miles of land in an underdeveloped country has been used for many years to grow beans. Further, the bulk of the land is owned, as it has been for centuries, by two wealthy landowners. Poorer members of the community work the land and receive a portion of the crop, a portion barely sufficient to satisfy nutritional needs. Next, imagine that a multinational corporation offers the two wealthy owners a handsome sum for the land, because it plans to grow coffee for export. Now *if*—and this, admittedly, is a crucial "if"—the corporation has reason to *know* that a significant number of people in the community will suffer malnutrition as a result, that is, if it has convincing reasons to believe that either those people will not be hired by the company or will not be paid sufficiently if they are hired, or that if forced to migrate to the city they will receive less than subsistence wages (wages inadequate to provide food and shelter), then the multinational may be said to have failed in its correlative duty to protect individuals from the deprivation of the right to subsistence. This is true despite the fact that the corporation would never have stooped to take food from workers' mouths, and despite the fact that the malnourished will, in Samuel Coleridge's words, "die so slowly that none call it murder."

Disagreements: The Relevance of Facts and Culture

The foregoing commentaries obviously are not intended to complete the project of specifying the correlative duties associated with fundamental international rights; they only begin it. Furthermore, here—

as in the matter of specifying specific correlative duties generally—disagreements are inevitable. Take the land acquisition case in the preceding section. One may claim that multinationals are never capable of knowing the consequences of land purchases with sufficient certainty to predict malnutrition or starvation. The issue obviously requires debate. Moreover, one may wish to argue for the moral relevance of predictions about the actions of other agents. If the corporation in question refrains from buying land, will not another corporation rush in with the same negative consequences? And might not such a prediction mitigate the former corporation's responsibility in buying land in the first place? Here both facts and metamoral principles must be weighed.

The same point arises in the context of an even more controversial issue concerning the right to subsistence. Critics have asserted that by promoting and developing high-technology agriculture in developing countries where wealthier farmers are preferred risks for loans to buy imported seeds and fertilizer, multinationals have encouraged the syndrome of land concentration and dependence upon imported food and fertilizer. They assert further that this occurs in situations where proceeds from cash crops are used to buy luxuries for the rich elite, and where poorer farmers must sell their small plots of land and move to the cities. Whether such practices do violate rights is obviously a subject of controversy. What is central to the resolution of such a controversy is the *empirical* question of whether such practices *do* lead to starvation and malnourishment. The problem may be positioned for solution, but it is certainly not solved, by establishing the right to subsistence and its correlative duties: facts remain crucial.

In general, the solution to most difficult international problems requires a detailed understanding not only of moral precepts, but of particular facts. The answer does not appear, as if by magic, simply by citing the relevant rights and correlative duties, any more than the issue of whether welfare recipients in the United States should be required to work disappears by appealing to the government's correlative duty to aid the disadvantaged. In the next chapter, an "ethical algorithm" will be proposed to aid multinational managers in making difficult trade-offs between home and host country values. The algorithm will supplement the account of fundamental international rights offered in this chapter, but neither it nor any other moral theory can draw conclusions when key facts are in dispute. Put simply, when crucial facts are in irreconcilable dispute, so too will be the moral outcome.

It is important to remember that "key" or "crucial" facts are being discussed here. The ten fundamental international rights are not to be eroded in every instance by the old·argument that "we don't have enough facts." Such a defense clearly has its limits, and these limits are overstepped by the demand that evidence be definitive in every sense. An excellent example of excess in this vein is that of cigarette companies who deny that their products are dangerous because we do not yet understand the causal mechanism whereby cigarette smoking is correlated with cancer.

It may be that some of the fundamental rights on our list would not be embraced, at least as formulated here, by cultures different from ours. Would, for example, the Fulanis, a nomadic cattle culture in Nigeria, subscribe to this list with the same eagerness as the citizens of Brooklyn, New York? What list would they draw up if given the chance? And could we, or should we, try to convince them that our list is preferable? Would such a dialogue even make sense?[38]

I want to acknowledge that rights may vary in priority and style of expression from one cultural group to another. Yet in line with the conclusions of the discussion of cultural relativism in Chapter 2, I maintain that the list itself is applicable to peoples even when those peoples would fail to compose an identical list. Clearly the Fulanis do not have to *accept* the ten rights in question for it to constitute a valid means of judging their culture. If the Fulanis treat women unfairly and unequally, then at least one fundamental international right remains unfulfilled in their culture, and their culture is so much the worse as a result.

Three specific rights are especially prone to varying cultural interpretation. These are the right to nondiscriminatory treatment (with special reference to the treatment of women), to political participation, and to the ownership of property. The latter two raise tendentious political issues for cultures with traditions of communal property and nondemocratic institutions. I wish simply to grant that the list has no pretensions to solve these age-old political problems. Though I happen to subscribe to a modified Lockean notion of property in which certain political systems incorporating social ownership violate individual rights, the right to property advanced in our list need not be so narrowly interpreted. It need not, in other words, rule out any instance of public ownership. For example, even primitive societies with communal property practices might be said to recognize a modified version of the right to property if those practices entail mutually agreed-upon, and fairly applied, rules of use, benefit, and liability. The account of rights in this chapter does not presume that each and every instance of public ownership violates the right to own property.

Even so, a point exists beyond which the public ownership of property violates the individual's right to own property. The point is passed when all land and movable property is owned by the state. Is it passed when a country nationalizes its phone systems? Its oil industry? Is that point passed when a primitive culture refuses to subordinate family to individual property? Although it is clear that such questions are of decisive significance, it is equally clear that establishing such a point is a task that cannot be undertaken satisfactorily here.

The same holds for interpreting the right to political participation. I happen to affirm the merits of a democratic electoral system in which representatives are chosen on the basis of one person one vote; yet the list of rights should not be interpreted to demand a photocopy of U.S.-style democracy. For example, one might imagine a small, primitive culture utilizing other fair means for reflecting participation in the political process—other than a representative electoral system—and thereby satisfying the right to political participation.

The Drug Lord Problem

One of the most difficult aspects of the proposed rights list concerns the fairness-affordability condition, a problem we can see more clearly by reflecting on what might be called the "drug lord" problem.[39] Imagine that an unfortunate country has a weak government and is run by various drug lords (not, it appears, a hypothetical case). These drug lords threaten the physical security of various citizens and torture others. The government—the country—cannot afford to mount the required police or military actions that would bring these drug lords into moral line. Or, perhaps, this could be done but only by imposing terrible burdens on certain segments of the society which would be unfair to others. Does it follow that members of that society do not have the fundamental international right not to be tortured and to physical security? Surely they do, even if the country cannot afford to guarantee them. But if that is the case, what about the fairness-affordability criterion?

Let us begin by noting the "affordability" part of the fairness-affordability condition does imply some upper limit for the use of resources in the securing of a fundamental international right (for example, at the present moment in history, kidney dialysis cannot be a fundamental international right). With this established, the crucial question becomes *how* to draw the upper limit. The argument advanced in this chapter commits us to draw that limit as determined by a number of criteria, two of which have special relevance for the present issue: first, compatibility with other, already recognized, international rights; and second, the level of importance of the interest, moral or otherwise, being protected by the right, that is, the first of the three conditions. In terms of the compatibility criterion, we remember that the duties imposed by any right must be compatible with other moral duties. Hence, a *prima facie* limit may be drawn on the certification of a prospective right corresponding to the point at which other bona fide international rights are violated. As for the importance of the right, trade-offs among members of a class of prospective rights will be made by reference to the relative importance of the interest being protected by the right. The right not to be tortured protects a more fundamental interest than, say, the right to an aesthetically pleasing environment.

This provides a two-tiered solution for the drug lord problem. At the first tier, we note that the right of people not to be tortured by the drug lords (despite the unaffordability of properly policing the drug lords) implies that people, and especially the drug lords, have a duty not to torture. Here the solution is simple. The argument of this chapter establishes a fundamental international right not to be tortured, and it is a right that binds all parties to the duty of forbearance in torturing others. For on the first application of the fairness-affordability condition, that is, when we are considering simply the issue of which fundamental international rights exist, we are only concerned about affordability in relation to *any* of the three classes of correlative duties. Here we look to determine only whether duties of *any* of the three classes of duties are fair and affordable, where "affordable" means literally capable of paying for. And with respect to the issue of affordability, clearly the drug lords, just as every other moral agent, can "afford" to refrain from actively depriving persons of their right not to be tortured. They can afford to refrain from torturing. (Earlier in this chapter, the fairness-affordability condition was interpreted to imply that any act of forbearance, of a kind involved in not violating a right directly, is "affordable" for any moral agent.) It follows that people clearly have the fundamental international right not to be tortured, which imposes at least one class of duties upon all international actors, namely the duty of forbearance.

At the second tier, on the other hand, we are concerned with whether the right not to be tortured includes a duty of the government to mount an effective prevention system against torture. Here the fairness-affordability criterion is used in a second application, which helps establish the specific kinds of correlative duties associated with the already-acknowledged-to-exist right not to be tortured. Surely all nation-states can "afford" under ordinary circumstances to shoulder duties of the second and third categories of helping prevent deprivation and of aiding the deprived, although the specific extent of those duties may be further affected by considerations of fairness and affordability. For example, in the instance described in the drug lord problem, it seems questionable that all countries could "afford" to *succeed* completely in preventing torture, and hence the duty to help prevent torture presupposed by a fundamental international right to freedom from torture probably cannot be construed to demand complete success. Nonetheless, a fairly high level of success in preventing torture is probably demanded by virtue of international rights since, as noted earlier, the ordinary protection of civil and political rights, such as the right not to be tortured, carries a negative rather than positive economic cost. We know that the economic cost of allowing the erosion of rights to physical security and fair trial—as an empirical matter of fact—exceeds the cost of maintaining them.

What the list of rights and correlative corporate duties establishes is that multinational corporations frequently do have obligations derived from rights when such obligations extend beyond simply abstaining from depriving directly to actively protecting from deprivation. It implies, in other words, that the relevant factors for analyzing a difficult issue, such as hunger or high-technology agriculture, include not only the degree of factual correlation existing between multinational policy and hunger, but also the recognition of the existence of a right to subsistence along with a specification of the corporate correlative duties entailed.

I have argued that the ten rights identified in this chapter constitute minimal and bedrock moral considerations for multinational corporations operating abroad. Though the list may be incomplete, the human claims that it honors, and the interests those claims represent, are globally relevant. The existence of fundamental international rights implies that no corporation can wholly neglect considerations of racism, hunger, political oppression, or freedom through appeal to its "commercial" mission. These rights are, rather, moral considerations for every international moral agent, although, as we have seen, different moral agents possess different correlative obligations. The specification of the precise correlative duties associated with such rights for corporations is an ongoing task that this chapter has left incomplete. Yet the existence of the rights themselves, including the imposition of duties upon corporations to protect—as well as to refrain from directly violating—such rights, seems beyond reasonable doubt.

6

Multinational Decision Making: Reconciling International Values

Jurisprudence theorists are often puzzled when, having thoroughly analyzed an issue within the boundaries of a legal system, they must confront it again outside those boundaries. For international issues, trusted axioms often fail as the secure grounds of legal tradition and national consensus erode. Much the same happens when one moves from viewing a problem of corporate ethics against a backdrop of national moral consensus to the morally inconsistent backdrop of international opinion. This chapter will examine the subclass of conflicts in which host country norms appear substandard from the perspective of the home country, and it evaluates the claim sometimes made by multinational executives that the prevalence of seemingly lower standards in a host country warrants the adoption by multinationals of the lower standards.

Is a worker justified in appealing to the standards of other countries when complaining about a corporate practice accepted within his or her country? Is a factory worker in Mexico justified in complaining about being paid three dollars an hour when a U.S. factory worker, employed by the same company, is paid ten dollars for the same work?[1] Is the worker justified when in Mexico the practice of paying workers three dollars an hour—and even much less—is widely accepted? Is an asbestos worker in India justified in criticizing the lower standards of in-plant asbestos pollution maintained by a British multinational relative to standards in Britain, when the standards in question fall within Indian government guidelines and, indeed, are stricter than the standards maintained by other Indian asbestos manufacturers?

What distinguishes these issues from ordinary ones about corporate practices is that they involve a conflict of norms, either moral or
legal, between home and host country. We shall be concerned specifically with cases of the following form:

> A multinational company adopts a corporate practice which is morally
> and/or legally permitted in the company's *host* country, but not in its *home*
> country.

We shall see that although an appeal to international rights (as specified in Chapter 5) frequently helps to interpret such conflicts, nonetheless, in certain key instances the strategy is ineffective. This chapter's aim is to design a conceptual test, or ethical algorithm, for
multinationals to use in distinguishing justified from unjustified applications of standards. As the chapter will attempt to show, the
presence of lower standards in the host country does sometimes justify the multinational company's adopting the lower standards, but
only in certain well-defined contexts.

If a company is a multinational rather than a national corporation,
then one may wonder why home country opinion should be a factor
in the multinational company's decision making. One reason derives
from an observation, made in Chapter 3, that although global companies are multinational in doing business in more than one country,
they lean toward uninationality in composition and character. And
while leading multinationals now rely increasingly on foreign nationals to lead host country operations, and while it is true, as also noted
in Chapter 3, that the evolution of interindustry, intergovernment,
and world-organizational codes of conduct tends to blur the home-
host distinction in some contexts, that distinction remains a formidable bench mark for moral deliberation. It is important to acknowledge, for example, that the moral presuppositions of managers at
corporate headquarters—the underlying assumptions of the top
managers which infuse corporate policies with a basic sense of right
and wrong—are tightly connected to the laws and mores of the home
country.

Modern textbooks dealing with international business consider
cultural differences to be a powerful factor in executive decision
making. Indeed they often use those differences to justify practices
abroad which, although enhancing corporate profits, would be questionable at home. One textbook, for example, remarks that "in situations where patterns of dominance-subordination are socially determined, and not a function of demonstrated ability, management
should be cautioned about promoting those of inferior social status
to positions in which they are expected to supervise those of higher
social status."[2] Referring to multiracial societies such as South Af-

rica, the same textbook offers managers some practical advice: "The problem of the multiracial society manifests itself particularly in reference to promotion and pay. An equal pay for equal work policy may not be acceptable to the politically dominant but racial minority group."[3]

We have already seen in Chapter 2 that cultural relativism fails as a plausible doctrine. But it does not follow that cultural differences are entirely irrelevant to the determination of which practices are, and which are not, permissible for multinationals to perform in host countries. Consider two actual instances of the problem at issue.

> Case A: A new American bank in Italy was advised by its Italian attorneys to file a tax return that misstated income and expenses and consequently grossly underestimated actual taxes due. The bank learned, however, that most other Italian companies regarded the practice as standard operating procedure and merely the first move in a complex negotiating process with the Italian internal revenue service. The bank initially refused to file a fallacious return on moral grounds and submitted an "American-style" return instead. But because the resulting tax bill was many times higher than what comparable Italian companies were asked to pay, the bank changed policy in later years to agree with "Italian style."[4]

> Case B: In 1966 Charles Pettis, employee of an American multinational, became resident engineer for one of the company's projects in Peru: a 146 mile, $46 million project to build a highway across the Andes. Pettis soon discovered that Peruvian safety standards were far below those in the United States. The highway design called for cutting through mountains in areas where rock formations were unstable. Unless special precautions were taken, slides could occur. Pettis blew the whistle, complaining first to Peruvian government officials and later to U.S. officials. No special precautions were taken, with the result that thirty-one men were killed by landslides during the construction of the road. Pettis was fired for his trouble and had difficulty finding a job with another company.[5]

THE MORAL POINT OF VIEW

One may well decide that home country standards were mandatory in one of the cases just described, but not in the other. One may believe that despite conforming to Peruvian standards, host country precautions in Peru were unacceptable, and, in the former case, one may acknowledge that however inequitable and inefficient Italian tax mores may be, a decision to file "Italian-style" is permissible.

Thus, despite claims to the contrary, one must reject the simple dictum that whenever the practice violates a moral standard of the home country, it is impermissible for the multinational company. Arnold Berleant has argued that the principle of equal treatment endorsed by most U.S. citizens requires that U.S. corporations pay workers in less developed countries exactly the same wages paid to U.S. workers in comparable jobs (after appropriate adjustments are made for cost of living levels in the relevant areas). But most observers, including those from the less developed countries, believe this stretches the doctrine of equality too far in a way detrimental to host countries. By arbitrarily establishing U.S. wage levels as the bench mark for fairness one eliminates the role of the international market in establishing salary levels, and this in turn eliminates the incentive U.S. corporations have to hire foreign workers. If U.S. companies felt morally bound to pay Korean workers exactly the same wages U.S. workers receive for comparable work, they would not locate in Korea. Perhaps U.S. firms should exceed market rate for foreign labor as a matter of moral principle, but to pay strictly equal rates would freeze less developed countries out of the international labor market.[6] Lacking, then, a simple formula that says "the practice is wrong when it violates the home country's norms," one seems driven to undertake a more complex analysis of the types and degrees of responsibilities multinationals possess.

We must remind ourselves that our aim here, as earlier, is to isolate not "maximal" but "minimal" duties. The difference, as noted in Chapter 4, is that "minimal" constitutes a duty such that the persistent failure to observe it deprives the corporation of its moral right to exist; a "maximal" duty is one whose fulfillment may be praiseworthy but not mandatory. It is the determination of minimal duties that stands as our task here, since in attempting to decide whether a practice is permissible for the multinational company in the host country, the notion of permissibility must eventually be cashed in terms of minimal standards. Thus, a practice is not permissible for the multinational company simply because it fails to achieve an ideal vision of corporate conduct; for example, a multinational company's failure to contribute generously to the United Nations is a permissible, if regrettable, act.

Because minimal duties are again our target, it is appropriate here, as in Chapter 5, to invoke the language of rights, for rights are entitlements that impose minimum demands on the behavior of others. Recall that in Chapter 5 ten fundamental international rights were specified which multinational corporations must observe. Hence it seems clear that one means of arbitrating conflicts of norms between home and host countries is by appeal to fundamental international rights. On this supposition, no action that violates such a right, whether conforming to host country law or opinion or not, would be permissible.

Notice that even if one were to reject the analysis of welfare rights offered in Chapter 5, and opt instead for a more libertarian, non-welfare-oriented interpretation of rights that utilizes personal liberty as the touchstone for determining the validity of all other rights, one would be compelled to view multinational corporations as having clear responsibilities to rights bearers in foreign countries. Such a view, while denying that anyone has a right to be provided an economic good by another, would nonetheless acknowledge that one's liberty is limited by the possibility of direct harm to another. "My right to swing my arm anywhere," as the saying goes, "is limited by the position of your nose." The informing principle of such a view has been often labeled by philosophers the "no harm" principle. Associated with John Stuart Mill and traditional liberalism, it reflects a rights-based approach emphasizing the individual's right to liberty, allowing maximal liberty to each so long as each inflicts no avoidable harm on others.

In an intriguing application of the "no harm" principle to the actions of U.S. multinationals abroad, Henry Shue confirms that observing the principle entails clear obligations for multinational corporations.[7] For example, he notes that one may by appeal to the "no harm" principle criticize a plan once proposed by a Colorado-based company to export millions of tons of hazardous chemical waste from the United States for processing and disposal in the West African nation of Sierra Leone (an instance of storing toxic waste similar to those discussed in Chapter 5).[8] Using the same principle, he is able to criticize any U.S. asbestos manufacturing corporation which, in order to escape expensive regulations at home, moves its plant to a foreign country with low or nonexistent standards.[9]

Considering an escape from the principle, Shue discusses whether inflicting harm is acceptable in the event that overall benefits outweigh the costs. Hence, dramatically increased safety risks under reduced asbestos standards might be acceptable insofar as the economic benefits to the country outweigh the costs. The problem, as Shue correctly notes, is that this approach fails to distinguish between the "no harm" principle and a naive greatest happiness principle. Even classical defenders of the "no harm" principle were unwilling to accept a simple-minded utilitarianism that sacrificed individual justice on the altar of maximal happiness. Even classical utilitarians, in other words, did not construe their greatest happiness principle to be a "hunting license."[10]

Hence, the rights-based approach laid out in Chapter 5 remains viable even were it possible to overturn—as I have argued it is not—the legitimacy of welfare rights. Chapter 5 advanced arguments on behalf of at least some welfare rights; nonetheless, it is worth noting that the claim that the concept of rights can be used to arbitrate disputes between conflicting standards in home and host country does not depend for its truth on the acceptance of the existence of welfare rights.

A different challenge to the claim that international rights are useful in arbitrating between conflicts of norms can be made by appealing to the rigors of international economic competition. Can we really expect firms to place themselves at a competitive disadvantage by installing expensive safety equipment in a market where other firms are brutally cost-conscious? Such policies, argue critics, could trigger economic suicide. The obligation not to harm, in turn, properly belongs to the government of the host country. Here, too, a rejoinder by Shue is on target. He notes first that the existence of an obligation by one party does not cancel its burden on another party; hence, even if the host country's government does have an obligation to protect its citizens from dangerous work place conditions, its duty does not cancel that of the corporation.[11] Second, governments of poor countries are themselves forced to compete for scarce foreign capital by weakening their laws and regulations, with the result that any "competitive disadvantage" excuse offered on behalf of the corporation would also apply to the government.

A rights-based approach recommends itself as one means for interpreting conflicts in international norms. For such a purpose, it is irrelevant whether the standards of the host country comply or fail to comply with home country standards; what is relevant is whether they meet a universal, objective minimum. In the present context, the principal advantage of a rights-based approach is to establish a firm limit to appeals made in the name of host country laws and morals—at least when the issue is a clear threat to workers' safety. Clear threats such as in-plant asbestos pollution that exceeds levels recommended by independent scientific bodies are incompatible with employees' rights, especially their right not to be harmed. It is no excuse to cite lenient host country regulations or ill-informed host country public opinion.

But even as a rights-oriented approach clarifies a moral bottom line for extreme threats to workers' safety, it leaves obscure not only the issue of less extreme threats, but of harms other than physical injury. The language of rights and harm is sufficiently vague so as to leave shrouded in uncertainty a formidable list of issues crucial to multinationals.

When refined by the traditions of a national legal system, the language of rights achieves a great precision. But left to wander among the concepts of general moral theory, the language proves less exact. Granted, the well-known dangers of asbestos call for recognizing the right to workers' safety no matter how broadly the language of rights is framed. But what are we to say of a less toxic pollutant? Is the level of sulphur-dioxide air pollution we should demand in a struggling nation, say one with only a few fertilizer plants working overtime to help feed its malnourished population, the same as the level we should demand in Portland, Oregon? Or, taking a more obvious case, should the maximal level of thermal pollution generated by a poor nation's electric power plants be the same as that in West Germany? Since thermal pollution raises the temperature of a given body of water, it lowers the capacity of the water to hold oxygen and depletes the number of "higher" fish species, such as salmon and trout. But whereas the trade-off between more trout and higher output is rationally made by the West German in favor of the trout, the situation is reversed for the citizen of Chad, Africa. This should not surprise us. It has long been recognized that many rights, such as the right to medical care, are dependent for their specification on the level of economic development of the country in question.[12]

Nor is it clear how a general appeal to rights will resolve issues that turn on the interpretation of broad social practices. For example, in the Italian tax case mentioned earlier, the propriety of submitting an "Italian" versus "American-style" tax return hinges more on the appraisal of the value of honesty in a complex economic and social system, than it does on an appeal to inalienable rights.

AN ETHICAL ALGORITHM

What is needed, then, is a test for evaluating a given practice which is more comprehensive than a simple appeal to rights. In the end nothing short of a general moral theory working in tandem with an analysis of the foundations of corporate existence is needed. As implied in Chapter 4, for the multinational executive there is ultimately no escape from merging the ordinary canons of economic decision making, of profit maximization and market share, with the principles of basic moral theory. Yet even the existence of a comprehensive theory of corporate morality does not preclude the possibility of discovering lower-order moral concepts to clarify the moral intuitions already in use by multinational decision makers. Apart from the need for general theories of multinational conduct we need pragmatic aids to help managers bring into focus the ethical implications of views already held. This suggests the possibility of generating an interpretive mechanism, or algorithm, which multinational managers could use in determining the implications of their own

moral views about cases stated in the following form: "Is the practice permissible for the multinational company when it is morally
and/or legally permitted in the host country, but not in the home
country?"

The first step in creating such an ethical algorithm is to isolate the
distinct sense in which the norms of the home and host country conflict. If the practice is morally and/or legally permitted in the host
country, but not in the home country, then the problem falls into
one of two types of conflict:

1. The moral reasons underlying the host country's view that the
   practice is permissible refer to the host country's relative level of
   economic development.
2. The moral reasons underlying the host country's view that the
   practice is permissible are independent of the host country's relative level of economic development.

Let us call the conflict of norms described in number 1 a type 1
conflict. In such a conflict, an African country that permits slightly
higher levels of thermal pollution from electric power generating
plants, or a lower minimum wage than that prescribed in European
countries, would do so not because higher standards are undesirable
per se, but because its level of economic development requires an
ordering of priorities. In the future, when it succeeds in matching
European economic achievements, it may well implement the higher
standards.

Let us call the conflict of norms described in number 2 a type 2
conflict. In such cases levels of economic development play no role.
For example, low-level institutional nepotism, common in many developing countries, is justified not on economic grounds but on the
basis of clan and family loyalty. Presumably the same loyalties will be
operative even after the country has risen to economic success—as
the nepotism prevalent in Saudi Arabia indicates. The Italian tax
case also reflects an Italian cultural style, a penchant for personal
negotiation and an unwillingness to formalize transactions, more than
a strategy based on level of economic development.

The most important reason for distinguishing between the two types
of conflict is that our powers of empathy are considerably greater in
instances where merely economic welfare is at stake, than in one
dominated by embedded cultural values. We are simply better able
to imagine ourselves in the position of citizens making trade-offs between more trout and more fertilizer than the same citizens making
deep-seated, Moslem- or Hindu-influenced judgments about the importance of clan and family loyalty. (The issue of the relative degree
of empathy will be discussed further in Chapter 7.) This, in turn,

suggests the need to utilize a different method when clarifying the ethical parameters of one type of case in contrast to the other.

When the conflict of norms occurs for reasons other than relative economic development (type 2), then the possibility is increased that there exists what Richard Brandt has called an "ultimate ethical disagreement." An ultimate ethical disagreement occurs when two cultures are able to consider the same set of facts surrounding a moral issue while disagreeing on the moral issue itself. An ultimate ethical disagreement is less likely in a type 1 case since after suitable reflection about priorities imposed by differing economic circumstances, the members of the home country may come to agree that given the facts of the host country's level of economic development, the practice is permissible. On the other hand, a type 2 dispute about what Westerners call "nepotism" will continue even after economic variables are discounted.[13]

The status of the conflict of norms between the home and host country, whether it is type 1 or 2, does not fix the truth value of the host country's claim that the practice is permissible. The practice may or may not be permissible whether the conflict is of type 1 or 2. This, however, is not to say that the truth value of the host country's claim is independent of the conflict's type status, for a different test is required to determine whether the practice is permissible when the conflict is of type 1 rather than type 2. In a type 1 dispute, the following formula is appropriate:

> The practice is permissible if and only if the members of the home country would, under conditions of economic development relevantly similar to those of the host country, regard the practice as permissible.

Under this type 1 test, excessive levels of asbestos pollution would almost certainly not be tolerated by the members of the home country under relevantly similar economic conditions, whereas higher levels of thermal pollution would be. The test, happily, explains and confirms our initial moral intuitions.

Yet, when as in type 2 conflicts the dispute between the home and host country depends upon a fundamental difference of perspective, the step to equalize hypothetically the levels of economic development is useless. A different test is needed. In type 2 conflicts the opposing evils of ethnocentricism and ethical relativism must be avoided. A multinational must forgo the temptation to remake all societies in the image of its home society, while at the same time it must reject a relativism that conveniently forgets ethics when the payoff is sufficient. Thus, the task is to tolerate cultural diversity while drawing the line at moral recklessness.

Since in type 2 cases the practice is in conflict with an embedded norm of the home country, one should first ask whether the practice is necessary to do business in the host country, for if not, the solution clearly is to adopt some other practice that is permissible from the standpoint of the home country. If petty bribery of public officials is unnecessary for the business of the Cummins Engine Company in India, then the company is obliged to abandon such bribery. If, on the other hand, the practice proves necessary for business, one must next ask whether the practice constitutes a direct violation of a basic human right. Here the notion of a fundamental international right outlined in Chapter 5, specifying a minimum below which corporate conduct should not fall, has special application. If Toyota, a Japanese company, confronts South African laws that mandate systematic discrimination against nonwhites, then Toyota must refuse to comply with the laws. Thus, in type 2 cases, the practice would be permissible if and only if the answer to both of the following questions is "no."

• Is it possible to conduct business successfully in the host country without undertaking the practice?

• Is the practice a clear violation of a fundamental international right?

What sorts of practice might satisfy both criteria of the type 2 test? Consider the practice of low-level bribery of public officials in some developing nations. In some South American countries, for example, it is impossible for any company, foreign or national, to move goods through customs without paying low-level officials a few dollars. Indeed, the salaries of such officials are sufficiently low that one suspects they are set with the prevalence of the practice in mind. The payments are relatively small, uniformly assessed, and accepted as standard practice by the surrounding culture. Here, the practice of petty bribery would pass the type 2 test and, barring other moral factors, would be permissible.

A further condition, however, should be placed on multinationals that undertake the practice in type 2 contexts. The companies should be willing to speak out against the practice. Even if petty bribery or low-level nepotism passes the preceding tests, it may conflict with an embedded norm of the home country, and as a representative of the home country's culture, the company is obliged to take a stand. This would be true even for issues related exclusively to financial practice, such as the Italian tax case. If the practice of underestimating taxes is (1) accepted in the host country, (2) necessary for successful business, and (3) does not violate any fundamental rights, then it satisfies the necessary conditions of permissibility. Yet insofar as it violates a norm accepted by the home country, the multinational company should make its disapproval of the practice known.

To sum up, then, two complementary tests have been proposed for determining the ultimate permissibilty of the practice in question. If the practice occurs in a type 1 context, then the practice is not permissible if:

> The members of the home country would not, under conditions of economic development relevantly similar to those of the host country, regard the practice as permissible.

If the practice occurs in a type 2 context, then the practice is not permissible if either one of the following criteria is true:

* It is possible to conduct business successfully in the host country without undertaking the practice.
* The practice is a direct violation of a fundamental international right.

Notice that the type 1 test or criterion is not reducible to the type 2 test. In order for the two tests to have equivalent outcomes, four propositions would need to be true: first, if the practice passes criterion 1, it passes criterion 2; second, if it fails criterion 1, it fails criterion 2; third, if it passes criterion 2, it passes criterion 1; and fourth, if it fails criterion 2, it fails criterion 1. But none of these propositions is true. The possibility matrix in Table 6.1 shows in rows A and B the only combinations of outcomes that are possible on the assumption that the two tests are equivalent. But they are not equivalent because the combinations of outcomes in C and D are also possible.

To illustrate, the practice may pass criterion 2 and fail criterion 1; for example, the practice of petty bribery may be necessary for business, may not violate fundamental rights, but may nonetheless be unacceptable in the home country under hypothetically lowered levels of economic development. Similarly, the practice of allowing a significant amount of sulphur-dioxide pollution (sufficient, say, to erode historic artifacts) may be necessary for business, may not violate fundamental rights, yet may be hypothetically unacceptable in the home country. Or, the practice may fail test 2 and pass test 1; for example, the practice of serving alcohol at executive dinners in a strongly Moslem country may not be necessary for business in the host country and thus impermissible by criterion 2 while being thoroughly acceptable to the members of the home country under hypothetically lowered economic conditions.

Table 6.1. Possible Outcomes of the Ethical Algorithm

	Criterion 1	*Criterion 2*
A	Fail	Fail
		equivalent outcomes
B	Pass	Pass
C	Fail	Pass
		nonequivalent outcomes
D	Pass	Fail

It follows, then, that the two tests are not mutually reducible. This underscores the importance of the preliminary step of classifying a given case as either type 1 or type 2. The prior act of classification explains, moreover, why all cases in row C or in row D do not have the same moral outcome. Consider, for example, the Fail-Pass case from row C concerning artifact-damaging, sulphur-dioxide pollution, mentioned earlier. It could happen that if properly classified under type 2, the practice would be permissible, but if under type 1, it would be impermissible.

PRACTICAL CONSIDERATIONS AND OBJECTIONS

The algorithm does not obviate the need for multinational managers to appeal to moral concepts both more general and specific than the algorithm itself. It is not intended as a substitute for a general theory of morality or even an interpretation of the basic responsibilities of multinationals. Its power lies in its ability to tease out implications of the moral presuppositions of a manager's acceptance of "home" morality and in this sense to serve as a clarifying device for multinational decision making. But insofar as the context of a given conflict of norms categorizes it as a type 1 rather than type 2 conflict, the algorithm makes no appeal to a universal concept of morality (as the appeal to fundamental rights does in type 2 cases) save for the purported universality of the ethics endorsed by the home country culture. This means that the force of the algorithm is relativized slightly in the direction of a single society. When the home country's morality is wrong or confused, the algorithm can reflect this ethnocentricity, leading either to a mild paternalism or to the imposition of parochial standards. For example, the home country's oversensitivity to aesthetic features of the environment may lead it to reject a given level of thermal pollution even under hypothetically lowered economic circumstances, thus yielding a paternalistic refusal to allow such levels in the host country, despite the host country's acceptance of the higher levels and its belief that tolerating such levels is necessary for stimulating economic development. Or, the home country's mistaken belief that the practice of hiring twelve-year-olds for full-time, permanent work, although happily unnecessary at its relatively high level of economic development, would be acceptable and economically necessary at a level of economic development relevantly similar to the host country's, and might lead it both to tolerate and to undertake the practice in the host country. It would be a mistake, however, to exaggerate this weakness of the algorithm; coming up with actual cases in which the force of the algorithm would be relativized is extremely difficult. Indeed, I have been unable to discover a single, nonhypothetical set of facts fitting this description.

The algorithm is not intended as a substitute for more specific guides to conduct such as the numerous codes of ethics now appearing on the international scene. A need exists for topic-specific and industry-specific codes that embody detailed safeguards against self-serving interpretations. Consider the Sullivan Standards, drafted by the black American minister Leon Sullivan for the purpose of ensuring nonracist practices by U.S. multinationals operating in South Africa.[14] Among other things, companies complying with the Sullivan Principles must:

- Remove all race designation signs.
- Support the elimination of discrimination against the rights of Blacks to form or belong to government-registered unions.
- Determine whether upgrading of personnel and/or jobs in the lower echelons is needed (and take appropriate steps).[15]

Despite the fact that during the summer of 1987, Leon Sullivan himself changed course and called for companies to end all commercial ties with South Africa, the Sullivan code, and its counterparts in Canada and the Common Market (which, in contrast to the Sullivan Principles, are administered by the governments) will continue to inform the decisions of many companies who decide to stay.[16]

As we saw in Chapter 3, a variety of other international codes are either operative or in the process of development. In addition to those already discussed, they include the European Community's Vredeling Proposal on labor-management consultations, the United Nations International Standards of Accounting and Reporting, the WHO Code on Pharmaceuticals and Tobacco, the World Intellectual Property Organization's Revision of the Paris Convention for the Protection of Industrial Patents and Trademarks, and the International Chamber of Commerce's Rules of Conduct to Combat Extortion and Bribery.[17]

Despite these limitations, the algorithm has important application in countering the well-documented tendency of multinationals to mask immoral practices in the rhetoric of "tolerance" and "cultural relativity." According to this algorithm, no multinational manager can naively suggest that asbestos standards in Chile are permissible because they are accepted there. Nor can a manager infer that the standards are acceptable on the grounds that the Chilean economy is, relative to the multinational's home country, underdeveloped. A surprising amount of moral blindness occurs not because people's fundamental moral views are confused, but because their cognitive application of those views to novel situations is misguided.

What guarantees that multinationals possess the knowledge or objectivity to apply the algorithm fairly? As Richard Barnet quips, "On the fifty-sixth floor of a Manhattan skyscraper, the level of self-protective ignorance about what the company may be doing in Colombia or Mexico is high."[18] Can Exxon or Johns Manville be trusted to have a sufficiently sophisticated sense of "fundamental rights," or to weigh dispassionately the hypothetical attitudes of their fellow citizens under conditions of "relevantly similar economic development"? My answer to this is "perhaps not," at least given the present character of the decision-making procedures in most global corporations. But this only serves to underscore the need for more sophisticated, and more ethically sensitive, decision-making techniques in multinationals. And I would add that from a theoretical perspective the problem is a contingent and practical one. It is no more a theoretical flaw of the proposed algorithm that it may be misunderstood or misapplied by a given multinational, than it is of Rawls's theory of justice that it may be conveniently misunderstood by a trickle-down Libertarian.[19]

What would need to change in order for multinationals to make use of the algorithm? Most of all, multinationals would need to enhance the sophistication of their decision making. They would need to alter established patterns of information flow and collection to accommodate moral information. They would need to introduce alongside analyses of the bottom line, analyses of historical tendencies, health, rights, and demography. And they might even find it necessary to introduce a new class of employee to provide expertise in these areas. However unlikely such changes are, I believe they are within the realm of possibility. Multinationals, the organizations capable of colonizing our international future, are no doubt also capable of applying—at a minimum—the same moral principles abroad that they accept at home.

7

The Ethics of Risk:
The Lessons of Bhopal

In India, the Philippines, Nigeria, and elsewhere, technology is spread thin on ancient cultures.[1] In 1984 in Bhopal, India, the devastating potential of technology's hazards in a nontechnological culture was brought home with awesome pain—more than 2,000 people died and more than 200,000 were injured when toxic gas seeped from a Union Carbide insecticide plant.[2] My aim in this chapter is to inquire about the justice of practices, like those in Bhopal, which subject foreign citizens to technological risks higher than those faced by either home country citizens or more favored foreign citizens. The object of exploration, hence, is the justice of the distribution of technological risks in and among nation-states. What moral obligations underlie, what extranational responsibilities should inform, the behavior of global actors such as Union Carbide and the United States? The question not only intrigues us, it demands answers on behalf of those who have been harmed or who are presently at risk. Yet it appears disturbingly clear that the question as framed eludes answers because we possess no viable interpretive scheme for applying traditional moral precepts to the moral twilight created by the juxtaposition of differing cultural norms and rapidly advancing technology.

The strategy in this chapter will be to interpret and extend the moral concepts developed in earlier chapters, especially in Chapter 6, to unravel the moral complexities of global risk. The key issue will be that of obligation. In particular, what are the obligations of macro-agents or macro-organizations regarding the risks of hazardous technology to third and fourth parties who are denied membership in those organizations? The terms "macro-agents" or "macro-organizations" will be used interchangeably. They refer to key organizational actors in the international economy, especially nation-states and multinational corporations. By "third-party victims" I mean persons who are placed at risk by a given macro-organization but who are not themselves members of that organization, for example, innocent bystanders or citizens of another country. By "fourth-party victims" I mean fetuses and future generations. In general, third- and fourth-party victims do not make policy decisions that affect the level or distribution of risk, and when harmed are entirely innocent. Both categories should be distinguished from those of first-party victims such as corporate managers or government leaders, and second-party victims such as rank-and-file employees or national citizens.[3] When harmed, these latter persons may or may not be innocent.

The point about nonmembership in macro-organizations is important. We expect corporations to honor certain responsibilities to their employees (no matter how frequently some may violate them), and when they fail to do so, we are able to appeal to accepted moral principles in criticizing their behavior. Similarly, we expect nation-states to exercise special care over their citizens, and indeed doing so is regarded as a sine qua non of a national legal system. Hence when states fail in this regard, we know what to say. But we do not know, or know as well, what to say about the responsibilities of the U.S. government to the citizens of Bangladesh, or of Dow Chemical Corporation to the man or woman in the street in Cubatao, Brazil.

BHOPAL: CULTURAL VARIABLES

Let us begin by sketching key elements of the disaster in Bhopal, India. Bhopal is by no means unique in the history of chemical catastrophes. In 1972 from 400 to 5,000 Iraqis were killed as a result of eating unlabeled, mercury-treated grain from the United States. In 1979 workers and livestock were poisoned in Egypt by the pesticide Leptophos; and, in 1984 hundreds died and were injured in Mexico City as a result of a liquified natural gas explosion.[4] But Bhopal is striking for the enormity of its scale and, more important, the lessons it teaches.[5]

About 12:40 A.M. on December 3, 1984, Suman Dey, the senior operator on duty at Union Carbide's Bhopal plant, went to investigate a leak of methyl isocyanate in the partially buried, number 610 storage tank. As he watched the small wisp of steam rising from a leak at the top of the tank, the platform on which he stood began to shake. As he turned and ran from the tank, he saw a slab of concrete, sixty-feet long and six-inches thick, rise and break apart. A tower of gas erupted through the stack connected to the tank and formed a white cloud; it floated slowly towards the southwest, toward the sleeping neighborhoods of the city of Bhopal.[6]

Although the entire story remains to be told, blame for the disaster is likely to be spread through a complex constellation of persons and acts. Cost-cutting measures had in the previous year severely weakened safety control at the Bhopal plant. The refrigeration unit designed to cool the methyl isocyanate had been ineffective for some time, and more than a score of crucial safety devices specified in the safety handbook prepared by Union Carbide in the United States were conspicuously absent.

The training, habits, and attitudes of Indian employees were lax and naive. Safety procedures specified in the handbook were routinely circumvented by technicians who, lacking adequate training, went on with their work blissfully ignorant of the dangers lurking behind their daily routines. In responding to the disaster, employees showed bad judgment and poor training: upon first learning of the initial leak, the officer in charge opted to think about it over tea. Outside the plant, government regulatory authorities and city officials were entirely at a loss either to inspect and regulate the plant on an ongoing basis, or to respond appropriately to a disaster once it occurred.

Finally, Union Carbide itself, despite holding a majority of its subsidiary's stock and accepting responsibility for all major economic and safety decisions, may not have maintained an adequate system of safety accountability, and consequently, may not have exercised appropriate control over its Indian subsidiary. This may be true even if it turns out that Union Carbide's claims of employee sabotage—a defense it has offered in courts of law—is able to withstand legal scrutiny.

The legal aftermath of the disaster was tangled. For over four years after the disaster, the victims and families of victims had failed to receive significant compensation. Attorneys for the victims pushed for a U.S. trial, but a U.S. judge finally ruled that the trial should be held in India on the condition that Union Carbide submitted to discovery under United States legal principles, principles which permit closer investigation of company-held information than under Indian law.[7] In December of 1987, Judge M. W. Deo in the Bhopal court ordered Union Carbide to donate an unprecedented $270 million as interim relief, and at roughly the same time, the Indian government decided to file criminal charges against Union Carbide. Throughout, Union Carbide's image has suffered at the hands of a skeptical public.[8]

Finally, on February 14, 1989, the Indian government announced

the settlement of claims against Union Carbide. Union Carbide agreed
to pay $470 million to the Indian government which, in turn, will
establish a commission to distribute the funds. In return, India agreed
to drop criminal charges. Nonetheless, many survivors of the gas
leak were unsatisfied and traveled to New Delhi to protest the settlement.[9]

Yet what happened at Bhopal is not only a story about tragedy
and human frailty, it may also be a story about injustice. The people
who died and suffered were not citizens of the nation whose corporation held responsibility. The people who suffered most were slum
dwellers, the poorest of India's poor, who had pitched their huts
literally next to the walls of the Union Carbide plant.

Cultural variables muddy moral analysis. Whereas in the context
of our own culture we can estimate with some assurance the value
of goods sacrificed or put at risk by undertaking a given act or policy, in a foreign case our intuitions are opaque. Our extracultural
vision may be sufficiently clear to allow us to understand a trade-off
between risk and productivity, between the dollar value of an increased gross national product on the one hand, and the higher dollar cost of the medical care necessary to accommodate higher levels
of risk; but our vision is blurred for more ethnocentric trade-offs.
In many less developed countries a higher gross national product is
only one of a handful of crucial goals informed by cultural tradition
and experience.

This is the principal reason why, in the preceding chapter, we distinguished between type 1 and type 2 tests for arbitrating conflicts
between cultural norms. Put simply, we must use different methods
of ethical analysis when our empathetic vision is blurred than when
it is clear. We are now in a position to refine the rationale that underlies the algorithm, and, having done so, give that rationale application to the specific issue of risk distribution.

Two cultural variables can sidetrack international risk analysis. The
first is the level of gross marginal improvement in health or economic well-being, as statistically measurable by universally accepted
norms of health and economic welfare. Let us call this marginal value
that of "statistical welfare." Since, as suggested earlier, the analyst is
free to factor cultural values into the determination of extranational
responsibilities, he is also free to integrate the concept of "statistical
welfare" into overall risk analysis, and to estimate trade-offs from
the standpoint of the foreign country. Furthermore, since the concept is by definition compatible with objective, quantitative methods
of analysis, the task is manageable. Armed with an appropriate statistical method, he may well conclude that the marginal welfare resulting from the use of a hazardous drug or piece of technology is

positive in the United States, while negative in another country, or vice versa. The notion of marginal statistical welfare thus aids in sidestepping one version of cultural myopia and in weighing the effect local conditions can have on the character of trade-offs between risks and benefits.

The second variable is that of marginal "cultural welfare." In contrast to marginal statistical welfare, it cannot be interpreted through standard norms of health or economic well-being. A citizen of Zimbabwe, Africa, may be willing to trade off a few marginal dollars in per capita gross national product for the nonquantifiable improvement in her nation's economic independence from earlier colonial powers. For the same improvement, she may even be willing to trade off a fraction of a percentage point in the nation's infant mortality rate. Similarly, a citizen of Pakistan may be more eager to preserve her country's Moslem heritage, a heritage with strict sexual differentiation in the division of labor, than to increase the country's economic welfare through integrating women into the work place.

The point is simply that in instances where trade-offs involve marginal cultural welfare it is doubtful how accurately a cultural stranger can estimate the value that a citizen of another culture places on key goods involved in social trade-offs. Short of abdicating risk analysis entirely to the other culture (a move that I will show later to be unwise), no decisive or even objective decision-making mechanism appears to exist for assessing risk trade-offs.

Further, cultural variables can aggravate weaknesses of traditional methods of risk analysis. This is especially true of most methods' tendency to focus on dollars and bodies at the expense of social and cultural criteria, a tendency which, while faulted in domestic contexts, becomes pernicious when the difference between two countries' social and cultural habits are marked.

Consider the twin issues of distributing risk and pricing risk. It is well known that the techniques of cost-benefit analysis are often mute regarding issues of distributive justice. They tend to bypass questions of the fairness of a practice from the perspective of its relative impact on social subclasses, such as the poor, the infirm, or the members of a minority ethnic group. Such silence is less neglectful in the context of a national legal system whose rules have as a central function the protection of individual rights.[10] But in the context of international transactions, where the legal strictures affecting a macro-agent's domestic activities do not (and in an important sense *cannot*) regulate its activities in a separate legal jurisdiction, the silence is morally corrupting. Obviously, pesticide risks to field workers must be weighed against the crying need of a poor country for greater food production; but when that development is carried entirely on the backs of the poor, when the life expectancy of the field worker is cut by a decade or more while the life expectancy of the urban elite *increases* by a decade, then distributive moral factors should override consequential cost-benefit considerations offered in the name of overall welfare.

The common and sometimes criticized distinction in risk analysis between voluntary and involuntary assumptions of risks is of little help. If we are uneasy over the assumption that the decision of a lower-class worker in the United States to take a high-risk job is "voluntary," despite that worker's limited technological sophistication and pressing financial needs, then surely we must reject the label of "voluntary" when applied to the starving, shoeless laborer in Bangladesh, who agrees to work in a pesticide-infected field.

Finally, the tendency in cost-benefit analysis to tie costs to market prices can distort risk trade-offs in less developed countries. The dominant assumption of most risk analysis—and of cost-benefit analysis in particular—that risks must be balanced against costs, means that in the instance of life-threatening risks human life must be assigned a price. Despite the apparent barbarity of the very concept, defenders point out that most of us are willing to assume nonzero risks to our lives for the sake of reducing cost; we frequently do so when we, say, buy a smaller car or accept a higher paying but riskier job.[11] Assigning a price to human life may have beneficial consequences against the backdrop of a single, developed country, because it may help policymakers better allocate scarce safety-promoting resources, but in developing countries it can unfairly relativize human worth. Since the market price of a life is tied to the capacity of a person to generate income, and since in most parts of the developing countries the absence of a capital infrastructure limits the average individual's productive capacity, it follows that in the developing countries a human life will be given a lower price.

If cultural variables confound risk analysis, then how can such analysis address international problems? One tempting solution must be abandoned, namely, reliance on international market pressures for acceptable risk distribution. What the market does unsuccessfully in a national context, it fails utterly to do in an international context. As Charles Perrow has pointed out, even in the developed countries "there is no impersonal fair market that rewards those that risk their lives with higher wages."[12] The "jumpers" or "glow boys" in the nuclear industry, temporary workers "who dash into a radioactive area to make repairs, will be hired for two or three weeks' work, at only six dollars an hour. . . . Textile workers are not compensated for brown lung disease, nor are chemical plant workers compensated for cancer showing up ten or twenty years after exposure."[13]

The average level of unemployment in the developing countries today exceeds 40 percent, a figure that has frustrated the application of neoclassical economic principles to the international economy on a score of issues. With full employment, and all other things being equal, market forces will encourage workers to make trade-offs between job opportunities using safety as a variable. But with massive unemployment, market forces in developing countries drive the unemployed to the jobs they are lucky enough to land, regardless of safety.

INTRANATIONAL RISK DISTRIBUTION

Does some criterion exist, itself not bound by culture or nation, that can give objectivity to intercultural assessments of risk distribution? At first glance nothing seems appropriate. The monumental analysis of distributive justice undertaken by John Rawls explicitly exempts international considerations from the reach of his famous two principles, (1) that everyone is entitled to maximal liberty, and (2) that inequalities in the distribution of primary goods are unjust unless everyone, including the average person in the worst affected group, stands to benefit.[14] Rawls's reasons for nationalizing distributive justice are tied to his belief that distributive claims can be evaluated meaningfully only against a background scheme of cooperation that yields goods subject to distribution. Since nation-states are customarily the agents that provide the mechanisms necessary for facilitating cooperative arrangements and for pooling and distributing the fruits of such arrangements, and since such mechanisms are conspicuously not provided on the international scale, it seems both idealistic and implausible to speak seriously of distributive justice on an international scale.

Yet, even if Rawls is correct in limiting the application of the two principles, it is noteworthy that many problems of risk assessment in a global context do not depend on *inter*national distributive comparisons (distributions *among* nations), but on *intra*national comparisons (distributions *within* a nation). Hence Rawls's principles have important application, even when international distributive comparisons are excluded. For example, in assessing the fairness of exposing a disproportionate number of poor Indians to the risks of chemical accidents, Union Carbide need not enter into the moral calculus of distributing risk between Indian citizens and U.S. citizens; it need only calculate the fairness of risk distribution among Indians. Insofar as Rawls's second principle (usually called the "difference" principle) implies that it is unfair to distribute risks disproportionately among citizens of any country without corresponding benefits for those at greatest risk (and it may sometimes be unfair even when there are corresponding benefits), it is unfair for any official, whether of the Indian government, the U.S. government, or Union Carbide, to undertake activities in India that unfairly distribute risks in such a manner.[15]

Hence Rawls's second principle would need to be modified only slightly to apply to problems of risk distribution within developing countries. The modification would take the following form: first, his difference principle would need to be adjusted to include freedom from risk as one of the primary goods normally covered by the principle. Second, the difference principle may—and this is less certain—need to be adjusted to relax the condition of "moderate scarcity" which limits the application of the principle to societies with sufficient material welfare to make the anticipation of cooperative ventures plausible.

Some may wish to argue that this latter modification is necessary because they believe that certain existing countries manifest poverty sufficiently harsh so that "fruitful ventures must inevitably break down."[16] Whether the condition must be relaxed—at least vis-à-vis the risk issues—is a question I wish to sidestep at this point. Side-stepping it, however, will not cripple our claim that the difference principle is relevant to intranational risk distribution. To begin with, there is a good chance that the "minimal scarcity" condition need *not* be relaxed, since no matter how poor they are by European or U.S. standards, most developing countries do not seem to be at a point where "fruitful ventures must inevitably break down." However, even if this were so, and the condition must be relaxed, the difference principle would maintain its application to risk problems in developing countries, since no matter how poor a country is in terms of material goods, it would not thereby be prevented from adopting cooperative strategies to help ensure a fair distribution of risk among is inhabitants.

INTERNATIONAL RISK DISTRIBUTION

Turning next to *inter*national issues, Rawls may be wrong about the scope of his own theory. As Brian Barry notes, no scheme of cooperation need exist in order to demonstrate the unjustness of allowing toxic air pollution, generated in one country for the benefit of that country, to waft into the unpolluted atmosphere of a second country.[17] And Charles Beitz points out that Rawls's argument for the inapplicability of his scheme seems to presuppose not only the current absence of such features as community and enforcement, but their long-term impossibility.[18] What makes assertions of distributive justice and injustice meaningful, according to Beitz, are the shared features of agents to whom such assertions apply, such as rationality and purposiveness. To put it another way, what makes it wrong for me to refuse to spend $10 in order to save the life of a starving Ethiopian is our shared humanity, a humanity that may someday prompt the emergence of international enforcement mechanisms.

A distributive criterion for risks, then, may be appropriate for evaluating the actions of macro-agents in international affairs, although the nature of that criterion remains unspecified. Giving precision to it is no easy matter, since Rawls's difference principle, even if applicable, probably must be weakened in the international context. It probably must be weakened because it is generally assumed that one has greater duties to one's fellow citizens than to foreigners in much the same way one has greater duties to one's own family members than to strangers. For example, the ordinary citizen may have a minimal duty to help the homeless in America, but the duty is usually believed to fall short of providing them personal attention and love, as one is bound to provide in the case of one's own children. And similarly, one may have a minimal duty to aid the hungry in Africa, but it probably does not extend to providing them social security benefits in old age, as it may in the case of one's fellow citizens.

For this and other reasons, I shall not attempt here the complex task of shaping Rawls's principle to fit problems of international risk distribution (despite my belief that such a project is promising).

Instead, I wish to approach the problem of international risk distribution by appeal to two non-Rawlsian concepts. The first is a fundamental distinction between two kinds of associations, those that are value-*intrinsic* and those that are value-*extrinsic*. The second is a precept entailed by the ethical algorithm discussed in Chapter 6 for arbitrating between conflicting cultural standards.

It will help to provide concrete contexts for the problem. Here are two incidents relevant to the issue of risk, the first involving the selling of banned goods abroad.

Case 1: Morally speaking, selling banned goods abroad seems a clear example of double standards.[19] Nonetheless, developing countries sometimes argue that a given banned product is essential to meeting their needs.[20]

The U.S. Congress in 1979 passed legislation amending the Export Administration Act which gave the president broad powers to control exports.[21] But just thirty-six days after President Carter signed the order, newly elected President Reagan revoked the order on February 17, 1981.[22] In a further move, President Reagan called for a repeal of the export restrictions affecting unapproved drugs and pharmaceutical products. (Banned pharmaceuticals, in contrast to other banned goods, have been subject to export restrictions since the 1940s.) In defense of the Reagan initiative, drug manufacturers in the United States argued by appealing to differing cultural variables. For example, a spokesman for the American division of Ciba-Geigy Pharmaceuticals justified relaxing restrictions on the sale of its Entero-Vioform, a drug he acknowledges has been associated with blindness and paralysis, on the basis of culture-specific, cost-benefit analysis. "The government of India," he pointed out, has requested Ciba-Geigy to continue producing the drug because it treats a dysentery problem that can be life-threatening."[23]

Let us consider a second instance of international risk distribution, this time involving the world's worst pollution.

> Case 2: A small triangle of land near Sao Paulo, Brazil, known as Cubatao, has more reported cases of cancer, stillbirths, and deformed babies than anywhere else in Brazil.[24] Factories, and especially petrochemical plants, dominate the landscape, where about 100,000 people live and work. Cubatao has air considered unfit on a record number of days and has the highest level of pollutants in the rainfall recorded anywhere. In 1983, one hundred slum dwellers living alongside a gasoline duct were killed when the duct caught fire. The town was constructed during the heyday of the so-called Brazilian miracle, a time when right-wing military rulers maintained pro-business labor laws, stable political conditions, and some of the highest profit margins in the world—conditions that allowed them to attract an enormous influx of foreign investment. Even today, with the Brazilian miracle in disrepute, substantial foreign investment remains: Cubatao's 111 plants are owned by twenty-three foreign and Brazilian companies.
>
> According to Marlise Simons of the *New York Times,* "Squatters have built rows of shacks above a vast underground grid of ducts and pipes that carry flammable, corrosive and explosive materials. Trucks lumber alongside loaded with poison, which has spilled in past accidents. . . . 'But we need the work,' one man said. 'We have nowhere else to go.' "[25]

Risk Sociocentrism

The neglected responsibilities of the importing countries to police more effectively incoming goods and of less developed countries in particular, such as Brazil, to improve pollution controls, are no doubt awesome. But without forgetting these responsibilities, I want for the moment to investigate the responsibilities of the exporting nations, and in particular of the developed nations. The first task is to consider a special challenge to the entire project of analyzing international risk distribution. The challenge is mounted from the perspective of a particular view that we shall call risk "sociocentrism"; this view asserts the existence of duties to fellow citizens, but not to foreigners. This view begins, innocently enough, by noting that all nations, including developing ones, have moral duties to tighten the inflow of dangerous goods and to ensure an acceptable level of industrial risks. Government and corporate officials have fiduciary duties to their fellow citizens either through the fact of mutual citizenship, or, as in the case of a government official, because of a public trust. So far so good. But, according to the sociocentric view, responsibilities for the citizens of other countries belong *exclusively to the officials and citizens of those countries.*

The sociocentric view shares a packet of problematic assumptions with a sister theory, the doctrine of realism, which we discussed and rejected in Chapter 2. Both adopt a convenient definition of the responsibilities of leaders which places overriding priority on the interests of citizens in contrast to foreigners. Unfortunately, sociocentrism (and some versions of realism) frequently relies upon an unstated premise to draw a questionable conclusion. The unstated premise is that we have stronger duties to those who are closer to us by virtue either of proximity or shared membership (for example, political or family associations), than to those who are not. The questionable conclusion is that our *moral* responsibilities to foreigners—responsibilities other than, of course, those defined by explicit covenants or role responsibilities—are either negligible or nonexistent. The premise, while probably not entirely false, is vague because it says nothing about possible distinctions among those who are owed duties, such as family members, nonfamily members, next-door neighbors, fellow citizens, and fellow noncitizens; nor does it speak to the possibility that some persons living abroad, such as members of the same religious organization, might be owed duties for the same moral reasons (whatever those are) as those living within our national borders.

What is more, neither the premise nor sociocentrism itself entails any limits upon the favoritism it endorses. For example, while it may be true that a father is morally permitted to spend a dollar to repair his own child's bicycle instead of sending it to a starving child abroad, or a congresswoman to spend millions on national park improvement instead of sending it to Afghan rebels, this in itself cannot be extended to an unlimited endorsement of *national* favoritism.

Good reasons do exist for limited favoritism. The first is that social arrangements which define memberships in associations as well as the specific fiduciary duties of certain members often turn out to be an *efficient* means of maximizing shared values. For example, the institution of the family is a remarkably efficient way to raise the young. It is more efficient for a single person, or a small group of persons (as in a kibbutz) to specialize in caring for a particular child or group of children, than it is for people in general to distribute love and

attention broadly. Nation-states, too, are efficient means of organizing judicial arbitration, military defense, and resource control.

The efficiency gained from organizing society in a manner in which
emotional and geographic realities are recognized through associations, and in which "each takes care of his own," recommends the
creation and development of *permanent* associations, whose habits and
rules cannot be changed at whim. Hence when a family or nation
finds itself in the happy position of possessing a relative abundance
of goods or a comparative international advantage, it is not necessarily true that the surplus should be shared equally with other nations
or families. To do so would necessitate the undoing of the very institutions and habits that benefit all persons in the long run.

Nonetheless, it is noteworthy that this is "limited" favoritism and
not the "absolute" favoritism implied by sociocentrism. It is limited
by the very fact that its final justification depends on appeal to the
welfare of *all* persons, citizens or not. Hence when the advantages
of institutional efficiency are outweighed by the pressing needs of
others (as in the case of potential life-threatening chemical disasters
such as Bhopal), the needs of others take priority.

Value-Intrinsic and Value-Extrinsic Associations

A second reason sometimes offered for favoritism also entails limited, not absolute, favoritism, although the reasons for the limits are
less obvious. It is the argument that some associations, including some
organizations and some personal relationships, are morally privileged and demand preferential treatment from their participants.
Marriage is a good example. Confronted with the choice of saving
the life of one's spouse or that of a stranger, few people, including
moral philosophers, will advocate flipping a coin.[26] Here the argument is not that favoritism is efficient, it is rather that it is morally
demanded—almost as a morally primitive consideration—in certain
associations. This is the underlying significance of Bernard Williams's quip that the man who must justify his decision to save his
wife's life before that of a stranger by citing impartial reasons has
had "one thought too many."[27]

But while this strategy may justify favoritism in certain well-
defined instances, its ability to justify the favoritism of one's fellow
citizens over foreigners is severely limited. The reason concerns the
distinction between "value-intrinsic" and "value-extrinsic" associations.[28] The distinction turns on the fact that not all such associations
from the perspective of intrinsic appeal are on equal footing. Some,
such as the nation-state, or the neighborhood car pool, depend for
their justification almost entirely on impartial reasons—reasons that

appeal to anyone else in a relevantly similar situation and which are transrelational in extending beyond particular persons and relationships.

Compare, for example, two prominent institutions: the family and the modern nation-state (I intentionally exclude the small Aristotelian polis.) Assuming equal levels of happiness (which is, of course, a strong assumption), a world devoid of nation-states or large cities seems preferable to one without friendship and families. The nation-state, unlike the family, has something in common with the neighborhood car pool or snow-removal squad—which, notably, are two other partiality-displaying organizations—all three draw much of their value from their capacity to deliver public and impartially recognized goods. To put it differently, the satisfaction of the ends the car pool and the snow-removal squad are designed to achieve does not logically entail the existence of those institutions. The end of the car pool is to conserve fuel, yet we can imagine this end being achieved without car pools (say, by superefficient gasoline engines).

Similarly, if one assumes—as traditional political theory would suggest—that the primary ends of nation-states are either the preservation of rights, the enhancement of general welfare, or the overcoming of class exploitation (and perhaps all three), then we can at least imagine such ends met without nation-states. Yet we cannot imagine the ends, or, alternatively, the value, of friendship and the family being met without friends and families. To be sure, we can imagine something other than the nuclear, biological family meeting the ends of the family, and we can perhaps imagine something other than the institutionalized form of friendship in our own culture meeting the ends of friendship; but in order to meet those ends we must have *some* form of family and *some* form of friendship.

We shall use the term "value-intrinsic" to characterize the extent to which an institution's ends are logically unobtainable without the existence of that institution itself,[29] and the term "value-extrinsic" to characterize the extent to which an institution's ends conceivably could be achieved by other means. On the basis of this distinction, some institutions such as family and friendship count as strongly value-intrinsic, while others, such as the nation-state, count as strongly value-extrinsic. As may be obvious, the value-intrinsic/value-extrinsic distinction is one of degree: almost any partiality-displaying institution contains elements of both.

It follows that not all institutions should be seen as "morally privileged," or, in other words, as warranting actions by their participants that overstep broadly the limits of impartial morality. The extent to which an institution is value-extrinsic is the extent to which it fails to be "morally privileged" in this manner. It follows that insofar as the nation-state, including the nationalism it entails, is strongly value-extrinsic, then it lacks status as a morally privileged institution, or, if it is morally privileged to some degree, then it is less so than institutions such as the family and friendship. Hence, to the extent that the nation-state does *not* qualify as a strongly value-intrinsic institution, the primary justification for favoring the interests of fellow citizens over strangers in distant lands must be cast in impartial terms. This is true at least when membership in the nation-state is not entangled with sentiments of religion and common experiences. (Note, however, that a state such as Israel may be an exception to the rule.) That is, the justification for partial treatment of fellow Americans, or fellow Germans, fellow Russians, or fellow Argentinians, must be provided impartial grounding to a much greater degree than the justification of partiality for friendship and family.

It is a short step to the conclusion that many policies now endorsed by key actors in the international arena may be morally suspect, especially those informed by a doctrine such as sociocentrism which accords *exclusive* concern in policymaking to the welfare of fellow citizens. The only way such exclusive concern for fellow citizens could be justified would be on the assumption that either the nation-state is a strongly, if not thoroughly, value-intrinsic institution, or that rampant state selfishness is the only practical means for achieving universally recognized political goals. Both seem implausible.

There are, no doubt, good reasons for putting citizens first in national policy calculations, but most of those reasons are impartial ones, reasons that could be used to provide a justification for a similar, citizen-first priorities in the policymaking of other nations.

We may conclude that the amount of permissible favoritism by nation-states or multinational corporations toward their own members in questions of international risk distribution is for the most part the amount that can be justified in the name of efficiency. To put the matter in what philosophers would call "rule-consequential" terms, a corporation or nation-state is justified in adopting policies exhibiting favoritism to the extent that such favoritism is a noneliminable aspect of policies which, if adopted by other relevantly similar states, would increase efficiency and thus maximize overall welfare.

The point is that precious little *risk* favoritism can be justified in this manner. It would stretch moral credibility, for example, to suppose that the toleration of frighteningly high levels of toxic pollution in Cubatao, Brazil, or of the export to developing countries of most banned products—acts that tend to distribute risk to the advantage of multinational corporations and First World citizens—could be justified in the name of rule-consequential sanctioned efficiency. It seems highly unlikely that these are noneliminable aspects of policies that will maximize global welfare; rather the policies seem quite eliminable and appear to be the sort which, if eliminated, would result in greater overall happiness. Hence, it is safe to conclude that the penchant for national egoism and for the favoring of fellow citizens over foreigners, or for favoring fellow employees and stockholders in the instance of the corporation, provides no justification for gross inequities in risk distribution.

Risk and the Test of Rational Empathy

Appeals to efficiency or to the duty to favor friends over strangers are not the only way to attempt to justify international risk inequities. A different, and in many respects more successful way is through appeal to a nation's special needs, such as economic development or the elimination of a particular problem. Lower safety and pollution standards are explicitly maintained by some countries to achieve special ends. In Brazil, for example, lax standards of pollution enforcement are justified in the name of Brazil's desperate need for greater productivity, and the claim has a persuasive edge in a country where malnutrition is so widespread that by some estimates one in every five Brazilian children will suffer permanent brain damage.[30] As mentioned earlier, special dysentery problems have prompted the Indian government to encourage the import of drugs which, without India's unique health problems, would be considered unacceptably risky.[31] It seems morally arrogant to suppose that acts that encourage or tolerate lower standards abroad undertaken by the macroagents of developed societies are impermissible simply for that reason. On the other hand, the convenient relativism of some corporate and government officials which excuses anything in the name of sociocentrism seems equally suspect.

In Chapter 6 I argued for the need to distinguish cases of conflicting norms where the norms accepted by citizens of a host country appear inferior to those of the home country. There I maintained that a key distinction should be drawn between those instances in which from the standpoint of the foreign country (1) the reason for tolerating the "lower" norms refers to the country's relative level of economic development, and (2) the reason for tolerating them is related to inherent cultural beliefs, as in religion or tradition. When an instance falls under the type 1 classification, a different analysis is required than when it falls under type 2. Here it makes sense to do what for cultural reasons cannot be done in the latter instance (where inherent cultural beliefs intrude), namely, to put ourselves in the shoes of the foreigner and engage in a test of rational empathy. To be more specific, it makes sense to consider ourselves and our own culture at a level of economic development relevantly similar to that of the other country. And, if, having done this, we find that *under such hypothetically altered social circumstances* we ourselves would accept the lower risk standards, then it is permissible to adopt the standards that appear inferior. Chapter 6 specified certain limitations upon the use of such a thought-experiment and noted that the experiment cannot substitute for a normative theory of ethics. Nonetheless, the chapter showed that the experiment can help to clarify the transcultural application of a given decision maker's moral intuitions.

It is worth noting that what lies behind the thought-experiment is the age-old philosophical insight that when considering the universality of moral principles, like must be compared to like, and cases must be evaluated in terms of morally relevant similarities. Hence, when considering the acceptability of practices abroad, the moralist must not err by applying wholesale principles relevant to her own nation, but instead must ask herself what those principles would imply under the relevantly altered circumstances of the foreign nation.

Now as a practical matter of moral psychology, some acts of rational empathy are easier than others. This is reflected in the distinction between lower standards justified in terms of relative economic development and those that are not. It is relatively easier for us to empathize with the need for economic development in a poor nation, since economic well-being is an almost universally shared value, than to empathize with the need for a purer form of Moslem government, or for a more African, less European, social system. Indeed, the general principle governing the psychological possibility of rational empathy seems to restrict empathy to situations wherein the fundamental values motivating the decision making of our object of empathy are values that we share.

Let us be more specific. Utilizing the conclusions of the preceding chapter, we can "test" the practices of shipping banned products abroad, and of operating multinational branch facilities in Cubatao, by a thought-experiment wherein we ask whether our own moral intuitions would find such practices acceptable were we at a state of social development relevantly similar to that of the country in question. The test works because the values that presumably prompt the lower standards in foreign countries are ones we share, economic and medical well-being. For example, it makes sense to ask whether we in the United States would find levels of pollution equal to those existing in Cubatao justified in the United States for the sake of economic progress, assuming that we were at Brazil's present level of economic development. If we answer "yes," then we may conclude that it is permissible for U.S. multinationals to adopt the lower pollution standards existing in Cubatao. If not, then the practice is not permissible. (I suspect, by the way, that we would *not* find Cubatao's pollution permissible.)

The same test is appropriate in the case of banned products. Were we at a hypothetically lowered state of economic development similar to Ghana or Colombia, would we allow Tris-treated sleepwear (sleepwear treated with a fire-retardant known to be highly carcinogenic and hence banned from the U.S. market) to be bought and sold? Probably not. Yet, lest one think that the test always returns negative results, consider the case mentioned earlier of India's special request for the drug Entero-Vioform. Dysentery, a widespread and virulent health problem, is often associated with undeveloped societies because of their lack of modern systems of food handling and sanitation. It may well be that as we imagine ourselves in a relevantly similar social situation, the trade-offs between the risks to sufferers and the widespread dysentery that would occur without the drug would favor the export of Entero-Vioform, despite its properly being banned in developed countries.

In instances where we fail to share the moral values that prompt lower safety standards, the test of rational empathy is inappropriate for reasons already stated. Here the final appeal can only be to a floor of fundamental international rights (see Chapter 5). With the presumption in favor of permitting the lower standards unless doing so violates a fundamental right or conflicts with standards of intranational risk distribution mentioned earlier. Unable to appeal to the values that must ultimately underlie social-welfare trade-offs, we must presume the validity of the foreign culture's stance except in the instance where a fundamental international right is at stake, or where we doubt the actual acceptance of the lower norms by rank-and-file citizens. Appealing to rights here has special validity because rights are, by definition, moral concepts that specify moral minimums and prescribe, as it were, the lowest common denominator of permissibility.

Moral and Social Autonomy

The preceding analysis has attempted to show, then, that there are firm limits to the extent to which macro-actors can impose risks on third and fourth parties in foreign countries, even when such risks fall within existing moral and legal guidelines operative in the foreign country. Hence, risk sociocentrism must be abandoned. Although reached by a different route, it is notable how similar in tone this conclusion is to that of Rawls's difference principle, wherein it is necessary to consider the welfare of those who are disadvantaged in order to justify a systematic inequality.

The only remaining defense possible for risk sociocentrism is an appeal to moral and social autonomy. The argument would run something like this: in individual affairs the value of freedom often overrides even that of moral propriety. Even if we believe it morally wrong for a person to risk his health by drinking excessively at home, we do not want the law to restrict his activity. If developing countries wish to expose themselves to unreasonable risks it is not our business.

This argument, however, is faulty. In its present form it falls prey to the obvious objection that coercion of others is not directly at issue here (as it is in the instance of a law proscribing home drinking). Were multinational corporations and First World nations to restrict voluntarily their risk-imposing activities which threaten the citizens of developing countries, they would be exercising *self-control*, not coercion. And though it would surely affect the actions of others, their decision to refuse to distribute risk in certain ways would merely limit the range of options available to others (for instance, they would no longer be able to purchase certain banned goods). The actions would be what John Stuart Mill thought of as "primarily self-regarding," not "primarily other regarding."[32]

Even if reformulated to refer to actions that may *discourage* (rather than coercively restrict) unreasonable risks, however, the argument fails. This is not only because in morality, as in law, aiding or abetting an irresponsible action is itself colored by the shadow of the action's irresponsibility. It is also because in the instance of most developing countries the agents who assume risks are surrogate ones, which is to say that they act on behalf of third parties to whom they are presumably responsible. Surrogate agency would be less damning were it true that both democracy and informed public opinion lay behind such agency. But in most developing countries this is not the case. Most are far from democratic in the sense familiar to democratic, developed nations; even when democratic, they possess a level of technological sophistication sufficiently low to rule out the possibility of rational risk assessment. In Bhopal, India, which happens to be a good-sized city, only one in a thousand households owns a telephone. It would be wrong for us to presume that people living there make rational decisions about exposing themselves to the risks of a modern technological product such as methyl isocyanate.

The idea of a culture "choosing" to undertake risks when that culture lacks a sufficient political and technological infrastructure seems confused. Again, consider Bhopal. Even the Indian employees of

Union Carbide were unaware of methyl isocyanate's toxicity; most thought it was chiefly a skin and eye irritant, and almost none knew it could kill outright. Outside the plant, the Indian regulatory apparatus was obviously unequal to its task. A few weeks before the disaster, the Union Carbide plant had been granted an "environmental clearance certificate." Enforcement was left not to the national government, but to the separate states. In Madhya Pradesh, the state in which Bhopal lies, fifteen factory inspectors were given the task of regulating 8,000 plants; those inspectors, sometimes lacking even typewriters and telephones, were forced to use public buses and trains to get from factory to factory. The two inspectors responsible for the Bhopal area held degrees only in mechanical engineering and knew little about chemical risks.[33] The regulators themselves confessed that chemical safety was an issue they left up to the plant managers. It should be added that India is considerably *more* advanced technologically, with a better technological infrastructure, than most of its counterparts in the developing world.

Bhopal offers many lessons about what developing countries must do to reduce irrational technological risks, among which are probably the need for suitable zoning ordinances, better inspection and regulation of hazardous factories, and the acceptance of only those technologies that the local infrastructure is capable of handling. There is little doubt that these same countries have unfulfilled responsibilities in other areas, including policies affecting the importation of banned products. Nicholas Ashford has offered a tidy list of recommendations: that such countries coordinate industrial development policy with environmental policy (frequently the Ministry of Industry does not exchange information with the Ministry of the Environment); that they develop a data base for the assessment of effects on productivity and safety of imported products; and, finally, that they maintain a centralized purchasing control mechanism for choosing products or technology that will enter the country.[34]

But realism demands that we also recognize the unlikelihood of such reforms in the near future. Surely it would be wrong to thrust the moral burden of technological risk on the shoulders of societies still adolescent in the age of technology.

To conclude, we can summarize the moral limitations upon the distribution of risk in the global economy identified in this chapter. Both market-dominated risk distribution and an "anything goes" policy were rejected as solutions. We found each to be excessively permissive. Next, the issues of intranational and international risk distribution were separated. For intranational issues, no convincing reason exists for deviating from traditional canons of distributive justice, for example, a modified version of Rawls's second ("difference") principle. International issues, on the other hand, are more recalcitrant. Sociocentrism, however tempting, is morally wrongheaded. Claims for state favoritism, while sometimes defensible, were shown to be limited to those justifiable in the name of institutional efficiency. Furthermore, the presence of surrogate agency and technological infrastructure in developing countries refutes defenses of sociocentrism made in the name of national autonomy and freedom. Finally, the ethical algorithm developed in Chapter 6 was interpreted and the results extended to risk trade offs in the context of developing countries.[35]

8

Disinvestment

This chapter, like the preceding one, confronts an issue of immediate concern for nation-states and multinational corporations.* The issue is whether multinational corporations are ever morally required to undertake business disinvestment in a host country. In other words, can nations such as South Africa be sufficiently corrupt that foreign companies should sell their holdings and refuse to transact further business? This chapter will answer the question in the affirmative. It will first identify a moral principle to use in making disinvestment decisions, and then apply that principle to the example of South African disinvestment in the late 1980s. Our approach, however, shifts strategically the focus of the ordinary disinvestment debate by acknowledging at the outset that the consequence of full disinvestment (of a kind that only a tiny handful of corporations have been inclined to take in South Africa) by foreign corporations *may* be to harm more than help innocent parties, for example, South African nonwhites. This acknowledgment bypasses the most controversial disinvestment issue: namely, whether on balance disinvestment will contribute to or detract from the welfare of innocents. For example, while I do not happen to believe that nonwhites in South Africa would suffer long-term harm, I shall assume in the present chapter that they might in order to demonstrate that even if the main argument of critics is granted, the matter of disinvestment is far from settled.[1] By appealing to the notion of a fundamental international right developed in Chapter 5, this chapter shows why firms

*A slightly different version of this chapter was originally published as "Disinvestment," *Public Affairs Quarterly* 2, 2 (April 1988): 37–56. Reprinted by permission.

Both this chapter and the original paper are indebted to many persons who commented on previous versions, including Anthony Appiah, Thomas Carson, Peter Madson, Howard McGary, and Vincent di Norcia.

with even enlightened practices sometimes violate a key moral principle regulating business conduct, and why such firms should not only leave such countries as South Africa, but refuse to buy from, or sell to, other companies chartered in such countries.

The meaning of the term *"disin*vestment" may be understood through the broader concept *"di*vestment." "Divestment" includes all forms of economic disengagement fashioned as a protest to policies or practices that occur within a host country. A striking example of such objectionable practices is the South African policy of apartheid. Divestment strategies range from relatively mild resolutions, such as the insistence that consumers withdraw funds from banks and other financial institutions that make loans directly to the government of a host country to strenuous ones, such as the demand that foreign corporations refrain from doing business with the host country.[2] I use "disinvestment" to refer to this latter sense of divestment, and I focus especially on the question of whether foreign multinationals operating in the late 1980s should have undertaken "full" disinvestment in South Africa, that is, whether they were obliged to undertake disinvestment involving the termination of all business transactions, the sale of local holdings, and a refusal to resume business transactions even through intermediaries until reform was evident.

By way of background, by the summer 1987 only one major U.S. manufacturing company, Eastman Kodak, had undertaken full disinvestment in South Africa in the sense just specified.[3] This was true despite the fact that in the five years following 1983 about 160 firms, roughly half of the 300 American companies operating there, "withdrew" from South Africa (the group of 160 included some of the most visible actors, such as IBM, Coca-Cola, General Electric, General Motors, and Xerox).[4] The products and services of most of these companies were still available[5] because most companies sold either to local companies, local managements, or companies of third nations, or created trusts with reacquisition options—arrangements that allowed many of them to establish franchise or dealer relationships through which they could distribute the very products sold previously through direct subsidiaries.[6] Only 21 of the "withdrawing" companies closed their operations and 7 of those 21 managed to keep their products and services available. Of the 14 that closed shop, all were small operations except for Kodak (whose products nevertheless remained available in South Africa, purchased by a local company from third parties.)[7]

Whether one is a critic or a defender of disinvestment, one must grant that one specific argument commonly heard against disinvestment is inconclusive. To say that corporations ought not disinvest because once having done so they would no longer constitute a force for reform may highlight a relevant moral consideration, but cannot by itself be decisive since the possibility of serving as a force for moral reform is only one of many moral factors that must be considered in a decision to terminate or maintain a relationship. Society frequently holds persons responsible for terminating relationships even when so doing hinders their efforts to reform associates. Criminals cannot justify their participation in organized crimes by avowing their sincere desire to modify their colleagues' behavior; and, more to the point, no one would try to justify the morality of, say, selling computers to Hitler, or investing capital in Hitler's Germany, on the grounds of a possible "reforming" effect.

THE CONDITION-OF-BUSINESS PRINCIPLE

The consideration just mentioned offers a clue to our moral intuitions about business. In ordinary life, in some circumstances we believe it morally wrong to do business with individuals whose character and actions are thoroughly reprehensible, even in instances where we are not forced to condone or abet their evil as a condition of the business relationship. The expression "I wouldn't do business with someone like that" is sometimes offered by market participants and almost always accepted by others as a reason for terminating commercial transactions. Sometimes the reasons behind such a remark are prudential, but frequently they are moral. Excepting unlikely scenarios (for example, where business might facilitate an undercover operation), engaging in business relations with Hitler, with the Mafia, or with smugglers of hard drugs are not activities open to moral debate. What principles lie behind this fundamental intuition that with persons, nations, or corporations of an especially reprehensible sort, one simply ought not conduct business?

As a first approximation, consider a principle, called the "condition-of-business" principle, which turns on the issue of the appropriate reaction to the violation of human rights: the principle states that *ceteris paribus (all other things being equal), business transactions by B with A are impermissible when A is a violator of rights*. A and B will stand for any person, state, or organization (including a corporation). When a multinational corporation engages in business with a South African-chartered corporation—as when General Motors sells parts for assembly to its old subsidiary now owned by white South Africans and chartered by the South African government—the company must also engage in transactions with the white-dominated nation of South Africa that charters and supports the South African corporation. It must, for example, fill out government forms, provide var-

ious proofs of legal compliance, and pay, and in some instances collect, government taxes. Hence, let us assume further that if either
the South African corporation or the South African nation that
charters that corporation is a violator of rights, then the condition-
of-business principle applies.

In its present form, the principle clearly embraces too much and
yields the severe conclusion that business relations with most states
and many organizations must be severed, since most states and many
organizations from time to time engage in rights violations. Surely
morality is unable to demand that we terminate business dealings
with *all* corporations that have at some time in their history engaged
in discriminatory hiring practices. It can, however, properly demand
that we terminate business transactions with the Mafia or known drug
traffickers. This suggests that the evil being committed must be of a
persistent and fundamental sort.

Let us stipulate that the rights violations that properly trigger the
termination of business transactions must be systematic violations of
the most basic human rights, that is of the sort of rights that were
called "fundamental international rights" in Chapter 5. These rights
include the rights to freedom of physical movement, freedom of
speech, ownership of property, physical security, political participation, subsistence, minimal education, freedom from torture, fair trial,
and nondiscriminatory treatment. In turn, violations of less than
fundamental rights, such as the right to clean air and water or to a
high school level of education, while independently significant, would
not be subject to the "condition-of-business" principle. Hence the
principle will be revised to read *ceteris paribus, business transactions by
B with A are impermissible when A is a systematic violator of fundamental
rights.*

But even to say that A is a rights violator of this sort is insufficient
to establish the impermissibility of all transactions with A. Under
ordinary circumstances, it would be permissible for B to argue with
A, to accept just compensation from A, or to cooperate with A in an
effort to save the life of C. We should ask, then, what is special about
doing business with A that gives *prima facie* credence to the
"condition-of-business" principle. A partial answer no doubt is that
B's doing business with A frequently tends both to *benefit A in consequence of A's rights violations,* and to *encourage directly or indirectly those
violations.* Morality both condemns evil in itself and the benefiting of
evildoers when the benefit comes as a consequence of their evil (for
example, we assume that practicing racists ought not benefit as a
result of their racist actions). Accordingly, one might infer—and
common sentiment tends to confirm—that if business transactions
tended to discourage rights violations and either to harm or, at a

minimum, to fail to benefit rights violators in consequence of their rights violations, then the transactions may be permissible.

Such a situation can be hypothesized. The sale of political science textbooks to South African companies supplying schools for non-white youths living in the Bantustans, books extolling the rights of all persons regardless of race to participate in the political process, might be morally justified, because we could reasonably predict that the long-term effects of such sales would be to undermine apartheid even as they weakened the privileges of the white minority. The same may be true of sales to the Ford Motor Company's South African subsidiary in light of Ford's decision to sell a significant portion of its South African production facilities to nonwhite workers (the rest of it being sold to white South Africans) while continuing to supply parts and provide advice to the new South African company.

Thus, the original "condition-of-business" principle must be revised again to exempt certain transactions. It should read *ceteris paribus, business transactions by B with A are impermissible when A is a systematic violator of fundamental rights, unless those transactions serve to discourage the violation of rights and either harm or, at a minimum, fail to benefit A in consequence of A's rights-violating activity.*

What does this principle entail when applied to South Africa? *If* the overall effect of U.S. business activity in South Africa were the undermining of apartheid and the undercutting of white privileges, and *if* disinvestment would fail to achieve those same results more efficiently and in a greater degree than not disinvesting, then U.S. business activity with South Africa might be morally justified. However, few observers continue to make the argument that the mere presence of foreign investment will, owing to its encouragement of the South African economy, help free nonwhites from apartheid through their labor becoming more valuable in an expanding economy. So if any argument holds promise in this direction it must be one that specifies a certain *kind* of business, for example, enlightened U.S. businesses in South Africa that adhere to progressive principles like those once advocated by the Reverend Leon Sullivan. I will set aside this important possibility for the moment, however, and return to it later.

Consistency is crucial. To say that any country that violates fundamental rights thereby becomes an immoral trading partner may seem correct in the instance of South Africa; but is the same true in the instance of the Soviet Union? Many observers would argue that better Superpower cooperation is the only avenue to world peace. Their claim reflects a broader concern, namely, the assertion that a wide range of exceptions to the principle must be tolerated, in particular, every instance in which adhering to it would generate, on balance, negative consequences. In this vein during the late 1980s some U.S. State Department officials and members of the Margaret Thatcher government argued that disinvestment in South Africa would be wrong since valuable economic goods would be lost.[8] And, making a similar appeal, many in the United States claimed that the United States had crucial national security interests at risk in South Africa.

Not all consequential exceptions to the condition-of-business principle can be precluded by appeal to the nature of principled moral reasoning. One need not be a consequentialist (someone who believes that all actions are evaluated in terms of the extent to which they achieve desirable results) to recognize that most principles can be overridden either by stronger principles or by the threat of moral catastrophe. That the threat of moral catastrophe can override principles is suggested by the insight that while rights and other moral principles may ordinarily "trump" consequential goals (to borrow Ronald Dworkin's expression),[9] their validity becomes suspect when extraordinary moral horrors could be expected to ensue from their exercise.[10] Consider again the notion of dealing with the Mafia. Suppose that only the Mafia had access to a drug needed to cure a large number of desperately ill patients suffering from cancer. Without buying from the Mafia, a moral catastrophe would occur: many patients would die needlessly from cancer. Here, all other things being equal, business with the Mafia would be justified.

When put improperly, as it sometimes is, the "extraordinary moral horror" caveat appears to make principled moral reasoning inconsistent; that is, it appears to create a theory that shuns simple calculations of the consequences of alternative, historically situated acts, then swallows its pride and does precisely that—so long, of course, as the particular consequences are sufficiently catastrophic. But when understood properly the caveat need imply no inconsistency. It may, for example, be understood as a second-level, organizing concept (of the sort that philosophers label "syncategormatic") which in the present instance signals a probable failure in the application of a set of moral principles to a particular context. To put it another way, when the consequence of following a principle is an extraordinary moral horror, it alerts the moral reasoner to the possibility that some other relevant, opposing principle should have been considered. Hence there need be no logical inconsistency in advising a person or corporation to follow a principle, such as the condition-of-business principle, while warning them that the principle may be invalid if moral horrors would result from its application.

To summarize the discussion so far, then, the "condition-of-business" principle, although revised to handle obvious counterexamples, nonetheless leaves open two important classes of exceptions. The first concerns the possibility that morally enlightened business activities, such as those conducted in accordance with the Sullivan Principles,[11] might escape the principle by serving to harm both apartheid and the racist individuals who support it; the second concerns the possibility that extraordinary moral horrors might follow from renouncing business ties to rights violators. If this were true then the *ceteris paribus* condition of the principle would fail to be met. The remainder of this chapter is devoted to examining the South African situation of the late 1980s in some detail and showing why it fails to qualify as an exception of either kind. The conclusion, then, will be that there exists at least one real-life, nonhypothetical case—that of South Africa—in which disinvestment is morally required.

"ENLIGHTENED" BUSINESS IN SOUTH AFRICA

Because of their response to criticisms of racism, some corporations operating in South Africa deserve the label "enlightened." Obvious examples are some, but not all, of the so-called Sullivan signatories, a group of approximately 170 U.S. corporations adhering to the code of conduct developed by the Philadelphia minister Leon H. Sullivan.[12] On June 3, 1987, Leon Sullivan himself called for companies to disinvest, to sell all investments and end all commercial ties with South Africa. Yet even without the blessing of the code's founder, many U.S. corporations continue to support the Sullivan Code, and it appears increasingly capable of sustaining an independent life.[13] In addition to the Sullivan code, two similar codes exist for foreign multinationals: one for Canada, and the other for the Common Market nations. As mentioned earlier, all are voluntary, but the Canadian and Common Market codes are administered by the respective governments, while the Sullivan Code is administered by the Sullivan Organization.[14] The codes prescribe among other things that signatory subsidiaries in South Africa pay equal wages for equal work, integrate previously segregated eating and rest room facilities, and, in some instances, take positive steps to discourage the maintenance of apartheid.[15]

Before we examine the question of Sullivan signatories, let us reexamine the revised condition-of-business principle to shed light on the more fundamental question of *why* parties ought not to benefit from rights violations or abet the rights violations of others.

Two aspects of the caveat section of the revised principle need separating: that of encouraging or discouraging rights violations on the one hand, and that of harming or benefiting rights violators on the other. In the South African context, the former concerns the question of whether ongoing business transactions tend to support or weaken the institution of apartheid. Here the moral issue is straightforward: all other things being equal, one ought not act in ways that support an unjust institution. This embodies the more general principle that one ought not facilitate the doing of evil, and this principle informs not only our moral traditions, as evidenced by notions such as "I wouldn't do business with a person like that," but also our laws. For example, law sometimes prohibits business activity in certain instances where the activity is normally considered lawful because the activity encourages the criminal activity of others—the most obvious case being that of buying or receiving stolen goods.

The latter issue of harming or helping rights violators is at stake when we ask whether ongoing business transactions benefit those responsible for maintaining apartheid. It is distinct from the earlier issue: for example, an action may benefit an individual evildoer while nonetheless harming the unjust institution in which he or she participates. (I reject for present purposes the deeper philosophical sense of "benefit," articulated by Plato, in which evildoers never benefit by way of their evil.) It is, moreover, an issue connected to traditional notions of retributive justice. We think that those who undertake evil acts, such as systematically violating others' rights, ought not to benefit in consequence of their evil.

Now with respect to the issue of encouraging or discouraging apartheid, the morality of disinvestment is inconclusive. No doubt a strong *prima facie* argument exists for saying that the presence of foreign business in South Africa helps erode apartheid or, at a minimum, prevents it from becoming worse. Foreign firms are said to be able to exert pressure for change, pressures stemming largely from the different traditions and moral expectations present in their home countries. Would not South African companies with racist managements rush to take the foreigners' place? And might not the fear and bitterness engendered by the exit of the representatives of the world's leading industrial powers encourage even stricter apartheid, in a conservative backlash? On balance, however, it seems implausible to suppose—and almost nobody is willing to argue—that rank-and-file, non–Sullivan signatory firms contribute significantly to the dismantlement of apartheid. The lip service paid to egalitarian policies is disavowed in practice by inequitable treatment, including discriminatory working conditions, which is typically afforded employees.

The leading possible exceptions, again, are the so-called enlightened firms such as the Sullivan Principle signatories and their

Canadian and Common Market counterparts. Nevertheless, we must recognize the obvious limits on their ability to achieve reform. The number of South African nonwhites working for U.S. firms is less than 1 percent of the nonwhite South African work force, and the total percentage of nonwhites working for foreign multinationals is less than 4 percent.[16] And while enlightened multinationals could conceivably press for more equitable wage ratios between nonwhites and whites—ratios estimated by some to be about 1:4 for comparable work—there are formidable pressures of competition. If company X, a mining firm, attempts to employ nonwhites at higher wages than company Z, a rival firm, then X puts itself at a competitive disadvantage. It does so because it must pay higher wages and, in turn, sell products at higher prices to receive a comparable return on investment; and without comparable return on investment the company will lose the confidence of the investment community, in particular the capital markets, and as a consequence will lessen its ability to finance future activities. Such situations of competitive disadvantage tend not to persist over the long term without government intervention, since disadvantaged firms are driven from business by competitors.

Now it must be granted that the prospect of equalizing wage rates is a complex economic issue. For example, many multinationals might finance reform in their South African operations by drawing capital and revenues away from other global operations, a possibility that looks brighter when we realize that South African operations usually constitute only a tiny fraction of any given multinational's business. Nonetheless, most will recognize that the willingness and ability of corporations to finance ongoing operations at a loss for moral reasons is severely limited; and it is worth reminding ourselves that most corporations use decentralized accounting techniques that emphasize the need for each separable unit to show a profit.

It also would be naive to suppose that because it is in the interest of employers to pay more in order to get more, the principles of free market competition will equalize wage rates between nonwhites and whites. Classical economic theory decrees that equal work should receive equal pay, yet economists agree that it frequently does not. Unemployment among nonwhites in South Africa is rampant, a fact signaling an excess supply of labor so severe that competition in the labor market for nonwhites is a fiction. Moreover, even free market principles do not pretend to guarantee equal pay for equal *effort*, but only for equal *productivity*. And since productivity is a function of many more variables than effort, for example, of education, skills, and capital, and since nonwhites lack these characteristics in dramatic abundance, it follows that they will inevitably lose in head-to-head market competition with whites. Our experience in the United States should serve as sobering testimony to this very fact, since over 200 years after the abolition of slavery, U.S. blacks earn barely more than half of what whites earn, and what is worse, possess only one tenth the personal wealth.

In short it is cheaper for foreign companies to pay nonwhites lower wages, and because it is cheaper, the practice will likely persist until South African law intervenes. This conclusion may appear pessimistic, but is not; indeed it is compatible with the relatively optimistic view that corporate actions are not always the simple product of market and other external forces. Companies do have important discretionary powers and can frequently resist market forces, but their ability to do so is sharply limited, and for labor-intensive industries— precisely the sort of industries for which nonwhites in South Africa tend to work—labor costs constitute such a large proportion of total costs that ability to pay above market wages, even for enlightened, labor-intensive firms—is severely limited. The road to social hell is frequently paved with the most rational of economic intentions.

What is true for the prospect of improving wage disparities is also true for any corporate reform costing money. It is true for corporate training programs, for boycotts of racist suppliers, for contributions to activist political programs (including contributions and fees paid to the Sullivan Organization), and for civil disobedience of a kind that breaks unfair laws while incurring fines and other legal penalties. Indeed, it is difficult to imagine corporate actions effective in combating apartheid that do not cost money, and this should raise doubts about the power of enlightened foreign business to turn the tide of South African racial history.

Hence, when asking whether the presence of foreign business, even of enlightened foreign business, makes the maintenance of apartheid more difficult, the most honest answer is that the matter is undecided. In the face of empirical uncertainties and plausible arguments both for and against, any attempt to base the moral case against disinvestment on the speculation that the long-term consequence of the presence of foreign firms is to undermine apartheid should be regarded with suspicion.

But the second of the two issues, that concerning benefit to individuals, is a different matter. Again, traditional moral notions hold that evildoers ought not to benefit as a consequence, direct or otherwise, of their evil. We may put aside for present purposes theoretical controversies over retributive versus utilitarian schemes of punishment, since both tend to converge in supposing that *if* racism or some other pernicious evil has fruits, those fruits should not be pleasant tasting. Even committed utilitarians can grant the efficacy on balance of negative reinforcement. Thus, insofar as insensitive whites may derive economic and social benefits through the very system of apartheid they struggle to maintain, those benefits are ill-gotten from the moral point of view.

Although most will grant the principle that evildoers ought not benefit by virtue of their evil, some may be reluctant to take the additional step of asserting that such considerations should be factors in corporate decision making. Yet we do consider rectification a proper end of business management in certain instances.[17] For example, we believe that the executives at Morton Thiokol, Inc., ought not reward those who attempted to camouflage safety problems in solid rocket boosters before the Challenger rocket disaster in 1986, and we believe that they ought not even if it could be shown (which I suspect it cannot) that the practice of camouflaging safety problems on the whole tends to advance rather than retard corporate profits.

Even granting that our actions ought not benefit racists when those benefits happen in consequence of the racists' rights-denying activities, how can it be supposed that our actions *do* benefit racist South Africans? Here, too, an appeal to principles of classical economic thought is possible. The rationale for supposing that South African whites benefit through business with even enlightened foreign firms is similar to the rationale of the market itself; in voluntary market transactions one assumes that parties will not participate unless they believe they will benefit. The South African company that buys from a U.S. hydraulic valve manufacturer engages in a transaction which according to classical theory is optimal from that company's perspective, since were it otherwise, the company would exercise its option to purchase from a rival supplier. This means that since market transactions between foreign multinationals and South African corporations are seldom forced, we may predict that doing business with foreign firms is beneficial to those corporations, and to individual South African consumers, at least in the long term. To question this logic, one must imagine oneself to possess more knowledge about the preferences and wants of South African whites, as well as the means necessary to satisfy them, than the whites themselves possess. Such knowledge may be possible in individual cases (for example, we may suppose to know more about the true benefits of "Odor Eaters" to a particular friend, or of a luxury automobile to a victim of insular poverty, than those persons themselves) but making such suppositions on a broad scale is risky at best. Consequently, particular instances may occur in which a South African firm's business with a foreign corporation serves to harm rather than help its interests, as when, say, the revolutionary books handled by a South African wholesaler are put to use by its nonwhite employees to formulate their labor demands. But we have no reason for supposing that such instances are more than exceptions to the rule.

So even though claims that enlightened firms encourage, or, alternatively, weaken, the institution of apartheid are open to reasonable doubt, the general claim that white South Africans, white-dominated South African corporations, and the white South African government are harmed, or fail to benefit, by transactions with foreign multinationals seems false. Hence, since for one side of the question we reach an inconclusive answer, and on the other side a conclusive one, applying the revised condition-of-business principle yields the conclusion that, *ceteris paribus*, foreign multinationals should exit South Africa. The revised condition-of-business principle states that transactions are impermissible unless "those transactions serve to discourage the violation of rights and either harm A or, at a minimum, fail to benefit A, in consequence of A's rights-violating activity." We have argued that although it is impossible to say with confidence that maintaining transactions will discourage the violation of rights in itself, it is possible to say that maintaining them will benefit A, and, as a result, *ceteris paribus*, maintaining them is impermissible.

EXTRAORDINARY MORAL HORRORS

But are all things equal—*ceteris paribus*? The remaining escape route from the foregoing argument is by way of the "extraordinary moral horrors" exception mentioned earlier. According to this exception it is sometimes argued that disinvestment may dangerously compromise NATO security. Three particular concerns are offered by U.S. State Department officials in defense of the strategic and geopolitical importance of South Africa. The first is South Africa's location at a critical juncture of shipping lanes for Middle Eastern oil. The second is South Africa's abundant mineral reserves; they note that half of South Africa's foreign earnings come from gold exports and that a large part of the rest comes from other strategic metals—indeed, South Africa is the world's largest supplier of platinum, chromium, and vanadium, all of which are considered vital to U.S. military industry. The third is South Africa's enormous diamond-producing capacity. Of these individual claims, only two touch on what might be considered a "moral horror," namely, the production of materials such as platinum and vanadium necessary for U.S. military production and South Africa's strategic sea-lane position.

But neither consideration suggests the significant possibility of moral horrors in the event of disinvestment.[18] Not only does the West have alternative sources for the strategic metals in question (although sometimes at higher prices),[19] but there is the possibility that a South Africa isolated from international business would reform its racist system in response. It might implement precisely the changes desired by reformers, and, in turn, renew its trade with the major developed countries.[20] It is also possible that disinvestment could contribute to the final downfall of white rule in much the way that the boycott of Rhodesia did.[21] Even if it did not, the second consideration, South Africa's strategic sea position, is unlikely to constitute a serious threat to NATO interests. The argument assumes that South Africa might switch to the Soviet camp and interfere, or threaten to interfere, with international shipping lanes. But as one of the very few governments in the world with a stronger professed hatred of communism than the United States, South Africa under white rule is unlikely to enter, either now or in the future, the Soviet camp. This conclusion is strengthened by the supposition, common among experts, that South Africa possesses atomic weapons.[22] With atomic capabilities a white South African government, antagonized by most Western governments, would have the luxury of avoiding the trade-off so common among smaller states of sacrificing either military security or nonalignment.

But a more serious "moral horror" must be considered. Might not full foreign disinvestment trigger a bloodbath between rebelling nonwhites and intransigent whites? This possibility must be taken seriously despite the fact that the weight of informed opinion in the late 1980s, including not only that of nonwhite leaders in South Africa but of foreign observers, appeared to reach the opposite conclusion, namely, that economic pressure was one of the last hopes for relaxing white intransigence and avoiding a bloodbath.

It is true that a number of writers, especially in the popular media, have invoked the possibility that sanctions will provoke catastrophic warfare.[23] At the heart of the charge seems to be the conviction that there is an absolute line beyond which the whites will not move. Some concessions, of course, are possible: all political prisoners could be released under suitable safeguards, the Group Areas legislation could be modified, a limited form of plural representation could be introduced, the labor market could be loosened, and a color-blind consumer society could be encouraged. But white control is another matter. As Dennis Austin has written, "No Afrikaner government is going to pull down the Vortrekker Monument or the national flag of the Republic." And "if 250,000 whites in Rhodesia were prepared to fight over a fifteen year period against odds of one to twenty-five, how much more probable it is that four and three-quarter million whites in South Africa at odds of one to five, will continue to use armed force?"[24] The likelihood of bloody warfare may be further

enhanced, some add, by the fact that the African National Conference (ANC) is united on the need to retain the option of using violence as a means to securing political change.[25]

Yet a closer examination tells a different story. Although white
resistance was long-lasting in Zimbabwe, it is important to remember
that Zimbabwe did successfully emerge from a political deal in which
full-scale civil war was avoided.[26] The peculiar circumstances of South
Africa make most parallels with other African states questionable,
however, although they also improve South Africa's prospects. Three
points of difference stand out: first, the period of white rule has
been long; second, the nonwhites' struggle for power has been protracted; third, the urban and industrial experience of a substantial
portion of the nonwhite population has been considerable and long-
lasting.[27] "No other sub-Saharan state has been forged in conditions
anything like this," write Buzan and Nazareth, "and they will give
Azania ["Azania" is the name accepted by many groups opposed to
apartheid for the new, projected South Africa state] some tremen-
dous advantages."[28] White incentives for a negotiated solution are
strong. A protracted conflict would put enormous strains on the limited white manpower base, and the whites would be forced to fight
on with no hope of ultimate victory. They would realize that international support would nearly all be on the other side. Furthermore,
the commitment to militarism by nonwhites discussed by conservative journalists is probably exaggerated. A key sign of the ANC's
moderation is its constant effort to enlist the cooperation of whites.
Even ANC violence directed against whites is explicitly intended not
to drive whites out, but, in Mandela's words, to "bring them to their
senses."[29] The ANC leaders, writes Mufson, "do not envision themselves rolling into Pretoria on top of a Russian tank."[30] The ANC
still appears to count on negotiating with the government.

It is also worth reminding ourselves that the central issue in the
overall context is not simply whether revolutionary bloodbath in South
Africa is likely, but whether its likelihood is enhanced through foreign disinvestment. And on this score, nonwhite opinion in South
Africa (as well as the majority of opinion outside it) favors the likelihood that sanctions will avoid, not encourage, bloodshed. Rather
than stiffening the back of the Afrikaner resistance, sanctions will,
many argue, promote reform. Bishop Desmond Tutu has said, "We
reject completely the argument that international pressure will force
the South African Government to withdraw into itself; . . . the Af-
rikaners have, in fact, only changed course when under extreme
pressure."[31] And in the highly acclaimed report prepared under the
auspices of the forty-nine member Commonwealth organization,[32] it
was agreed that "if the South African government comes to believe

that no economic measures will be taken against it, the process of change will stall and the descent into violence will hasten."[33] The report concluded that the South African government is not ready, and does not intend, to negotiate in good faith and that economic sanctions "may offer the last opportunity to avert what could be the worst bloodbath since the Second World War."[34]

It is also worth noting that extraordinary moral horrors predicted by those who oppose South African disinvestment are not predicted out of concern for nonwhites: rather their concern is about milder possibilities, for example, that jobs would be scarcer and commodities more expensive.[35]

The arguments predicting a bloodbath are not decisive: we may conclude that there is at least one instance—that of South Africa in the late 1980s—where full disinvestment is the right step. Doing business with South African firms and, indirectly, the white-led nation that charters and supports them, is wrong because it benefits those who ought not benefit: namely, individuals and organizations determined to preserve privileges defined by apartheid. For this reason a corporation's merely divesting itself of its South African subsidiaries is inadequate: the wrong people still benefit. Such a corporation should take the additional step of refusing to buy from, or sell to, previous subsidiaries and other South African-chartered corporations.

None of this is to deny that some real world instances properly fall under the "extraordinary moral horrors" exception. For example, termination of all trade with the Soviet Union could have a chilling effect on relations between the Superpowers, and could step up tensions in the nuclear standoff, so that perhaps even Soviet violations of fundamental rights should take second place in evaluating the morality of bilateral trade. But the stakes in the South African debate are neither so gargantuan nor crucial.

For other countries, the answer is less clear. Should the United States and other developed democracies refuse to engage in commerce with Vietnam, Chile, and Turkey? On the basis of the preceding reasoning, only one thing can be said with confidence: arriving at an answer implies a determination of whether systematic violations of the most fundamental sort of rights are occurring, and whether the facts justify either one of the two exceptions to the condition-of-business principle as outlined in this chapter.

The preceding discussion does not imply that individual foreign corporations or individual foreign investors should bear the entire burden of the financial losses engendered by disinvestment. Indeed, insofar as the leading argument for disinvestment relies on the obligation to respond appropriately to a systematic violation of fundamental rights, and since this obligation falls on all moral agents, just the reverse is suggested. At the very least, individual governments in the developed democracies should probably cushion the blow of disinvestment and make what is morally mandatory practically achievable. In the instance of South Africa, the average U.S. corporation with South African business connections in the mid 1980s generated less than 1 percent of its overall revenue from such business. For a handful of small foreign corporations deciding to exit South Africa, however, the move could have been tantamount to bankruptcy. It seems less than gracious for indignant onlookers to demand that these companies fulfill their international moral obligations at the cost of financial suicide.

In this chapter we defined and applied a norm to govern disinvestment decisions. This norm, the condition-of-business principle, asserts that unless one of two well-defined exceptions obtain, it is immoral to transact business with certain individuals and organizations disposed to violate fundamental rights systematically—a conclusion that applies to South Africa in the late 1980s. The principle is meant to be a refinement of a more common precept, one often expressed in business circles by the words "I wouldn't do business with someone like that." As we have seen, the principle applies even in instances where the termination of transactions tends to harm more than help innocents, unless that harm encompasses what has been labeled "extraordinary moral horrors."

9

Conclusion

This book has argued that multinational corporations and nation-states must recognize the ethical import of their commercial decisions with an eye to relevant empirical and moral complexities. Our aim, then, has been to rescue and restructure the old-fashioned idea that moral concepts can and should inform international economic activity. We began by attempting to provide a "breathing space" for international ethics. Such a space reflects the presence of human factors in a realm whose cultural diversity and interest-dominated policies have for many implied a moral wasteland. We argued that both traditional Hobbesians and cultural relativists are unduly pessimistic, and that while it is clear that moral philosophy in application to the international economic realm does not tolerate simplistic projections of home country values abroad, neither does it encourage a skeptical nihilism in which anything goes. The so-called realists were shown in this regard to be profoundly unrealistic.

Perhaps the single most important concept articulated in this book is that of a fundamental international right. It is the determinate concept of a right lying midway between the general, abstract concepts of moral philosophy and the more specific, demanding precepts of individual nations. The ten fundamental international rights (Chapter 5) serve to establish a moral minimum for the behavior of all international economic agents. In other words, whatever else an international business organization does, it must respect these ten rights. Honoring them, as we saw, means not only refraining from directly depriving people of rights, but sometimes indirectly protecting the rights from deprivation. This is not a simple matter. It often requires a sophisticated moral and empirical analysis incorporating the truth that multinational corporations are not responsible for honoring international rights in precisely the same manner as nation-states or individuals. Especially complex, as shown by the ap-

plication of the ethical algorithm (Chapter 6), are situations where
home and host country norms conflict. When host country standards
for pollution, discrimination, and salary schedules appear substandard from the perspective of the home country, it is not always true
that the manager should take the high road and implement home
country standards, because the high road sometimes implies a failure to respect a country's cultural traditions or its relative level of
economic development. Nonetheless, cultural integrity and level of
economic development were shown to be no excuse for moral nihilism; they offer no comfort for the view that "if our practice doesn't
break one of their laws, it's OK."

Hence this book offers a framework for viewing moral problems
in international business which incorporates three principal analytic
devices: a social contract analysis of the multinational corporation, a
set of ten fundamental international rights that entail correlative duties for multinational corporations, and an ethical "algorithm" for
use in arbitrating conflicts between home and host standards. From
the perspective of each of these analytic devices, moral, not prudential reasons, justify moral conclusions.

This should not be taken to mean that prudential reasons are irrelevant. Indeed, it is likely that significant convergence exists between ethics and long-term self-interest in global business, just as it
exists in domestic business and personal affairs. Of course, corporate
self-interest and ethics do not always coincide, even in the long term;
further, the *reason* for global business ethics clearly is not prudence.
Yet without ethics certain practical goods become less certain, and
few doubt that ethics can play a positive and contributory role in
multinational business in some instances. As Adam Smith argued years
ago, the free market requires the moral cooperation of its participants to help in honoring contracts, reducing market externalities,
and making the entire system run smoothly.

One part of the story about the prudential advantages of ethics is
told through the obvious interrelations among a business's public image, its ethics, and its profits. Media revelations about unethical practices make public relations a critical economic task for most multinationals, and it is no doubt true, as Farr and Stening have noted,
that whether such criticisms are warranted or not, multinationals must
devise appropriate responses for the charges laid against them.[1]

Anecdotes from foreign nationals who run branches of U.S. multinationals tell another part of the story. I have spoken to executives
in charge of the branches of U.S. companies abroad who argue, surprisingly enough, that rules against bribery entailed by the U.S. Foreign Corrupt Practices Act (rules that prevent them from bribing in

instances where other multinational managers are able to do so),* actually offer them a competitive advantage. When asked for a bribe, a ready response is available. The employee, who is usually a citizen of the host country, can say to the would-be bribee, "You know the U.S. types—their law simply does not permit bribery." The result is a competitive advantage for the U.S. firm. Its competition must pay not only the costs of production and distribution, but the costs of bribing local officials and executives as well. To take another example, heads of large multinational corporations with whom I have talked insist that their corporation's strong reputation for ethical practice is a business asset in host countries. Because of good reputation, they say they are trusted in foreign countries, especially by foreign governments, in instances where their competitors are not.

Admittedly, such evidence is anecdotal and sketchy. This does not mean, however, that we should abandon hope for establishing correlations between ethics and multinational business success; nor does it imply that we must adopt a position of perfect neutrality about the possible contributions that ethics might sometimes make in achieving specific business goals. It merely reflects the fact that in global as well as domestic contexts, the puzzle of empirically tracking the fruits of ethical behavior is nearly impossible. How does one isolate the variable of "ethical integrity," much less define it operationally?

But there is a deeper reason why this book does not attempt to establish empirical connections between ethics and international business success, a reason that explains the subtle error committed by many well-intentioned defenders of business ethics. Those who attempt to establish a correlation between good ethics and successful business, and then use it as the principal reason for taking ethics seriously, forget that the economic downside of, say, bribing a publicly elected official, cannot count as a *moral* reason for refusing to bribe. They forget, in other words, that the moral reason for not giving a large bribe to a publicly elected official in Brazil is simply that it is wrong; to be more specific (in line with the reasoning of Chapter 5), such a bribe conflicts with a multinational's obligation to honor the individual's right to political participation which, in turn, requires cooperation by the multinational in the protection of the right. They forget, in short, that moral reasons are required in support of moral conclusions.

In this vein it may be helpful to consider the analogy to our per-

---

*In contrast, West German law counts bribes as legitimate tax deductions, although one must be able to prove that the bribes were actually paid, by providing a receipt or other proof of the bribe to West German tax authorities.

sonal lives. We may agree with Bishop Buttler's point in *Ten Sermons Preached at Rolls Chapel* that a life of egoism is unnatural, unsatisfactory, and unhappy.[2] But it is a further step to say that *because* living nonegoistically makes us happier, doing so is therefore the *morally* best course of action. What is morally right and prudentially effective cannot be assumed, at least without further argument, to be identical. Immanuel Kant, the German philosopher, virtually made a career out of this simple, yet crucial, distinction.

On a broader scale, practice suggests that the realists' cry to eschew moralizing in international corporate and economic policy is futile. For the citizens of the world's developed countries—countries that serve as bases for the most powerful multinational corporations—are well known for the depth of their moral sentiment.[3] They will reliably introduce moral concerns into international business whether skeptics like it or not. In the United States, economic ties to the Soviet Union have been criticized on moral grounds, even as they have been defended on moral grounds. The issue of trade with South Africa, as we observed in Chapter 8, is understood primarily from the perspective of our moral views about discrimination, censorship, and apartheid. From the standpoint of this and other international issues, national self-interest constitutes only one of many considerations propelling public discussion, and it must take its place alongside those of fairness, cultural imperialism, democratic values, and rights.

For this reason, economists and business experts who attempt to disabuse us of the tendency to apply moral notions to international business perform a disservice, for they leave the moral part of international business unexamined. They insulate it from the rigors of clarity, consistency, and good causal analysis which make for informed business policy. One version of shallow moralizing, then, ironically, is to assert that morals play no role whatsoever in international business.

How might multinational corporations improve their moral performance and come to embody the normative conclusions advanced in this book? Two classes of remedies suggest themselves: external remedies that rely on international associations or agreements on the one hand, and internal remedies that rely on corporate initiative on the other.

Chapter 3 discussed the dramatic expansion of external remedies in the form of international laws, agreements, and codes of conduct. Although many of these are nonbinding in the sense that noncompliance fails to trigger sanctions, as a group they are coming to exert significant influence on multinational conduct. One of the principal advantages of such global and industrywide initiatives is that they distribute costs more fairly than initiatives undertaken by individual corporations. When, in line with the WHO Code of Marketing Breast Milk Substitutes, Nestle curtails questionable marketing practices for the sale of infant formula, it does so with the confidence that the other signers of the WHO code will not enjoy unfair advantage by undertaking the same questionable practices, for they, too, must adhere to its provisions. Still another advantage of external remedies stems from the fact that many nation-states, especially developing ones, are unable to gather sufficient information about, much less control, the multinational corporations that operate within their borders. Thus, supranational entities, whether of an international or interindustry form, can sometimes augment, or supplement the developing countries' power and information. It seems difficult to deny that the growth and maturation of such entities can enhance the ethical conduct of multinational business.

The issue of nonvoluntary sanctions is more difficult. As we have seen, the realm of what is called "international law" is largely a realm of voluntary associations, with agreed-upon rules and few sanctions. Because the sanctions that attach to domestic law, even in the enforcement of contracts, eventually imply the use of state force, and because the prospects of a global governing body with a monopoly on internationally administered force seem remote, so too the prospects for regulating business by international rules backed by sanction seem dim. George Ball and others have recommended the international chartering of global corporations, but the issues of the proper international agency to effect such chartering, and the imposition of penalties in the event the conditions of charter are violated, are thorny. Most corporations balk immediately at the suggestion that the United Nations become the chartering agency, since they perceive that body as being dominated by the interests of developing countries. Advocates of international chartering speak convincingly about the need for a new international agency established for the task of implementing multinational accountability; yet to date no concrete proposal has emerged. Whatever the merits of a global business policeman, the likelihood of its emergence seems small, and this dooms most discussions of such a prospect to academic irrelevance. For purposes of this book, the issue has been largely moot for a different reason. As mentioned at the very beginning, we have been concerned with determining the moral obligations of international business, not its legal obligations. We have been concerned with rules without laws. That many moral obligations are properly also legal obligations is certain, but determining what the law should be has not been our task.

The most important internal change likely to enhance the ethical

behavior of multinationals is for multinationals themselves to undertake ethical deliberation; to introduce factors of ethics into their
decision-making mechanisms. That they should do so is a clear implication of the discussion of the previous chapters, yet it is a conclusion some will resist. Those who place great confidence in the efficacy of the market may, for example, believe that a corporate policy
of moral disinterest and profit maximization will—*pace* Adam Smith's
"invisible hand"—maximize overall global welfare.

This kind of ideological confidence in the international market may
have been understandable decades ago. But persisting in the belief
that market mechanisms automatically ensure adequate moral conduct today seems recklessly idealistic. Forces such as Islamic funda-
mentalism, the global debt "bomb," and massive unemployment in
developing countries have drastically distorted the operation of the
free market in international commerce. Even though a further selec-
tive freeing of the market forces may enhance global productivity, it
cannot solve automatically questions of fair treatment, hazardous
technology, or discrimination. One of the aims of this book is to
highlight the depth and intractability of certain international business problems. It seems reasonable to ask, if domestic problems arising against a backdrop of the domestic legal system frequently elude
market solutions, can we be more optimistic about international
problems that straddle legal boundaries?

Even adopting the minimal guidelines for corporate conduct advanced in this book would involve dramatic changes in the decision-
making mechanisms of multinational corporations. Such firms would
need to alter established patterns of information flow and collection
to accommodate new forms of morally relevant information. The
already complex parameters of corporate decision making would become more so. Even scholarly research about international business
would need to change. At present, research choices tend to be dic-
tated by the goals of higher profits, long-term access to basic commodities needed for manufactured items, and increased global market share; obviously these goals sometimes conflict with broader moral
ends, such as refraining from violating human rights. Revised goals
call for a revised program of research. And although we have rejected the view that multinational corporations must shoulder the
world's problems of poverty, discrimination, and political injustice
because, as economic entities, they have limited social missions, their
goals must include the aim of not impeding solutions to such problems.

Are such changes in the decision making of multinational corporations likely or even possible? Resistance will be intense; clearly, there
should be no delusions on this score. Yet, without ignoring the dif-

ficulties, I do not think the task impossible. At a minimum, corporations are capable of choosing the more ethical alternative in instances where alternative courses of action yield equal profits—and I believe they are capable of even more. Corporations are run by human beings, not beasts. As multinational corporations continue to mature in the context of an ever-expanding, more powerful global economy, we have reason to think they can look beyond their national borders, and recognize the same minimal claims made in the name of our shared humanity that they accept at home.

APPENDIX

Neo-Hobbesianism: David Gauthier's *Morals By Agreement*

Gauthier takes certain of Hobbes's failings and attempts to turn them to ironic advantage. Pursuing the theory in its prescriptive rather than analytic application Gauthier utilizes a presupposition from traditional Hobbesianism: namely, that rational, exclusively self-interested individuals have reason to restrain self-interest and that the resulting principles of self-restraint qualify as moral norms. Yet he claims to discover advantage where Hobbes found moral impossibility. Whereas Hobbes concluded that the absence of a sovereign enforcer restricts morality both by requiring such an enforcer's presence for its emergence, and when the enforcer is present, by limiting it to principles that the enforcer could enforce, Gauthier jettisons the requirement of a sovereign and thus allows the boundaries of rational morality to expand broadly. In effect he rejects Hobbes's analytic application of his argument in order to bolster and brighten its prescriptive application. One consequence is to encourage the prospects of international morality and to strengthen the likelihood that moral norms can have transnational application, at least when the term "moral" is construed to include rational principles of self-interested cooperation.

Of course, Hobbes himself was the forerunner of the bold, ongoing effort to square rational self-interest with morality and to show that what helps me—at least in the long run—coincides with, and perhaps even defines, what is moral.[1] Hobbes believed that the limits of rational prudence were the limits of morality. By "right reason" Hobbes meant the "act of reasoning, that is, the . . . true ratiocination of every man concerning those actions of his, which may either

redound to the damage or benefit of his neighbors."[2] Hobbes abro-
gated in advance the appeal to fear of divine punishment or guilt
feelings and in doing so made his own task more difficult. Nonetheless, he believed that no genuine conflict between morality and rational prudence is possible, especially given the crucial need of rational agents to avoid disastrous outcomes triggered by sanctions from
others, such as the withdrawal of all future cooperation.

Leading Hobbesian commentators seem agreed that Hobbes's own
attempt to prove this falls short for a variety of reasons, not the least
of which is his unrealistic assumption that by undertaking an offen-
sive violation of moral rules, a person risks the total withdrawal of
future cooperation by others.[3]

But in Gauthier's neo-Hobbesianism, modern concepts are used to
mount a new and striking defense of rational prudence. Gauthier
relies on two prominent twentieth-century paradigms, the economist's notion of rationality, and the emerging field of decision theory, a reliance which has the effect of supporting Hobbes's age-old
perspective with new tools. Gauthier updates Hobbes by incorporating concepts of "maximizing" and "economic rationality" into the
Hobbesian prescriptive strategy.[4] Also notable for our purposes is
Gauthier's unblushing application of his theory to international contexts.

Gauthier's efforts occur at the end of a long line of attempts—the
wreckage of which litters the history of philosophy—to prove that
morality can be derived from reason. Whether from the Roman Stoics,
Kant, or more recently Alan Gewirth, arguments purporting to illuminate the rational source of our feelings of duty and charity frequently fail to satisfy fully; like proofs for the existence of God, they
sometimes bedazzle without convincing. In *Morals By Agreement* Gauthier attempts to show that interest-maximizing rationality and morality are not in conflict, and that, indeed, their courses are precisely
parallel. Individuals, nation-states, and corporations possess moral
responsibilities not despite, but because of, their wish to pursue their
own interests successfully. To this end he adopts the presupposition
that "a person acts rationally if and only if she seeks her greatest
interest of benefit."[5] The notion of seeking one's greatest interest or
benefit is not logically reducible to the meaning of the word "selfishness," or even "self-interest," since for Gauthier it is possible—although not at all necessary—that one's interests or preferences may
make reference to the states of affairs of others.[6] The formal language Gauthier uses to express his meaning is that of the economist's notion of "maximizing preference satisfaction."[7]

The logical tapestry woven from this presupposition consists of
three primary components: the economist's notion of a perfectly

competitive market (called a "moral free zone" by Gauthier); decision theoretic concepts of "rational agreement" and "mutual benefit"; and the notion of an "initial bargaining position" in which no person is assumed to be worse off than in a nonsocial context of no interaction. Gauthier's objective is to show that the very presumption against morality entailed by the competitive market concept, the idea that rational agents choose optimally by making direct calculations designed to maximize preference satisfaction, is defeated by adding to the concept of a competitive market the possibility of "contracting" or agreeing" with one another about constraints on the maximization of individual interests: hence the title of his book, *Morals By Agreement.*

Gauthier's view does not presume, as does that of Kant or Gewirth before him, that impartiality is built into the nature of rationality; rather he intends to show how impartiality is an outcome of rational choice.[8] In saying that it is "rational" to override one's individual interests on occasion and choose impartially, Gauthier appears to be contradicting himself; for, again, he wishes to define rationality in terms of seeking one's greatest interest or benefit (where this is understood as maximizing one's preference satisfaction). But the apparent contradiction is resolved when one understands Gauthier to mean that a broader, contractual approach to the seeking of one's benefit sometimes demands the overriding of more narrow, noncontractually construed interests. Indeed, such overriding is what morality, or at least a rational version of morality, amounts to for Gauthier.[9] In one of his most intriguing arguments, Gauthier attempts to show how in a particular instance someone who refuses to constrain the pursuit of her own interests, and who chooses instead on the basis of what is likely to give the greatest expectation of utility simply considered, will be worse off than she need be. Hence, a rational person chooses on an agreed basis of cooperation, rather than according to what appears to give the greatest expectation of value. For Gauthier, as for Hobbes, then, it is the fruits of cooperation, and, alternatively, the fear of noncooperation, that provide the crucial incentives for contract.

The first step toward an agreement whereby persons can share the fruits of a future cooperative surplus is accomplished by "moralizing" the "pure" or Hobbesian state of nature. A Lockean-style proviso with Nozickian modifications[10] is introduced which serves as a constraint on prospective cooperative agreements. The proviso allows each person a "basic endowment" (what one person can make use of and which no one else could make use of in her absence),[11] which, in turn, entails a preagreement right to the benefits of one's labor. Hence, moralizing the state of nature effects a framework of common use among interacting persons in which full compensation is required should one person interfere with the use another makes of that person's material goods.[12] The basis for accepting the Lockean proviso is anticipation of a possible agreement wherein the fruits of cooperative interaction will be shared. The remaining step is to reach agreement about the sharing of the cooperative surplus, a problem in bargaining theory which is ultimately resolved through acceptance of Gauthier's two novel principles, the "minimax relative concession principle" and the "constrained maximization principle."

The "minimax relative concession principle" affirms that the rational joint strategy, both in bargaining and in cooperating after the bargain is reached, is through a bargain among cooperators in which each advances his maximal claim to the surplus of cooperative action and then offers a concession no greater than that of the greatest concession that he supposes some rational person is willing to entertain.[13] The "constrained maximization principle" asserts that it is rational to keep the agreement, even in situations where the utility-maximizing course appears to entail violating it, at least so long as others can be expected to keep it. Those who act in accordance with "constrained maximization," says Gauthier, are more rational than those who do not because their resulting disposition will open more opportunities to them for mutually beneficial interaction.

Again, Gauthier explicitly applies his contractual analysis of morality, derived from an inquiry into individual rational agents, to peoples and nations; and it is undeniable that his analysis has powerful applications at the international level. It is capable of offering a rationale not only for the present self-restraint evident in international law, but for the enormous cooperation, both past and present, that characterizes international politics and commerce. We have already spoken of international law, of treaties, and of fundamental normative precepts that guide nations even in the absence of explicit sanctions. Perhaps even more striking, however, is the level of cooperation among international business entities such as multinational corporations. Even in the absence of global policemen and a body of commercial law backed by sanctions, billions of dollars change hands daily in globe-shaping transactions. To be sure, such market leviathans as Sony, BASF, and IBM sometimes have recourse to the courts of law that operate in the countries they inhabit; and to be sure, they sometimes renege on contractual duties. But a surprising amount of their business is transacted smoothly without explicit sanctions to guide it. Deals are made, renegotiated, and honored; and through it all, the motive for restraint, the impulse toward moral behavior, does not rely entirely upon the insecure foundation of goodwill; rather, it relies upon the more trustworthy contemplation by market participants of their broadly considered, rational self-interest.

The price of fraud and immorality, of breaking contracts and lying about prices, is high for corporations wishing to be future players in international business. Indeed, the price is as steep as the anticipation of the fruits of the future cooperative ventures themselves; and for a going concern contemplating an uninterrupted future, the costs are staggering. No company wants to deal with another who has a reputation for ethical shenanigans, and in hotel dining rooms or in silk-appointed conference rooms in Paris, London, Bonn, and Tokyo, as well as in countless newspapers and trade journals, the word is passed regarding the reliability of major corporate actors. This word itself is remarkably reliable. It is a striking image: thousands of market participants cooperating to refine, clarify, and understand the limits appropriate to profit-maximizing multinational organizations, all undertaken, ironically, from the motive of profit-maximizing. One is moved to adjust Adam Smith's famous line to read: "It is not from the benevolence of the Bechtels, the Batuses, and the Tokyo bankers that we expect our foreign trade, but from their regard of their self-interest."

All this Gauthier's analysis helps us to understand. The extent of cooperation in international affairs, especially in international commerce, is a predictable outcome of a theory which, like Gauthier's, refuses to conceive international activity as reflecting a vicious, uniterated Prisoner's Dilemma. Gauthier's adaptation of Hobbesian strategy serves to underscore the extent of cooperation required by the pursuit of self-interest, and, in turn, the fact that the international scene is not, as Hobbes's own theory predicts it will be, a war of all against all. In this manner, Gauthier, a neo-Hobbesian, is an even stronger champion of the moral implications of self-interested rationality than Hobbes himself. He applies Hobbes's principles in a greater variety of ways, and to a broader spectrum of cases, than does Hobbes.

Yet while Gauthier's international optimism far exceeds Hobbes's, it remains notably pessimistic on certain issues, and this is a clue to a key weakness in Gauthier's work. When considering the issue of international aid, Gauthier argues that a nation need have no reason to consider itself obliged to worsen its own situation in order to improve that of another. To give perspective he considers a hypothetical world in which "purples" and "greens" live widely separated existences in an international state of nature. No contact or cooperation between the two peoples has yet occurred. The purples have developed an ideally just society: in their society the free market is dominant and all market imperfections or "externalities" are countered by policies and practices that satisfy the minimax relative concession principle. The greens, on the other hand, live in total chaotic squalor. "Heedless of both their fellows and their future, they have exhausted themselves in strife, squandered their resources, propagated themselves without constraint, so that they are on the brink of catastrophic collapse."[14] After learning of the green people's situation, the purples reach a consensus that maximization of either the average or the minimum level of well-being for the two peoples would require a worsening of the purple people's situation.

Gauthier next asks, do the purple people have an obligation to help the greens at their own expense, say by maximizing the overall utility of the two peoples? Not necessarily, he replies, because morality must be understood in relation to the potential fruits of cooperation, and with no expectation of gain—even in the long term—there can be no reason for obligation. He writes that "the purples neither would nor could have reason to consider themselves obliged to worsen their own situation in order to maximize overall average utility."[15]

In another passage Gauthier makes the same point, this time in reference to clever, strong, energetic Robinson Crusoes who discover the existence—on other islands—of stupid, weak, lazy Crusoes. "Would," he asks, "an impartial principle require the better situated Crusoes to contribute to the worse situated ones, or the able Crusoes to the less able ones . . . ? Would it require equalizing contributions when possible? Or would it set out needs and require that these be met when possible?" "No," he answers, "any principle other than the one allowing each Crusoe to benefit himself would be unfair and partial, in requiring some to give free rides to others, or to be hosts for their parasitism."[16]

Gauthier's problem, however, is not that he aims at weakening our sense of international guilt. It is not that he takes the sterner side of the international charity dispute;[17] it is rather that he can find no reason for international charity at all, even in catastrophic rescue cases, at least so long as rescuing nation fails to anticipate eventual net benefit to itself. Imagine, for example, that the greens are in an even worse condition than described. They are not merely living chaotically, they are starving to death as the result of a dramatic but temporary crop famine. Millions of green men, women, and children—just as recently occurred in Sub-Saharan Africa—are dying for want of bare nutrition. Let us suppose further that the purple people are even far richer than today's Western industrialized nations. For the purple people to rescue the greens from their apocalypse, it costs them hardly anything, a hundredth of a percentage point of their gross national product, a mere flick of the hand—but it *will* cost them something for which they will not be reimbursed even in the long term. Now the point is that on the basis of Gauthier's analysis, and absent the existence of strong, independently motivated preferences by purples toward rescue, failing to rescue the greens is not only permitted but rationally required.

The seriousness of this conclusion conceals a still deeper and more disturbing problem in the analysis, namely, the absence of a mechanism or principle capable of condemning outright national exploitation. We have seen that Gauthier finds no reason to accept a duty of national charity irrespective of its ability to enhance the welfare of the donor nation. It may appear, however, that he can block unilateral national exploitation by appeal to the rights inherent in the original bargaining position. Hence, harming others, because it violates their rights in the state of nature, is seemingly *proscribed* even as helping them is not *prescribed*. But appearances, as we shall see, are misleading.

Many passages do encourage the more charitable impression. When speaking of the state of nature, Gauthier writes that "the idea of morals by agreement may mislead, if it is supposed that rights must be the product or outcome of agreement." He continues, "Were we to adopt this account, we should suppose that rights were determined by the principle of minimax relative concession . . . [But] rights provide the starting point for, and not the outcome of, agreement; . . . they are what each person brings to the bargaining table, not what she takes from it."[18] Hence, presumably naked aggression through force by one nation over another is ruled out even if parties are unable to agree on principles for dividing the cooperative surplus of social interaction. Later he illustrates this point by considering a hypothetical case in which one group of "fisherfolk" harms another by polluting a jointly used river in the state of nature. Because of its effect on the terms of trade between them, the first group's use of the river for waste disposal is said to violate proviso.[19] This point is generalized in the expression that "the proviso is violated by an action that betters the actor's situation through worsening the situation of another."[20]

It appears that straightforward exploitation is ruled out, even in the state of nature, through the Lockean proviso. The problem, however, is that the Lockean proviso, the introduction of which raises the "pure" or Hobbesian state of nature into a modified or "pre-agreement" state of nature, is contingent for its introduction on rational calculations made by agents with an eye to their eventual gain. "The proviso," Gauthier writes, "is a rational constraint on the interactions of nations *only* if there is the prospect of an international order of co-operation [my emphasis]."[21] This theme is repeated again and again in the book: in chapter 7 he warns that it is only *if* one views agents as "potential partners in social relationships, in market competition and in co-operation, [that] the [Lockean] proviso forbids the imposition of any costs upon them without appropriate compensation."[22] And still later he addresses the issue in a broader context when he states that "the moral claims that each of us makes on others, and that are expressed in our rights, depend, neither on our affections for each other, nor on our rational or purposive capacities, as if these commanded inherent respect, but on our actual or potential partnership in activities that bring mutual benefit."[23]

A little reflection reveals why, for Gauthier, rights even in the state of nature *must* be conditioned by the prospect of eventual gain in this manner. To have it any other way would be to undermine the fundamental presumption of *Morals By Agreement* which is that advantage grounds practical rationality, and that rationality, in turn, can be used to generate morality. As Gauthier puts it in the introduction, "Moral restraint, or not taking advantage, then, is a rational step taken in order to facilitate the emergence of society, an event from which every self-interested individual stands to gain."[24] The catch, however, is that every *nation*, in contrast to every *individual*, may not gain, since the desirability, or even existence, of international society is a matter of dispute. This means that in a pure state of nature, international or otherwise, even adherence to the Lockean proviso that respects other peoples' "basic endowments" of the right to the free use of their capacities for physical and mental activities is jeopardized.

Gauthier seems at one point to anticipate the problem, asking what would prevent the purples from utilizing thoroughly noncooperative policies, or, as he labels it, from "treating them [the greens] as animals." He argues that there are several grounds on which purples might defend constrained maximization, adherence to the proviso, and acceptance of minimax relative concession in their relationship with the greens. First, they might believe that whatever the short-term prospects are, in the long term they would benefit from constraint. Second, they might already be inclined to such cooperation through already introduced patterns of socialization disposing them to constrained maximization with all human beings. Or, third, they might possess a certain measure of sympathy for other humans.[25]

The important thing to note is that all of these responses turn on the word "might." The purples *might* anticipate long-term benefits to themselves, they *might* have developed habits of cooperation that resisted rational reform, and they *might* have sufficient sympathy even for distant peoples who have what they regard as a disgusting lifestyle, to overcome their other preferences. But—and this is the point—

they also might not; and that makes the most fundamental of moral proscriptions, of not exploiting, enslaving, or even killing others, hostage to empirical chance. There is no *a priori* claim in Gauthier's argument to the effect that long-term benefits will follow from co-operation with others, or that ingrained habits or sympathy will overcome either rational calculation or nonsympathetic, that is, egoistic, preferences. Indeed, he denies certainty on the matter and for this reason carefully chooses the word "might" in discussing the existence of dispositions that would constrain the purples to treat the greens with respect. But even as he adds to the number of possible dispositions that might incline the purples to humane action, his case weakens; for the commonest moral imagination affirms the truth that not enslaving, not murdering, and not treating people as animals are principles that should not be overridden even by the most rational of long-term, contractually informed forecasts of overall net benefit to oneself.

Nor can the problem be dismissed by saying that the present state of international relations, in contrast to hypothetical purples, greens, or Robinson Crusoes, is a condition beyond the state of nature in which cooperation is mandated. "The present international order," Gauthier remarks, "may not afford a rational and fair basis for co-operative interaction among the world's peoples," and by so saying he affirms that the existing international order may approximate a state of nature.[26] And while he does not identify the real world with the one of the greens and the purples, neither does he refrain from drawing lessons from their imaginary world. He notes, for example, that some contemporary moral thinkers argue in a way that masks a key truth of the purple-green story in holding that the developed countries are obliged to make sacrifices for the benefit of the less developed, and he argues that the European appropriation of America might, with a few modifications, have satisfied the rational requirements of morals by agreement.[27]

Gauthier's strategy is to assume the economic model of rationality, a model that ties rationality to anticipated benefit to the reasoner, or to be more precise, to the maximization of utility conceived of as preference satisfaction. This economic model, then, is used to generate morality, or at least a rational morality—the morality of the economic man. Morality, almost magically, appears to be extracted from a seemingly nonmoral source. In the story he tells, it is a happy accident that the fruits of interaction are significantly great to compel enormous constraints on the actions of individuals. This happens because isolated man is productively impotent without the aid of his fellows. As Adam Smith's thought-experiment of the pin factory in the *Wealth of Nations* shows, one person working alone can only produce a material pittance; together with her fellows she can produce a fortune. Hence this happy fact of coincidence between one's relative impotence as an individual and what is required of one by others to maximize one's individual welfare, turns out, for Gauthier, to be sufficient for generating rational morality.

But an individual nation is not so impotent as an individual person. Hence Gauthier's fundamental problem, made more obvious by its effects in an international setting, is that were the incentives he invokes less attractive then the reasons for being moral would dissolve. And there is the rub; for we suppose that our reason for behaving morally is more than the existence of a happy coincidence. The inadequacy of Gauthier's approach is thus highlighted in international contexts where the fruits of interaction are less certain, and where for the first time the possibility is realized that a nation or people may choose simply not to maximize on the basis of an anticipated cooperative surplus.

Gauthier's own candor in addressing the question is refreshing. In the final chapters of his book he wonders aloud about the theory's ability to capture the depth of moral feeling.[28] Here he seems to grant that the rational morality generated from the concept of economic man is a minimal and second-best version. A richer version, one held by the "liberal individual," he asserts, shares important features with the notion of morality most of us accept: in particular, it assigns important roles to one's sociability, interest in the welfare others, and the valuing of social participation for its own sake. An unsupplemented morality of economic man would make the future of morality precarious, he adds, because it inevitably treats constraints on the self-interest as a regrettable evil, as a "form of drudgery." Here he takes seriously Glaucon's argument to Socrates in Plato's *Republic* that a contractarian account of justice ought to be rejected because it implies that we care for morality, "not for its own sake, but because we lack the strength to dominate our fellows or the self-sufficiency to avoid interaction with them."[29] Nonetheless he persists here—as throughout the book—in supposing that the only rationally defensible moral theory is the one he has derived from the concept of economic man. Furthermore, he asserts that this "rational" morality plays the crucial role of grounding a broader, affective morality.

Let us leave aside the extent to which the "rational" grounding of morality can only be that stemming from economic man, and begin, instead, to assess the success of the revised Hobbesianism offered by Gauthier. Let us first remind ourselves that while Gauthier's theory is less pessimistic than the traditional Hobbesianism because it argues for the rationality of constraints on action without an international sovereign, it nonetheless mirrors traditional Hobbesianism in defining the limits of rationally defensible international constraints as the limits of enlightened self-interest.

As should be apparent, the project fails to offer a rational defense of basic moral constraints by way of appeal to the maximized self-interest of agents, at least in the international order. The basis it provides, as we have seen, is simply too weak to sustain even commonly accepted truisms about international behavior, ones dealing, for example, with the need to rescue foreigners from starvation in instances where it costs virtually nothing, as well as to refrain from exploiting life and property. By denying the analytic thesis of traditional Hobbesianism, Gauthier appears to lend credence to its prescriptive thesis—that the single and ultimate reason for moral restraint is self-interest—but the result is to leave the prescriptive thesis more in doubt than ever. As we have seen, Gauthier himself is driven in the end to acknowledge the relevance of a morality broader than the rational, contractarian theory he constructs in *Morals By Agreement*. He wishes, however, to view his rational, contractarian theory as crucial for a richer, noncontractarian morality, in that it offers a rational foundation for the latter. Yet, again, his own account of contractarian principles in the international realm can support neither minimal, bottom-line moral considerations, nor a broader concept of international justice. It is true that his ingenious appeal to rational maximization by economic man shows the surprising extent to which cooperative international activity *can* be justified through appeal to self-interest. This is good news. The bad news is that the international cooperative activity that he justifies fails to reflect precepts both he and others grant are necessary.[30]

NOTES

Preface

1. Rogene A. Buchholz, *Business Environment and Public Policy* (Englewood Cliffs, N.J.: Prentice-Hall, 1982); Stephen L. Wartick and Philip L. Cochran, "The Evolution of the Corporate Social Performance Model," *Academy of Management Review* 10 (1985): 758–69; Edwin Epstein, "The Corporate Social Policy Process: Beyond Business Ethics, Corporate Social Responsibility, and Corporate Social Responsiveness," *California Management Review* 29 (Spring 1987) pp. 99–104; William C. Frederick, "Toward CSR3: Why Ethical Analysis is Indispensable and Unavoidable in Corporate Affairs," *California Management Review* 28 (1986); 126–41; R. Edward Freeman, *Strategic Management: A Stakeholder Approach* (Boston: Pitman Press, 1984), and *Corporate Strategy and the Search for Ethics* (Englewood Cliffs, N.J.: Prentice-Hall, 1988); and S. Prakash Sethi, "Corporate Law Violations and Executive Liability," in Lee Preston, ed., *Corporate Social Performance and Policy, Vol. 3* (Greenwich, Conn.: JAI Press, 1981), pp. 72–73, and S. Prakash Sethi et al., *Corporate Governance: Public Policy-Social Responsibility Committee of Corporate Board* (Richardson, Tex.: Center for Research in Business and Social Policy, 1979).

2. International political issues have been the focus of an interesting joint venture between a philosopher and a political scientist in J. E. Hare and Carey B. Joynt, *Ethics and International Affairs* (New York: St. Martin's Press, 1982).

3. An exception is Duane Windsor's "Defining the Ethical Obligations of the Multinational Enterprise," in W. M. Hoffman et al., eds., *Ethics and the Multinational Enterprise* (Lanham, Md.: University Press of America, 1986).

4. See, for example, Thomas Poynter, *Multinational Enterprises and Government Intervention* (New York: St. Martin's Press, 1985); Thomas Moran, ed., *Multinational Corporations; The Political Economy of Foreign Direct Investment* (Lexington, Mass.: Lexington Books, 1985); and J. N. Behrman, *Decision Criteria for Foreign Direct Investment in Latin America* (New York: Council of the Americas, 1974).

5. W. J. Keegan, "Multinational Scanning: A Study of Information Sources Utilized by Headquarters Executives in Multinational Companies," *Administrative Science Quarterly* (1974): 411–21; and D. Cray, "Control and Coordination in Multinational Corporations," *Journal of International Business Studies* 15 (1984): 85–98.

6. See Lee Preston, "The Evolution of Multinational Public Policy Toward

Business: Codes of Conduct," paper presented at the Annual Meeting of the Academy of Management, New Orleans, August 1987.

7. One of the best summaries of this literature may be found in Larry May, *The Morality of Groups* (Notre Dame, Ind.: Notre Dame University Press, 1988). Moreover, the book offers a challenging reinterpretation of the moral agency issue.

Chapter 1

1. Albert O. Hirschman, "Morality and the Social Sciences," in *Essays in Trespassing: Economics to Politics and Beyond*, ed. Albert O. Hirschman (Cambridge: Cambridge University Press, 1981), pp. 305–6. Reprinted by permission.

2. Paul Lewis, "Economic Parley Termed a Success," *New York Times*, August 3, 1987, p. 5.

3. Thomas Donaldson, *Corporations and Morality* (Englewood Cliffs, N.J.: Prentice-Hall, 1982); see especially chapter 3.

4. See, for example, John Kultgen, "Donaldson's Social Contract for Business," *Business and Professional Ethics Journal* 5 (1987): 28–39.

5. Louis Turner, *Multinational Companies and the Third World* (New York: Hill and Wang, 1973), p. 22.

6. Andrew Pease, "Technology and Peasant Production: Reflection on a Global Study," *Development and Change* 8 (1977): 211. Clearly, developing countries are places where such technological or agricultural wonders are welcome. Developing countries contain 70 percent of the world's population, but only 30 percent of its income. See Brian Barry, "Humanity and Justice in Global Perspective," in J. Roland Pennock and John W. Chapman, eds., *Ethics, Economics, and the Law: Nomos Vol. XXIV* (New York: New York University Press, 1982), pp. 219–52.

7. For example, the economist W. Arthur Lewis believes that the growth of developing countries would be unaffected even if "all the developed countries were to sink under the sea." Lewis, *The Evolution of the International Economic Order* (Princeton, N.J.: Princeton University Press, 1978), p. 71.

Chapter 2

1. Thucydides, *The Peloponnesian War* (New York: Modern Library, 1934), p. 334.

2. In more modern times, one of the best-known modern defenders of realism has been Hans J. Morgenthau. See Morgenthau, *Dilemmas of Politics* (Chicago: University of Chicago Press, 1958), and *Politics in the Twentieth Century, Volume I: The Decline of Democratic Politics* (Chicago: University of Chicago Press, 1962).

3. George Kennan, *American Diplomacy* (New York: Mentor Books, 1952), p. 82.

4. See for example, Hans J. Morgenthau, *A New Foreign Policy for the United States* (New York: Praeger, 1969). See especially Morgenthau's comments on

the nature of realism in Chapter 5, "To Intervene or Not to Intervene," pp. 111–156.

5. Joseph S. Nye, Jr., "Ethics and Foreign Policy," paper presented at the Aspen Institute Conference on Ethics and Foreign Policy, Wye Plantation, Wye, Maryland, October 15–16, 1983, p. 1.

6. Jacques Barzun, *Is Democratic Theory for Export?* (New York: Carnegie Council on Ethics and International Affairs, 1986), pp. 1–27.

7. Ibid., p. 26.

8. Nye, "Ethics and Foreign Policy," p. 2.

9. Standard writings on cultural relativism include Walter T. Stace, *The Concept of Morals* (New York: Macmillan, 1937); Richard Brandt, *Ethical Theory* (Englewood Cliffs, N.J.: Prentice-Hall, 1959); William Graham Sumner, *Folkways* (Boston: Ginn and Co., 1907); and Carl Wellman, "The Ethical Implications of Relativity," *Journal of Philosophy* 60 (1963): 169–84.

10. This was most recently articulated by Michael Walzer in *Just and Unjust Wars* (New York: Basic Books, 1977).

11. Brandt, *Ethical Theory.*

12. To investigate aspects of the relativist versus nonrelativist debate that are not discussed here, the reader may wish to read Gilbert Harman's *The Nature of Morality* (New York: Oxford University Press, 1977), especially his treatment of nihilism and relativism in chapters 2, 3, and 4.

13. Thomas Hobbes, *Leviathan; or, The Matter, Form and Power of a Commonwealth, Ecclesiastical and Civil,* ed. Michael Oakeshott (Oxford: Basil Blackwell, 1946). See also Hobbes, *The Elements of Law Natural and Politic,* ed. Ferdinand Tonnies (London: Simpkin, Marshall, 1889), and *Philosophical Rudiments Concerning Government and Society: Volume 2* in *The English Works of Thomas Hobbes of Malmesbury,* 11 vols., ed. William Molesworth (London: Bohn, 1839–45).

14. Charles R. Beitz, *Political Theory and International Relations* (Princeton, N.J.: Princeton University Press, 1979), p. 64.

15. Ibid., p. 62.

16. Ibid., p. 64. An aspect of Beitz's criticism that we shall not explore concerns his rejection of Hobbes's assumption of the moral agency of nation-states. He writes, "The Hobbesian view invites a justification of international principles in terms of the interests of states; but even if Hobbes's metaethics were accepted, it is the interests of *persons* that are fundamental, and 'national interests' are relevant to the justification of international principles only to the extent that they are derived from the interests of persons." Ibid., p. 64.

17. Terry Nardin, *Law, Morality, and the Relations of States* (Princeton, N.J.: Princeton University Press, 1983), p. 72.

18. John Locke, *Second Treatise. Two Treatises of Government,* ed. Peter Laslett (New York: New American Library, 1965), pp. 367–96.

19. Jean Jacques Rousseau, *Oeuvres completes,* 4 vols., Editions de la Pleiade (Paris: Librairie Gallimard, 1959–69), p. 610. Cited in Nardin, *Law, Morality, and the Relations of States,* p. 72.

20. Aspects of this issue are taken up by D. F. Vagts, in *The Question of a Reference to International Obligations in the United Nations Code of Conduct on*

Transnational Corporations: A Different View (New York: UNCTC Current Studies, 1986), series A, no. 2.

21. *The Universal Declaration of Human Rights, 1948*. A publication of the United Nations signed by virtually every nation in the world, the declaration lays down a floor of basic rights that supports claims and entitlements regardless of nationality or culture.

22. Stanley Hoffmann, *Duties Beyond Borders* (Syracuse: Syracuse University Press, 1981), pp. 13, 14. Stanley Hoffmann also discusses Rousseau's criticism of the instinct for sociability in "Rousseau on War and Peace, in Hoffmann, *The State of War* (New York: Praeger Press, 1965).

23. Nardin, *Law, Morality, and the Relations of States*, p. 19.

24. Ibid., p. 233.

25. Voltaire, *Siecle de Louis XIV. Oeuvres completes*, vols. 14–15. 52 vols. Paris: Garnier Freres, 1877–1885, p. 159. Cited in Nardin, *Law, Morality, and the Relations of States*, p. 61.

26. Gregory Kavka, "Hobbes' War of All Against All," *Ethics* 93 (January 1983): 291–310.

27. For discussions of the theory of games, see R. D. Luce and H. Raiffa, *Games and Decisions* (New York: Wiley, 1957).

28. Kavka, "Hobbes' War," pp. 299–304.

29. David Lewis, *Convention* (Cambridge, Mass.: Harvard University Press, 1969), pp. 53–58.

30. Kavka, "Hobbes' War," p. 301.

31. Anatol Rapoport and Albert Chammah, *Prisoner's Dilemma* (Ann Arbor: University of Michigan Press, 1965), pp. 63–66.

32. Kavka, "Hobbes' War," p. 303.

33. Taking an approach not explored in this chapter, Marshall Cohen argues that ethical principles have meaningful application even in the state of nature. See Cohen, "Moral Skepticism and International Relations," *Philosophy and Public Affairs* 13 (Fall 1984): 299–346.

34. Hoffmann, *Duties Beyond Borders*, pp. 14–15.

35. Charles Beitz reaches a similar conclusion. He writes that Hobbes's pessimism obscures the fact that "the interactions that comprise international relations take a variety of nonviolent forms many of which require cooperative maintenance of common rules." Beitz, *Political Theory and International Relations*, p. 64.

36. Gregory S. Kavka, *Hobbesian Moral and Political Theory* (Princeton, N.J.: Princeton University Press, 1986); David Gauthier, *Morals By Agreement* (Oxford: Clarendon Press, 1986).

37. Another important contribution in this vein is Russell Hardin's *Morality Within the Limits of Reason* (Chicago: University of Chicago Press, 1988).

Chapter 3

1. J. Coates, "Towards a Code of Conduct for Multinationals," *Personnel Management* 10 (April 1978): 41.

2. J. R. Simpson, "Ethics and Multinational Corporations vis-à-vis Developing Nations," *Journal of Business Ethics* 1 (1982): 227–37.

3. I have borrowed these categories from researchers Lisa Farr and Bruce W. Stening, "Ethics and the Multinational Corporation," p. 4. Department of Management, The University of Western Australia, Nedlands, Western Australia.

4. See Mark Pastin and Michael Hooker, "Ethics and the Foreign Corrupt Practices Act," *Business Horizons* 23 (December 1980): 43–47.

5. Richard Barnet and Ronald Muller, *Global Reach: The Power of Multinational Corporations* (New York: Simon and Schuster, 1974), p. 363.

6. P. P. Gabriel, "MNCs in the Third World: Is Conflict Unavoidable?" *Harvard Business Review* 56 (March–April 1978): 83–93.

7. Barnet and Muller, *Global Reach*, p. 72.

8. Ibid., p. 60.

9. William Robertson, *View of the Progress of Society in Europe* (London, 1769, rpt. Chicago: University of Chicago Press, 1972).

10. Quoted in Barnet and Muller, *Global Reach*, p. 19.

11. Richard D. Robinson, *International Business Management: A Guide to Decision Making*, 2d ed. (Hinsdale, Ill.: Dryden Press, 1978).

12. This point is documented throughout Terutomo Ozawa's *Multinationalism, Japanese Style* (Princeton, N.J.: Princeton University Press, 1979).

13. Barnet and Muller, *Global Reach*, p. 282.

14. Ibid., p. 90.

15. Ibid., p. 143.

16. Richard Barnet, "Human Rights Implications of Corporate Food Policies," in Paula R. Newberg, ed., *The Politics of Human Rights* (New York: New York University Press, 1980), pp. 183–84.

17. Ozawa, *Multinationalism, Japanese Style,* p. 231.

18. An analysis of such reasons, one which also contains many observations on the evolution of international public policy, is contained in Lee E. Preston's "The Evolution of Multinational Public Policy Toward Business: Codes of Conduct," paper presented at the Annual meeting of the Academy of Management, New Orleans, August, 1987. The brief account of multinational public policy I sketch in the following pages is heavily indebted to the more comprehensive account given by Professor Preston in his paper.

19. Jon R. Luoma, "A Disaster That Didn't Wait," *New York Times Book Review*, November 29, 1987, p. 16.

20. I have coined the terms "interindustry," "intergovernment," and so on, but the basic fourfold division of international initiatives is drawn from Preston, "The Evolution of Multinational Public Policy Toward Business: Codes of Conduct."

21. See, for example, Robert J. Myers, ed., *The Political Morality of the International Monetary Fund* (New York: Transaction Books, 1987), especially chapters 1–4, 8, and 10.

22. See, for example, Francesco Giavazzi, Stephano Micossi, and Marcus Miller, eds., *The European Monetary System* (Cambridge: Cambridge University Press, 1988).

23. Preston, "The Evolution of Multinational Public Policy Toward Business: Codes of Conduct," p. 11.

24. Preston, "The Evolution of Multinational Public Policy Toward Business: Codes of Conduct, p. 14.

25. Nardin, *Law, Morality, and the Relations of States,* especially the first chapter.

26. Michael Porter, *Competitive Advantage* (New York: Free Press, 1980).

27. See Yair Aharoni, *The Foreign Investment Decision Process* (Boston: Division of Research, Graduate School of Business Administration, Harvard University, 1966); J. R. Piper, "How U.S. Firms Evaluate Foreign Investment Opportunities," *MSU Business Topics* (Summer, 1971): 11–20; and S. J. Kobrin, *Managing Political Risk Assessment: Strategic Response to Environmental Change* (Berkeley: University of California Press, 1982).

28. J. J. Boddewyn, "International Political Strategy: A Fourth 'Generic' Strategy," paper presented at the Annual Meeting of the Academy of Management, New Orleans, August 1987, and at the Annual Meeting of the International Academy of Business, November 1986, p. 1 (abstract). See also J. J. Boddewyn, "Political Aspects of MNE Theory," *Journal of International Business Studies* 19 (Fall 1988): 341–63.

29. Boddewyn, "International Political Strategy," pp. 4, 1.

30. Ibid., p. 25.

31. See Y. L. Doz, "Strategic Management in Multinational Companies," *Sloan Management Review* 21 (Winter 1980): 27–46.

32. C. K. Prahalad, "Strategic Choices in Diversified MNCs," *Harvard Business Review* 54 (July–August 1976): 67–78.

33. I was greatly aided in understanding the implications of Doz's models for multinational political risk by a paper presented at the 1987 Academy of Management Conference in New Orleans, by Kunal K. Sandhu, "Incorporating Political Risk Analysis in MNC Strategic Decision Making—A Contingency Framework."

34. H. W. Lane and D. G. Simpson, "Bribery in International Business: Whose Problem Is It?" *Journal of Business Ethics* 3 (Spring–Summer 1980): 118–37.

35. H. G. Johnson, "The Multinational Corporation as a Development Agent," *Columbia Journal of World Business* 4 (1985): 25–30.

36. M. J. Francis and C. G. Manrique, "Clarifying the Debate," in Lee A. Tavis, ed., *Multinational Managers and Poverty in the Third World* (Notre Dame, Ind.: Notre Dame University Press, 1982), pp. 68–90.

37. M. J. Ulmer, "Multinational Corporations and Third World Capitalism," *Journal of Economic Issues* 14 (June 1980): 458.

Chapter 4

1. See Thomas Donaldson, *Corporations and Morality* (Englewood Cliffs, N.J.: Prentice-Hall, 1982), especially chapter 2; and Thomas Donaldson, "Personalizing Corporate Ontology," in Hugh Curtler, ed., *Shame, Responsibility, and the Corporation* (New York: Haven Publishing, 1986), pp. 99–113. For classic articles discussing the issue of moral agency see those included in part II of Thomas Donaldson and Patricia Werhane, eds., *Ethical Issues in Business: A Philosophical Approach,* 3d ed. (Englewood Cliffs, N.J.: Prentice-Hall, 1987).

2. Milton Friedman, *Capitalism and Freedom* (Chicago: University of Chicago Press, 1962), p. 133.

3. Ibid.

4. Quoted in Warren A. Law, "A Corporation Is More Than Its Stock," *Harvard Business Review* 64 (May–June 1986): 82.

5. Ibid., p. 83.

6. David Lyons has challenged the assumption that respect for rights is incompatible with utilitarianism. He maintains, for example, that in his espousal of utilitarianism, John Stuart Mill recognized moral obligations other than maximizing the general welfare, and that to argue for a right is simply to justify a social rule calculated to achieve some benefit or liberty. See Lyons, "Rights, Claimants, and Beneficiaries," *American Philosophical Quarterly* 6 (July 1969): 173–85. See also Lyons's discussion of this issue in his introduction to David Lyons, ed., *Rights* (Belmont, Calif.: Wadsworth, 1979), pp. 1–13.

7. Edward Freeman has engaged in the task of enhancing the sophistication of the stakeholder model from the perspective of both strategic and moral theory. See R. Edward Freeman, *Strategic Management: A Stakeholder Approach* (Boston: Pitman Press, 1984).

8. See Donaldson, *Corporations and Morality*, especially chapter 3.

9. Bradford Cornell and Alan C. Shapiro, "Corporate Stakeholders and Corporate Finance," *Financial Management* 16 (Spring 1987): 5–14.

10. Ibid., pp. 5–6.

11. Ibid., p. 6.

12. Ibid., p. 5. Cornell and Shapiro extend their analysis to show how such implicit claims can be recognized in a new form of balance sheet.

13. This implicit agreement is argued by Warren Law to have been operative for virtually all U.S. corporations regarding their domestic employees. See Law, *A Corporation Is More Than Its Stock*, p. 82.

14. See Jeff McMahan, "The Ethics of International Intervention," in Anthony Ellis, ed., *Ethics and International Relations* (London: Manchester University Press, 1986), pp. 24–51.

15. Such a criticism of my own version of the social contract has been made by John Kultgen, "Donaldson's Social Contract for Business," *Business and Professional Ethics Journal* 5 (1987): 28–39.

16. Ibid., pp. 12, 18. Even as a heuristic device the contract is not an unmixed blessing from Kultgen's perspective. He writes that "the fiction of contractors devising a social contract has the disadvantage of misleading the unwary into thinking that an actual binding contract resembling the imaginary one somewhere somehow exists" (p. 18).

17. Moore argued that a fallacy was involved in defining "goodness" in terms of any natural objects or properties. "If . . . [a man] confuses 'good,' which is not in the same sense a natural object, with any natural object whatever, then there is a reason for calling that a naturalistic fallacy" G. E. Moore, *Principia Ethica* (Cambridge: Cambridge University Press, 1903) p. 13. The error, in Moore's view, was like defining the color "yellow" through its physical equivalent, say, as a certain kind of light vibration. Doing so, Moore protested, fails to capture what we *mean* by the term "yellow." Goodness,

like yellow, denotes a simple, indefinable property. See Moore, *Principia Ethica*, pp. 10, 18–20, 38–39, and 124–25.)

18. Immanuel Kant, *The Critique of Practical Reason*, trans. Lewis White Beck (Chicago: University of Chicago Press, 1949). See especially book II, chapter 2, "The Dialectic of Pure Reason in Defining the Concept of the Highest Good," pp. 214–48.

19. Sir Ernest Barker, *Social Contract* (Oxford: Oxford University Press, 1947), pp. ix–viii.

20. It must be said that Kultgen is painstaking in his interpretation of my position, always careful to assume no more than is warranted by the text. He does not, for example, as many commentators have, make the critical mistake of treating the classes of corporations and productive organizations as equivalent. Kultgen, "Donaldson's Social Contract," p. 18.

21. Immanuel Kant, *The Metaphysical Principles of Virtue*, trans. James Ellington (New York: Bobbs-Merrill, 1964), p. 48.

22. Barnet and Muller, *Global Reach*, p. 32.

23. Overseas Development Council, *U.S. Policy and the Third World: Agenda 1985–86* (Washington, D.C.: 1985).

24. United Nations, Food and Agricultural Organization (FAO), *Dimensions of Need* (Rome: FAO, 1982), E9.

25. *Fellowship* magazine (of the Fellowship of Reconciliation), February 1974, p. 1.

26. See Barnet and Muller, *Global Reach*, p. 162.

27. Some of the ideas presented in this chapter may be found in Thomas Donaldson, "Fact, Fiction, and the Social Contract: A Reply to Kultgen," *Business and Professional Ethics Journal* 5 (1987): 40–47.

Chapter 5

1. James LeMoyne, "In Central America, the Workers Suffer Most," *New York Times*, October 26, 1987, pp. 1, 4.

2. Ibid.

3. Ronald Dworkin, *Taking Rights Seriously* (Cambridge, Mass.: Harvard University Press, 1977). For other standard definitions of rights see James W. Nickel, *Making Sense of Human Rights: Philosophical Reflections on the Universal Declaration of Human Rights* (Berkeley: University of California Press, 1987), especially chapter 2; Joel Feinberg, "Duties, Rights and Claims," *American Philosophical Quarterly* 3 (1966): 137–44. See also Joel Feinberg, "The Nature and Value of Rights," *Journal of Value Inquiry* 4 (1970): 243–57; Wesley N. Hohfeld, *Fundamental Legal Conceptions* (New Haven, Conn.: Yale University Press, 1964); and H. J. McCloskey, "Rights—Some Conceptual Issues," *Australasian Journal of Philosophy* 54 (1976): 99–115.

4. Maurice Cranston, *What Are Human Rights?* (New York: Tamlinger, 1973), p. 67.

5. H. J. McCloskey, for example, understands a right as a positive entitlement that need not specify who bears the responsibility for satisfying that entitlement. McCloskey, "Rights—Some Conceptual Issues," p. 99.

6. Feinberg, "Duties, Rights and Claims"; see also Feinberg, "The Nature and Value of Rights," pp. 243–57.

7. James Brooke, "Waste Dumpers Turning to West Africa," *New York Times,* July 17, 1988, pp. 1, 7.

8. Ibid. Nigeria and other countries have struck back, often by imposing strict rules against the acceptance of toxic waste. For example, in Nigeria officials now warn that anyone caught importing toxic waste will face the firing squad. Ibid., p. 7.

9. James W. Nickel, *Making Sense of Human Rights,* pp. 107–8.

10. See Ian Brownlie, *Basic Documents on Human Rights* (Oxford: Oxford University Press, 1975).

11. For a contemporary analysis of the Universal Declaration of Human Rights and companion international documents, see Nickel, *Making Sense of Human Rights.*

12. James W. Nickel, "The Feasibility of Welfare Rights in Less Developed Countries," in Kenneth Kipnis and Diana T. Meyers, eds., *Economic Justice: Private Rights and Public Responsibilities* (Totowa, N.J.: Rowman and Allenheld, 1985), pp. 217–26.

13. James Sterba, "The Welfare Rights of Distant Peoples and Future Generations: Moral Side Constraints on Social Policy," *Social Theory and Practice* 7 (Spring 1981): 34.

14. Henry Shue, "Exporting Hazards," *Ethics* 91 (July 1981): 579–80.

15. Sterba, "Distant Peoples," p. 116.

16. Henry Shue, *Basic Rights: Subsistence, Affluence, and U.S. Foreign Policy* (Princeton, N.J.: Princeton University Press, 1980), p. 65.

17. Ibid., pp. 34, 20–23.

18. Ibid., p. 78.

19. Ibid., p. 71.

20. Ibid., p. 76.

21. Ibid., p. 170.

22. Ibid., p. 157.

23. Ibid., p. 91.

24. Ibid., pp. 37–38.

25. I am indebted to Alan Gewirth who made this point in a conversation about Shue's theory of basic rights.

26. Shue, *Basic Rights,* p. 20.

27. Ibid., p. 19.

28. Nickel, *Human Rights,* pp. 108–19.

29. Ibid., p. 112.

30. Ibid., pp. 113–14.

31. I am indebted to Lynn Sharp Paine who, in critiquing an earlier draft of this chapter, made me see the need for a clearer definition of the "fairness–affordability" criterion.

32. Shue, *Basic Rights,* p. 19.

33. Nickel, "Welfare Rights," pp. 217–26.

34. Some material in the following five paragraphs was first presented in Thomas Donaldson, "Trading Justice for Bread: A Reply to James W. Nickel," in Kipnis and Meyers, eds., *Economic Justice: Private Rights and Public Respon-*

sibilities, pp. 226–29. Reprinted by permission. See my response to Nickel's argument in its full version there.

35. Shue, *Basic Rights,* p. 57.

36. I am indebted to Edwin Hartman for establishing this point. Hartman has suggested that this warrants establishing a fourth significant kind of duty, i.e., "avoiding helping to deprive." For a more detailed account of this interesting suggestion, see Edwin Hartman, "Comment on Donaldson's 'Rights in the Global Market,' " in Edward Freeman, ed., *The 1988 Ruffin Lectures* (New York: Oxford University Press, forthcoming).

37. Brian Barry, "Humanity and Justice in Global Perspective," in J. Roland Pennock and John W. Chapman, eds., *Ethics, Economics, and the Law: Nomos Vol. XXIV* (New York: New York University Press, 1982), pp. 219–52. Companies are also charged with undermining local governments, and hence infringing on basic rights, through sophisticated tax evasion schemes. Especially when companies buy from their own subsidiaries, they can establish prices that have little connection to existing market values. This, in turn, means that profits can be shifted from high-tax to low-tax countries with the result that poor nations can be deprived of their rightful share.

38. Both for raising these questions, and in helping me formulate answers, I am indebted to William Frederick.

39. I am indebted to George Brenkert for suggesting and formulating the "drug lord" problem.

Chapter 6

1. An example of disparity in wages between Mexican and U.S. workers is documented in the case study by John H. Haddox, "Twin-Plants and Corporate Responsibilities," in Patricia Werhane and Kendall D'Andrade, eds., *Profit and Responsibility* (New York: Random House, 1985), pp. 223–237.

2. Richard D. Robinson, *International Business Management: A Guide to Decision Making,* 2d ed. (Hinsdale, Ill.: Dryden Press, 1978), p. 241

3. Ibid., p. 241.

4. Arthur Kelly, "Case Study: Italian Bank Mores," in Thomas Donaldson, ed., *Case Studies in Business Ethics* (Englewood Cliffs, N.J.: Prentice-Hall, 1984), 37–39.

5. Charles Peters and Taylor Branch, *Blowing the Whistle: Dissent in the Public Interest* (New York: Praeger, 1974), pp. 182–85.

6. Arnold Berleant, "Multinationals and the Problem of Ethical Consistency," *Journal of Business Ethics* 3 (August 1982): 185–95. Some have argued that insulating the economies of the less developed countries would be advantageous to the less developed countries in the long run. But whether correct or not, such an argument is independent of the present issue, for it is independent of the claim that if a practice violates the norms of the home country, then it is impermissible.

7. Henry Shue, "Exporting Hazards," *Ethics* 91 (July 1981): 579–606.

8. Ibid., pp. 579–80.

9. Ibid., p. 601.

10. Ibid., pp. 592–93.

11. Ibid., p. 600.

12. Sterba himself reflects this consensus when he remarks that for rights "an acceptable minimum should vary over time and between societies at least to some degree." Sterba, "Distant Peoples," p. 112.

13. Richard Brandt, "Ethical Relativism," in Thomas Donaldson and Patricia Werhane, eds., *Ethical Issues in Business*, 2d ed. (Englewood Cliffs, N.J.: Prentice-Hall, 1983), pp. 40–45.

14. See "The (Sullivan) Statement of Principles," published by the International Council for Equality of Opportunity Principles, Inc., Philadelphia, Penn., 1984.

15. See "Dresser Industries and South Africa," by Patricia Mintz and Kirk O. Hanson, in Donaldson, ed., *Case Studies in Business Ethics*, pp. 212–39.

16. Barnaby J. Feder, "Sullivan asks end of business links to South Africa," *New York Times*, June 4, 1987, pp. 1, 28. For an account of the business activities of countries other than the United States in South Africa, see Nicholas D. Kristof, "The Pressure on South Africa," *New York Times*, August 7, 1985, p. 7. *New York Times*, June 4, 1987, pp. 1, 28.

17. For a concise and comprehensive account of the various codes of conduct for international business see Lee E. Preston, "The Evolution of Multinational Public Policy Toward Business: Codes of Conduct," in Lee E. Preston, ed., *Research in Corporate Social Performance and Policy: Volume 10* (Greenwich, Conn.: JAI Press, 1988); see also "Codes of Conduct: Worry Over New Restraints on Multinationals," *Chemical Week* 129 (July 15, 1981): 48–52.

18. Barnet and Muller, *Global Reach*, p. 185.

19. An earlier version of this chapter appeared as Thomas Donaldson, "Multinational Decision-Making: Reconciling International Norms," *Journal of Business Ethics* 4 (1985): 354–67; and in Anthony Ellis, ed., *Ethics and International Relations* (London: Manchester University Press, 1986), pp. 127–41.

Chapter 7

1. The memorable phrase "technology spread thin on an ancient culture" appeared in a subheading from Stuart Diamond's article in the *New York Times*, February 3, 1985, p. 7.

2. Two books discuss Bhopal and the so-called Bhopal Syndrome in some detail. Dan Kurzman, *A Killing Wind: Inside Union Carbide* (New York: McGraw Hill, 1987); and David Weir, *The Bhopal Syndrome: Pesticides, Environment and Health* (San Francisco: Sierra Club Books, 1987).

3. I have adapted this set of distinctions between first-, second-, third-, and fourth-party victims from a somewhat different set appearing in Charles Perrow's *Normal Accidents* (New York: Basic Books, 1984), p. 67.

4. Nicholas A. Ashford, "Control the Transfer of Technology," *New York Times*, December 9, 1984, p. 2F.

5. The information used to construct the following description comes largely from a series of four articles in the *New York Times,* January 28, January 30, January 31, and February 3, 1985. These articles, as well as a preliminary article that appeared in the *New York Times* on December 9, 1984, shortly after the disaster, were written by Stuart Diamond. Diamond's account comes largely from interviews with workers, including Mr. Suman Dey, who was the senior officer on duty at the Union Carbide Bhopal plant.

6. This description of Mr. Dey's reaction is adapted from the description given by Stuart Diamond in his article, "Disasters in Bhopal: Workers Recall the Horror," in the *New York Times,* January 30, 1985, p. 1. Diamond's account comes largely from interviews with workers, including Mr. Suman Dey, who was the senior officer on duty.

7. Paul Shrivastava, *Bhopal: Anatomy of a Crisis* (Cambridge, Mass.: Ballinger, 1987), p. 81.

8. Wil Lepkowski, "Carbide faces key decisions in Bhopal litigation," *Chemical & Engineering News,* January 4, 1988, p. 8. In July 1985, Union Carbide tried to get the case dismissed in U.S. court on the grounds that the United States was not the proper location for the trial. Union Carbide had tried to reach settlements with victims who were privately represented, but when a $200 million settlement was offered in August, it was staunchly refused by the Indian government (Shrivastava, p. 81). Approximately one year after the disaster, Union Carbide hired the firm of Arthur D. Little to investigate the cause of the disaster. Union Carbide had contended that employee sabotage was the cause and was thus reluctant to admit to the liability that the Indians were trying to assign to it. Although the report on the accident did support the sabotage theory, Indians maintained that the plant design was unsafe and that this issue was itself indicative of Union Carbide's liability (Wil Lepkowski, *Chemical & Engineering News,* May 16, 1988, p. 6).

9. "Damages for a deadly cloud." *Time,* February 27, 1989, p. 53.

10. The view that the primary function of a legal system is the protection of rights is articulated systematically by Ronald Dworkin in *Taking Rights Seriously* (Cambridge, Mass.: Harvard University Press, 1978).

11. For an insightful account of the moral assumptions involved in risk analysis see Kristin S. Shrader-Frechette, *Risk Analysis and Scientific Method: Methodological and Ethical Problems with Evaluating Societal Hazards* (Hingham, Mass.: D. Reidel, 1985).

12. Perrow, *Normal Accidents,* p. 68.

13. Ibid.

14. John Rawls, *A Theory of Justice* (Cambridge, Mass.: Harvard University Press, 1971).

15. Ibid. Here I do not mean to assert the unquestioned propriety of applying Rawls's principle to *intra*national risk assessment, since to do so would necessarily involve a comparative assessment of Rawls's distributive approach in contrast to his competitors'. I want to claim only that *if* one accepts Rawls's principle as applying to analyses of one's own society, then one should also accept it in application to other societies. My own sympathies are Rawlsian, but I shall not presume their accuracy here.

16. Rawls's explicit characterization of the "moderate scarcity" proviso

(which he borrows from Hume) is that "natural and other resources are not so abundant that schemes of cooperation become superfluous, nor are conditions so harsh that fruitful ventures must inevitably break down." See ibid., pp. 127–28.

17. Brian Barry, "Humanity and Justice in Global Perspective," in J. Roland Pennock and John W. Chapman, eds., *Ethics, Economics, and the Law: Nomos Vol. XXIV* (New York: New York University Press, 1982), pp. 219–52.

18. Beitz also notes that a common error prompting the denial of international distributive justice is the assumption that international mechanisms of community and enforcement must exactly resemble existing ones at the national level. Other arrangements, while different from those associated with nation-states, would be capable of giving substance to distributive claims. Charles Beitz, *Political Theory and International Relations* (Princeton, N.J.: University Press, 1979), parts II and III; see also Charles Beitz, "Cosmopolitan Ideals and National Sentiment," *Journal of Philosophy* 80 (October 1983): 591–60.

19. A 1979 United Nations resolution stressed the need to "exchange information on hazardous chemicals and unsafe pharmaceutical products that have been banned in their territories and to discourage, in consultation with importing countries, the exportation of such products." Quoted in "Products Unsafe at Home Are Still Unloaded Abroad," *New York Times,* August 22, 1982, p. 22.

20. The problem, by the way, is not limited to the United States, since Europe exports greater amounts of hazardous products to developing countries than does the United States. See Ashford, "Control the Transfer of Technology," p. 2F.

21. With this as his basis, President Carter issued on January 15, 1981, an executive order that asked for a comprehensive approach to hazardous exports. The complex notification schemes for alerting foreign countries about hazards were to be coordinated and streamlined. An annual list of all products banned in the United States was to be compiled and made available, and government officials were empowered to seek international agreements on hazardous exports. Finally, the order required the creation of export controls on those "extremely hazardous substances" that constituted "a substantial threat to human health or safety or the environment." See Ashford, "Control the Transfer of Technology," p. 2F.

22. Industry opposition, which was described as "massive" by Edward B. Cohen, executive director of the Carter Administration's Task Force on Hazardous Exports Policy, probably was what killed the Carter plan. See "Products Unsafe at Home," p. 22.

23. Quoted in ibid.

24. Most of the information about Cubatao described here is from Marlise Simons, "Some Smell a Disaster in Brazil Industry Zone," *New York Times,* May 18, 1985, p. 4.

25. Ibid.

26. Charles Fried first discusses this example to illuminate the issue of why one might give priority of resources to actual and present sufferers over absent or future ones. See Fried, *An Anatomy of Values* (Cambridge,

Mass.: Harvard University Press, 1970), p. 227. Bernard Williams puts the example to a different use, to illustrate why "deep attachments to other persons will express themselves in the world in ways which cannot at the same time embody the impartial view." Williams, "Persons, Character and Morality," in Bernard Williams, ed., *Moral Luck: Philosophical Papers 1973–1980* (Cambridge: Cambridge University Press, 1981), p. 74.

27. Williams, "Persons, Character and Morality," p. 78.

28. See Thomas Donaldson, "Morally Privileged Relationships," *Journal of Value Inquiry*, forthcoming (1989).

29. This distinction resembles in some respects Alasdair McIntyre's separation of goods "internal" to a practice from goods "external" to a practice. A good is "internal," according to McIntyre for three reasons: (1) it can only be specified in terms of the practice itself; (2) it can only be identified and recognized by the experience of participating in the practice; and (3) it can only be obtained through the practice. McIntyre, *After Virtue* (Notre Dame, Ind.: Notre Dame University Press, 1981), p. 176. McIntyre's third criterion, but not necessarily his first and second, would apply to key goods obtainable through what I have called "value-intrinsic institutions."

30. See *Controlling Interest*, a film produced and distributed by California Newsreel, (San Francisco, 1977).

31. "Products Unsafe at Home," p. 4.

32. See John Stuart Mill, *On Liberty* (New York: Liberal Arts Press, 1956), p. 16.

33. Robert Reinhold, "Disaster in Bhopal: Where Does Blame Lie?" *New York Times*, January 31, 1985, p. 1.

34. Ashford, "Control the Transfer of Technology," p. 2F.

35. An earlier version of this chapter was published as "The Ethics of Risk in the Global Economy," *Business and Professional Ethics Journal* 5 (1988): 31–49.

Chapter 8

1. I shall use the term "nonwhites" to refer to South African blacks, Indians, and coloreds. Most published articles dealing with divestment focus on the consequences of divestment for nonwhite South Africans. This is true even of the few articles published by philosophers. See, for example, Kenneth Bond, "The Moral Dilemma of Divestment of South African Assets," *Journal of Business Ethics* 7 (1988): pp. 9–18; and William H. Shaw, "Boycotting South Africa," *Journal of Applied Philosophy* 3 (1986): pp. 59–72. And it is to a lesser extent true of the section entitled "U.S. Multinationals in South Africa," in Richard De George, *Business Ethics* (New York: Macmillan, 1986), pp. 373–80.

2. *Apartheid* is an Afrikaans word meaning "separateness." In this book, I use "apartheid" to refer to the entire system of regulations and laws that allows the white minority of South Africa of less than 3 million to maintain economic and political control over the nonwhite majority population of which nonwhite Africans number over 22 million. These include laws forcing re-

location in Bantustans or "homelands," laws forbidding nonwhites to vote, laws permitting detention of nonwhites without trials, and proscriptions on nonwhites owning guns; using white schools, hospitals, buses, recreational facilities, trains; and possessing property of significant value. My definition follows closely the interpretation of apartheid offered by Peter Madson in "The South African Divestment Debate: A Summary and Analysis," an unpublished paper prepared for the YWCA of Greater Pittsburgh, Pittsburgh, Pa., 1987, pp. 1–2.

For a discussion of what I have termed the "milder" forms of divestment, and in particular, of questions regarding the responsibility of investors in U.S. corporations operating in South Africa, see John Simon, Charles Powers, and Jon Gunnemann, *The Ethical Investor* (New Haven, Conn.: Yale University Press, 1972); and C. W. Powers, *Social Responsibility and Investment* (Nashville, Tenn.: Abingdon, 1971); and Richard De George, *Business Ethics*, pp. 373–80.

3. See John D. Battersby, 'U.S. Goods in South Africa," *New York Times*, July 27, 1987, pp. 21, 25. For related articles, see also *New York Times*, August 3, 1985, p. 4; and February 9, 1987, pp. 21 and 26.

4. Susan F. Rasky, "What Can Congress Do About Apartheid?" *New York Times*, June 12, 1988, p. 2E.

5. In the summer of 1988, the U.S. Congress prepared to force the commercial issue by passing new legislation to strengthen government sanctions passed in 1986. The 1986 sanctions included bans on new investment and new bank loans, a prohibition on oil and arms exports, and a partial ban on computer exports. Imports of South African agricultural products, uranium, krugerrands, iron, and steel were also banned. The new legislation proposed to ban most trade between the United States and South Africa and force U.S. companies and individuals to divest themselves of their South African holdings. Agricultural products from the United States as well as stategic minerals from South Africa in the new legislation would be exempt. Rasky, "What Can Congress Do?" p. 2E.

6. It is also noteworthy that the percentage of U.S. companies undertaking even such "paper" transactions is only about 10 percent. *New York Times*, August 3, 1985, p. 4; and February 9, 1987, pp. 21 and 26.

7. Battersby, "U.S. Goods in South Africa," p. 25.

8. For England the negative consequences of divestment would be harsher than for the United States, both because England is less healthy than the United States economically, and because England has over twice the invested capital in South Africa. Estimates of direct British investment in factories and equipment in South Africa range from 4.5 billion to 7 billion dollars, more than double American investment and 40 percent of the total foreign investment in South Africa. See Nicholas D. Kristof, "The Pressure on South Africa," *New York Times*, August 7, 1985, p. 7.

9. Ronald Dworkin, *Taking Rights Seriously* (Cambridge, Mass.: Harvard University Press, 1977).

10. See Amartya Sen's discussion of the possibility of such catastrophic conditions in "The Moral Standing of the Market," *Social Philosophy and Policy* 2 (Spring 1985): 1–19.

11. See "The (Sullivan) Statement of Principles," published by the International Council for Equality of Opportunity Principles, Inc., Philadelphia, Penn., 1984.

12. Reverend Leon Sullivan, "Agents for Change: The Mobilization of Multinational Companies in South Africa," *Law and Policy in International Business* 15 (1983): 427–44.

13. *New York Times*, June 4, 1987, pp. 1, 28.

14. For an account of other countries' business presence in South Africa, see Kristof, "The Pressure on South Africa," p. 7.

15. By 1987 over half of all U.S. corporations doing business in South Africa subscribed to the Sullivan Principles, although the level of their compliance is a matter of dispute. Even the Sullivan Organization confessed that approximately 20 percent of the signatories failed to achieve full compliance. See *Eighth Report on the Signatory Companies to the Sullivan Principles*, prepared by Arthur D. Little, Inc., Cambridge, Massachusetts, for Reverend Leon H. Sullivan, Zion Baptist Church, Philadelphia (Philadelphia: International Council for Equality of Opportunity Principles, Inc., 1984).

16. *South Africa Perspectives*, published by the Africa Fund, New York, no. 4, 1981, p. 2.

17. Donaldson, *Corporations and Morality*, pp. 1–2.

18. This conclusion is reached by way of a different set of arguments in William H. Shaw, "Boycotting South Africa," *Journal of Applied Philosophy* 3 (1986), pp. 59–72.

19. Robert Dale Wilson, head of the Office of Strategic Resources in the U.S. Commerce Department, remarked recently that it is highly unlikely that sanctions will prompt South Africa to cut off its supply of vital metals to the United States. See *New York Times*, July 21, 1986, p. 4. And the Commonwealth Group of Eminent Persons concluded that "even so-called strategic minerals could in our view be banned without harm to the West or without requiring purchase from the Soviet Union." "Supplies are available in other countries," the report argues, "and technological change is reducing the demand for some minerals." Malcolm Fraser and Olusegun Obasanjo, "What to Do About South Africa," *Foreign Affairs* 65 (Fall 1986): 159. See note 32 of this chapter.

20. Most experts agree that the ability of South Africa to hold out in the face of a general trade boycott is greater than most countries, but far from unlimited. Estimates on their ability to do so range from three to ten years, with the most serious deprivations occurring in areas where South Africa cannot efficiently produce on its own, such as big computers and large machinery. See Neil A. Lewis, "Circling the Wagons: South Africa and Sanctions," *New York Times*, July 21, 1986, p. 4.

21. Jeffrey Davidow, "Zimbabwe Is a Success," *Foreign Policy* 49 (Winter–Spring 1982–83): 93–106.

22. Lewis A. Dunn, *Controlling the Bomb: Nuclear Proliferation in the 1980s* (New Haven: Yale University Press, 1982).

23. See, for example, Simon Jenkins, "How Sanctions Help Apartheid," *The Spectator*, 10 August, 1985, pp. 10–12.

24. Dennis Austin, "A South African Policy: Six Precepts in Search of a Diplomacy?" *International Affairs* 62 (Summer 1986): 399.

25. The "Freedom Charter" adopted by the ANC in 1955 declares that "South Africa belongs to all who live in it, non-white and white," and advocates an end to restrictions on labor, equal opportunities in commerce, free compulsory education, land redistribution, a minimum wage, and a forty hour week. See Steven Mufson, "Who Is the ANC?" *New Republic* 195 (August 25, 1986): 21–24.

26. The parallel with Zimbabwe is instructive because several similar issues are involved—in particular the desire of nonwhites to maintain effective agricultural and industrial sectors, and the necessity for the whites to choose between emigration and accepting a radical nonwhite leadership which they have hitherto opposed by force. See Barry Buzan and H. O. Nazareth, "South Africa versus Azania: The Implications of Who Rules," *International Affairs* 62 (Winter 1985–86): 35.

27. Ibid., pp. 36–37.

28. Ibid.

29. Mufson, "Who Is the ANC?" p. 24.

30. Ibid.

31. Quoted in Trevor Huddleston, "A Hard Road for Tutu," *The Tablet* 18 (October 1986): 1103–4.

32. The Commonwealth Group of Eminent Persons was established to encourage a process of political dialogue in South Africa. The group was cochaired by Malcolm Fraser, past minister of Australia, and Olusegun Obasanjo, head of the Federal Military Government of Nigeria, 1966–79. The resulting report was published as *Mission to South Africa: The Commonwealth Report* (London: Penguin, 1986).

33. Fraser and Obasanjo, "What to Do About South Africa," p. 157.

34. Ibid., pp. 155, 158.

35. The experience of Rhodesian boycott is encouraging in this respect. See Robin Renwick, *Economic Sanctions* (Cambridge, Mass.: Center for International Affairs, Harvard University, 1981). The concern that, for example, employment would be scarcer and goods more expensive is sometimes doubted by critics in light of the repeated call by nonwhite South African leaders and the sentiment among rank-and-file nonwhites for external sanctions. This, in turn, suggests the possibility of adding a "nonpaternalism" principle to the condition-of-business principle already articulated. This principle would affirm that even if one's calculations showed that a political victim would be harmed more than helped by a given act, under certain circumstances the act would be justified if the person facing harm both understood the possible consequences of the act and encouraged its undertaking for reasons of justice.

Admittedly, statistics about nonwhite sentiment are open to controversy, in part because they must be gathered in a context where it is against the law to endorse sanctions. Nonetheless, surveys indicate that over 70 percent of all South African nonwhites favor the imposition of foreign sanctions upon the white African business. See *New York Times,* July 23, 1986, p. 6.

Furthermore, the much-touted resistance to sanctions of Chief Mangosuthu Gatsha Buthelezi, leader of the KwaZulu homeland and head of Inkatha, a nonwhite political party, has found little acceptance among nonwhites generally. According to a number of surveys, in the urban areas around Johannesburg and Pretoria, nonwhite support for Buthelezi and Inkatha declined from 28 percent in 1977 to 5 percent in 1985. Lars Waldorf, "Life in the Crossroads," *New Republic* 195 (August 25, 1986): 25. With the exception of Buthelezi, nonwhite leaders have supported sanctions. Tutu's own stand is well known, and Oliver Tambo, president of the ANC, has said, "What we in the African National Congress want to see is what the people of South Africa want to see . . . the total isolation of the racist regime—no investment and withdrawal of existing investment." Quoted in *South Africa Perspectives*, published by the Africa Fund, New York, no. 4, 1981, p. 2. Evidence attests to the willingness even of nonwhite workers in American-run South African companies to suffer short-term economic losses in the event multinationals leave South Africa. See David T. Beaty and Oren Harari, "South Africa: White Managers, Black Voices," *Harvard Business Review* v.65 (July–August 1987): 103. Nonetheless, consideration of such a "nonpaternalism" principle must await another occasion.

Chapter 9

1. Lisa Farr and Bruce Stening, "Ethics and the Multinational Corporation" (unpublished paper, Department of Management, The University of Western Australia, Nedlands, Western Australia), p. 4.

2. Bishop Butler, *Fifteen Sermons Preached at Rolls Chapel* (1726; rpt. London: Thomas Tegg & Son, 1835); see especially Sermons I and XI.

3. The Japanese, interestingly enough, are among the most strident.

Appendix

1. For an account of Hobbes's own attempt to square prudence with morality, see Gregory S. Kavka, "Right Reason and Natural Law in Hobbes's Ethics," *The Monist* 66 (January 1983): 120–34.

2. Thomas Hobbes, *The Philosophical Rudiments Concerning Government and Society: Volume 2* in *The English Works of Thomas Hobbes*, 11 vols. William Molesworth, ed. (London: Bohn, 1839–45), p. 16n.

3. Kavka, "Right Reason and Natural Law," p. 131.

4. Another important contribution in this vein is Russell Hardin's *Morality Within the Limits of Reason* (Chicago: University of Chicago Press, 1988).

5. David Gauthier, *Morals By Agreement* (Oxford: Clarendon Press, 1986), p. 7. The full quote is "Insofar as the interests of others are not affected, a person acts rationally if and only if she seeks her greatest interest or benefit." This may appear to imply that in those instances where others' interests are affected, rationality does not involve seeking one's greatest interest or benefit. That this is not Gauthier's meaning is made clear in the sentences

that follow. He writes, "[the essential difference between our view and others] . . . appears when we consider rational action in which the interests of others are involved. Proponents of the *maximizing* conception of rationality, which we endorse, insist that essentially nothing is changed; the rational person still seeks the greatest satisfaction of her own interests" (p. 7).

6. Gauthier notes that his conception of rationality does not require that practical reasons be self-interested.

> On the maximizing conception [i.e., Gauthier's own] it is not interests in the self, that take oneself as object, but interests of the self, held by oneself as subject, that provide the basis for rational choice and action. On the universalistic conception [which is opposed to Gauthier's view] it is not interests in anyone, that take any person as object, but interests of anyone, held by some person as subject, that provide the basis for rational choice and action. If I have a direct interest in your welfare, then on either conception I have reason to promote your welfare. But your interest in your welfare affords me such reason only given the universalistic conception." (*Morals By Agreement*, p. 7)

Nonetheless, Gauthier assumes that for the economic conception of man, i.e., the conception used to generate morals by agreement, individual utility functions are independent, or to put it another way, that "persons be conceived as not taking an interest in the interests of those with whom they exchange" (p. 87). He calls this the "non-tuism" assumption. Later, he refines this:

> The condition for asocial valuation is simply non-tuism; the non-tuist takes no interest in the interests of those with whom he interacts. His utility function, measuring his preferences, is strictly independent of the utility functions of those whom he affects. But non-tuism does not ensure asocial motivation. Even if one takes no interest in others' interests, one may take an interest in states of affairs that cannot be specified except with reference to others." (p. 311)

7. "One chooses rationally," Gauthier writes, "in endeavouring to maximize the fulfillment of those preferences that one holds in a considered way in the choice situation." Ibid., p. 32.

8. Ibid., p. 17.

9. Gauthier affirms the existence and importance of a non-"minimal" morality, yet doubts that it can ever find "rational" justification. He speaks of his theory of morals by agreement as developing from presuppositions about "economic man," yet notes that human beings are surely more than economic creatures. See *Morals By Agreement*, pp. 315–29; and Gauthier's "Reason and Maximization," *Canadian Journal of Philosophy* 4 (1975): 433. He writes:

> Economic man lacks the capacity to be truly the just man. He understand[s] the arguments for moral constraint, but he regards such constraint as an evil from which he would be free. . . . Morals by agreement have a non-tuistic [i.e., mutually disinterested] rationale. Their constraints bind rationally, and independently of all particular preferences. But it does not follow that morals by agreement bind only non-tuists." (*Morals By Agreement*, pp. 328–29)

A better person than economic man, according to Gauthier, is the "liberal individual." The liberal individual, unlike economic man, is "tuistic" in that he takes an interest in the interests of others. But his distinguishing feature, which encompasses sociability and a valuing of social participation for its own sake, is presumably only an affective, and not rationally justified characteristic.

10. For Locke, acquisitions in the state of nature are constrained by the proviso that "enough and as good" be left for others. Nozick has modified the proviso to allow it to accommodate situations in which there may not literally be "enough and as good" available for others, but where those who acquire property compensate others to the extent that they have worsened the position of others. See Robert Nozick, *State, Anarchy, and Utopia* (New York: Basic Books, 1974).

11. Gauthier, *Morals By Agreement*, p. 100.

12. Ibid., p. 214. The proviso requires what, following Nozick, is called "full compensation," and not "market compensation." "Full" in contrast to "market" compensation guarantees that a person is left without any net loss in utility. See ibid., p. 211.

13. Ibid., pp. 140–44.

14. Ibid., p. 282.

15. Ibid., p. 283.

16. Ibid., pp. 218–19.

17. Gauthier's rejection of any duty of international charity may be viewed in light of the ongoing controversy over international obligations. Philosophers such as Peter Singer, Brian Barry, and Henry Shue have urged a stricter interpretation of our duties to strangers, while others, including both traditional political realists and recent critics of Rawlsian liberalism such as James Fishkin, resist this raising of the moral stakes. See Peter Singer, "Famine, Affluence and Morality," *Philosophy and Public Affairs* 1 (1972): 229–43; James Fishkin, *Practical Ethics* (Cambridge: Cambridge University Press, 1980), especially chapter 8, pp. 158–81; and Brian Barry, "Humanity and Justice in Global Perspective," in J. Roland Pennock and John W. Chapman, eds., *Ethics, Economics, and the Law: Nomos Vol. XXIV* (New York: New York University Press, 1982), pp. 219–52. Henry Shue, *Basic Rights* (Princeton, N.J.: Princeton University Press, 1980). James Fishkin, *The Limits of Obligation* (New Haven: Yale University Press, 1982), and his "Theories of Justice and International Relations: The Limits of Liberal Theory," Anthony Ellis, ed., *Ethics and International Relations* (London: Manchester University Press, 1986), pp. 1–12. For an analysis of current arguments concerning our duties to the poor abroad, see Susan James, "The Duty to Relieve Suffering," *Ethics* 93 (Oct 1982): 4–21.

18. Gauthier, *Morals By Agreement*, p. 222.

19. Ibid., p. 212.

20. Ibid., p. 213.

21. Ibid., p. 282.

22. Ibid., p. 214.

23. Ibid., p. 222. Still another passage emphasizing this point is found in chapter 7 where Gauthier writes: "It is rational for utility-maximizers to accept the [Lockean] proviso as constraining their natural interaction and their individual endowments, in so far as they anticipate beneficial social interaction with their fellows" (p. 193).

24. Ibid., p. 16.

25. Ibid., p. 201.

26. Ibid., p. 280. Elsewhere Gauthier reaffirms this interpretation, remarking that "in so far as the state of nations remains a state of nature, those who profit at the expense of their neighbors are behaving in a straightforwardly maximizing manner in circumstances in which constrained maximization would not be reciprocated" (pp. 281–82).

27. Ibid., p. 287. In general, Gauthier holds that appropriations by "advanced" peoples of the land belonging to nonadvanced peoples, while not resting on consent, may be morally justified. "[I] wish to rescue from the indiscriminate obloquy that has fallen upon the imperial idea," he writes, "that very real and significant strand in which the more advanced power seeks to better its own situation in a manner that makes effectively available to others the prospect of increasing their numbers, prolonging their lives, adding to their material goods, and enlarging their opportunities." Ibid., pp. 297–98.

28. Ibid., chapters 10 and 11.

29. Ibid., p. 307.

30. An early version of the material in this appendix was presented at the 1988 International Studies Association Meeting, and at the 1988 Western Division American Philosophical Meeting. I am indebted to the many constructive criticisms offered there and elsewhere, and especially to those from Raymond Frey, Russell Hardin, Gregory Kavka, Christopher Morris, Terry Nardin, Julius Sensat, and Carl Wellman.

INDEX